PUTTING SOCIAL JUSTICE AND EQUITY AT THE HEART OF READING FOR PLEASURE

This essential book discusses what reading for pleasure is and what it is not, introducing some fundamental ideas about how we learn to read and how this process can impact a child's identity as a reader in classrooms that promote equality, inclusion and diversity.

The profile and importance of Reading for Pleasure has grown significantly over the last few years and is now firmly embedded in both government policy and the Ofsted framework. Developing a Reading for Pleasure school that is truly inclusive of the whole school community, however, can require a culture shift in relation to the teaching of reading, representation in the reading environment and the knowledge, and attitudes of the school community. This book seeks to use the current research, teacher case studies and the voices of children to address some of the issues that teachers and pre-service teachers encounter when trying to develop an inclusive Reading for Pleasure culture within their schools. Each chapter is co-authored by teachers and researchers and includes case studies and children's perspectives.

It provides practical and evidence-based advice, lesson ideas and creative ideas to both support and challenge all school leaders, staff and student teachers in their journey to create readers rather than children that can just read.

Jane Carter was a primary school teacher for many years before starting work as a senior lecturer and researcher at the University of the West of England, UK. She has a passion for literacy, language and learning with research interests from phonics and early reading to engaging families with reading.

'This accessible book, written by experienced educators views reading for pleasure through a social justice lens. Foregrounding opportunities for all, it actively highlights issues of inclusion in texts and contexts, and offers strategies, case studies and questions that will help teachers nurture volitionally engaged and motivated readers.'

Teresa Cremin, *Professor of Education (Literacy), the Open University, UK*

'This excellent, well-informed and influential book is a must read for students, teachers and academics who want to explore the intrinsic links between reading for pleasure and the context of social justice and equality. Each chapter takes a familiar theme but explores it from a social justice stance, thereby bringing fresh insight and encourages the reader to critically reflect on their own teaching. The book is packed with ideas and resources for the reader to explore as well as a 'call to action' which will no doubt lead to readers being empowered to develop a reading culture that is inclusive, empowering, and reflective of the diverse identities and experiences of the children they teach.'

Roger McDonald, *Associate Professor in Primary Education (Literacy) Faculty of Education, Health & Human Sciences School of Education, University of Greenwich, UK*

'This book is an essential read for anyone entering the teaching profession and indeed all those working in primary education. Research is expertly interwoven with practical ideas, case studies and resources to support all teachers to make well-informed decisions that will put social justice and equity at the heart of their classroom reading practices.'

Hannah Baker, *Literacy Consultant*

'This book delves deeply into the world of reading for pleasure and depicts what this means for all children and young people. It is an absolutely essential read for educators who are passionate about all learners enjoying their reading journeys. Whilst it draws extensively on research and theory, it provides educators with the perfect backdrop on which to understand and then demonstrate the values and factors involved for groups of learners in deepening their enjoyment of reading. It is what every teacher needs to know.'

Cerys Stevens, *Senior Lecturer and Primary Literacy Consultant*

'Putting Social Justice and Equity at the heart of RfP invites us to frame our thinking around the complexities defining the human experience of what it means to Read for Pleasure. Rooting social justice and equity at the heart of each chapter enables future teachers of readers to employ their professional agency through a multifaceted, intersectional lens - being considered, curious and critically engaged with the ever evolving theoretical, social and political landscape. Quite simply, this book has the child's voice and best interest at the heart of it.'

Kiran Satti, *Deputy Principal at Oasis Academy Woodview, UK*

'This book provides a timely lens on the power of reading for pleasure in developing equitable pedagogical practices in schools. Each chapter is carefully written to evidence the child's voice which is impactful on the reader's perception of school development. Each author skilfully ensures that the focus of their chapter brings new perspectives on reading for pleasure and, importantly for practitioners, evidence as to why this development is needed and how to weave this through classroom practice. With reading as a key lever to bring about equality that is vital for the future prosperity of our society, the book is a clarion call for schools to harness the power of reading for pleasure now. I, indeed, feel both 'affirmed and challenged' - always the sign of a great read!'

Joanna Farbon, *Fellow Charted College of Teaching, Chartered Teacher (Leadership), Headteacher and Chair of Luton Nursery & Primary Headteachers' Association*

PUTTING SOCIAL JUSTICE AND EQUITY AT THE HEART OF READING FOR PLEASURE

Tools, Tips and Research to Support Professionals in Primary Classrooms

Edited by Jane Carter

LONDON AND NEW YORK

Designed cover image: © Getty Images

First published 2025
by Routledge
4 Park Square, Milton Park, Abingdon, Oxon OX14 4RN

and by Routledge
605 Third Avenue, New York, NY 10158

Routledge is an imprint of the Taylor & Francis Group, an informa business

© 2025 selection and editorial matter, Jane Carter; individual chapters, the contributors

The right of Jane Carter to be identified as the author of the editorial material, and of the authors for their individual chapters, has been asserted in accordance with sections 77 and 78 of the Copyright, Designs and Patents Act 1988.

All rights reserved. No part of this book may be reprinted or reproduced or utilised in any form or by any electronic, mechanical, or other means, now known or hereafter invented, including photocopying and recording, or in any information storage or retrieval system, without permission in writing from the publishers.

Trademark notice: Product or corporate names may be trademarks or registered trademarks, and are used only for identification and explanation without intent to infringe.

British Library Cataloguing-in-Publication Data
A catalogue record for this book is available from the British Library

Library of Congress Cataloging-in-Publication Data
Names: Carter, Jane, editor.
Title: Putting social justice and equity at the heart of reading for pleasure : tools, tips and research to support professionals in primary classrooms / Edited by Jane Carter.
Description: Abingdon, Oxon ; New York, NY : Routledge, 2025. | Includes bibliographical references and index.
Identifiers: LCCN 2024046493 (print) | LCCN 2024046494 (ebook) | ISBN 9781032530543 (hardback) | ISBN 9781032530529 (paperback) | ISBN 9781003409939 (ebook)
Subjects: LCSH: Reading (Primary) | Social justice and education. | Children--Books and reading--Sociological aspects. | Children--Books and reading--Psychological aspects. | Identity (Psychology) | Inclusive education. | Educational equalization.
Classification: LCC LB1525 .P88 2025 (print) | LCC LB1525 (ebook) | DDC 372.4--dc23/eng/20241218
LC record available at https://lccn.loc.gov/2024046493
LC ebook record available at https://lccn.loc.gov/2024046494

ISBN: 978-1-032-53054-3 (hbk)
ISBN: 978-1-032-53052-9 (pbk)
ISBN: 978-1-003-40993-9 (ebk)

DOI: 10.4324/9781003409939

Typeset in Interstate
by KnowledgeWorks Global Ltd.

CONTENTS

List of contributors — vii

1. **Introduction to reading for pleasure** — 1
   Jane Carter and Kalpa Ghelani

2. **What counts as reading?** — 15
   Dan Northover

3. **Not reading for pleasure but "purposefully positive": Understanding the difference between reading for pleasure and using great texts for teaching** — 37
   Jane Carter

4. **Connecting people and planet through reading for pleasure** — 55
   Verity Jones and Amanda D Webber

5. **Representation in children's literature** — 69
   Karan Vickers-Hulse, Kalpa Ghelani, Emma Thomas and Nick Latham

6. **Engaging and re-engaging readers: Innovative approaches that can help reignite the spark** — 85
   Ros Steward, Catherine Delor and Leah Dowty

7. **Family engagement: Who are your influencers?** — 106
   Jane Carter

8. **The importance of teachers' knowledge of children's literature to develop children's reading for pleasure** — 126
   Ann Cowling, Ros Steward and Laura Manison

9 **The pleasure of reading against: Embedding lifelong critical literacy from picturebooks to social media** 140
Ann Alston and Jane Carter

10 **Conclusion: A call to action for social justice and equity in reading for pleasure** 159
Jane Carter and Ann Cowling

Appendices 163
Index 168

LIST OF CONTRIBUTORS

Ann Alston is a senior lecturer in Children's Literature at The University of the West of England, UK. She has published on the family in children's literature, co-edited and contributed to collections on Dahl, and is interested in climate literature, critical literacy and Welsh children's literature.

Ann Cowling is a lecturer at the University of the West of England in Bristol, UK. Ann taught English in secondary schools for fifteen years. She enjoys reading children's and Y.A. fiction and running Book Clubs for students training to be teachers, designed to introduce them to the richness of children's literature.

Catherine Delor has spent thirty years working in Primary education, and has now come full circle and is working at the University of the West of England, UK, teaching trainee teachers. She specialises in English subject knowledge and children's literature.

Leah Dowty is a Senior Lecturer and PGCE Programme Co-Lead at UWE. She is passionate about every child having the opportunity to find pleasure in reading and is particularly interested in how teachers can boost the self-efficacy of struggling readers in the classroom.

Kalpa Ghelani has taught in primary schools for 13 years. During this time, she was Disabilities Coordinator (SENDCo) and a specialist leader of education (SLE) in Primary English. She has interests in neurodivergent trainee teachers and engaging all students and children with reading for pleasure.

Verity Jones is an Associate Professor of Education at UWE, Bristol. Her research explores the intersections between social and environmental justice through education.

Nick Latham teaches on the undergraduate and PGCE ITE programs at UWE with a focus on humanities, science, English and professional development. He has been teaching for 10 years in primary schools in London, Bristol and Kuwait. His research interests are focused on curriculum, equity, representation, social justice and anti-racist practice.

Laura Manison is a senior lecturer in education at UWE Bristol, UK. Previous to that she worked in schools in Cardiff, London and Bristol as a teacher and deputy headteacher. She has 30 years of experience in the area of primary education with a particular interest in how children's learning and school experiences are impacted by social class.

Dan Northover is a Senior Lecturer at UWE Bristol. His main areas of interest and expertise are related to Primary English, and he has a particular passion for children's literature and supporting the development of reading for pleasure in schools.

Ros Steward was a primary school teacher for over 20 years in an inner-city school in Bristol before joining the University of the West of England as a senior lecturer in primary education with an English specialism. She is a passionate reader with a soft spot for picturebooks!

Emma Thomas is a Senior Lecturer in Primary Education at the University of the West of England in Bristol, UK.

Karan Vickers-Hulse is the Associate Director in Education at UWE Bristol. Before joining UWE, Karan worked as a primary school teacher, English leader and senior leader in schools. She is an early career researcher and her research interests focus on professional identity, social and emotional learning and issues of equity and inclusion.

Amanda D Webber is an anthropologist whose research is at the interface between people and nature, considering how we can effectively communicate around biodiversity conservation and the environment. She is also programme leader for UWE's MSc Science Communication.

1 Introduction to reading for pleasure

Jane Carter and Kalpa Ghelani

Why this book?

You may be wondering how another book about reading for pleasure can be written: there are already so many on the bookshelves of every school and teacher training institution, not to mention an array of fabulous websites available at the click of a button. However, this book will be approaching the subject through a slightly different lens. Many books include a chapter on children's literature and diversity and sometimes a chapter on reading for pleasure and inclusion, but this book attempts to put social justice and the consideration of children from minoritised groups and (what are often referred to as) more "vulnerable learners," at the centre of the approaches suggested and the research highlighted. Children's literature, in its widest sense, which can support the development of reading for pleasure in primary classrooms, will be considered through the eyes of these different groups of children and their teachers, as well as through the research literature. Later in this chapter, we will identify what we mean specifically by the terms diversity and inclusion.

The authors of this book are experienced early years, primary and secondary teachers, most of whom now work in Initial Teacher Education, but the authors also include scientists and an English literature expert. However, all have in common a passion for reading, for children's books and a desire to ensure children not only become readers but readers who read for pleasure and purpose. Social justice is at the core of our practice, and we are keenly aware that we rarely "get it right" for every child. We hope that this book will open and continue discussions in schools and teacher education institutions about how we, as teachers, recognise the diversity of needs in our classrooms that are as many and varied as there are children. This book will draw on the voices of the researcher, teachers and in particular the voices of children who often hold valuable nuggets of wisdom about learning and teaching. Their voices are sometimes not amplified loudly enough for us to hear, and this book aims to remedy this. Throughout the book, you will find case studies drawn from classrooms which will focus on what children say about their experiences of becoming readers for pleasure - or not! Case studies will also feature the exemplary practice of teachers, as well as raise questions about common approaches and ideas that we need to reflect on to ponder the possible range of meanings and messages that they give distinct groups of children in our classes. Moxnes and Osgood (2018) call this "diffraction" rather than reflection and urge us to consider and reconsider everyday actions and their intended messages and consequences, as well as the

DOI: 10.4324/9781003409939-1

possible unintended consequences of those same actions. For example, when reading aloud a story about refugees, the teacher may feel they are providing children with the opportunity to step into the shoes of others and see the world of others reflected in the story. The teacher may feel that the story enables children to explore difficult and complex issues, and all of this may be true, but what if the class has children who are, or who have families that are refugees, what is the message being given to them? What if the Black and brown children in the class only ever see Black and brown children in books who are refugees, what message does it give these children? How is the empathic child positioned – will they see themselves as the dominant group who can "gift" asylum to refugees? What if the only message given is that the children in the book are "just the same as" all children – without recognising the unique experience of the refugee and their particular circumstances and culture?

Even in these first paragraphs, a whole host of terms have been used and this introduction will aim to explore these key terms and set out how they will be further developed and operationalised in the chapters that follow. But first, it is useful to begin with the big picture of reading – what do we mean by reading and how do we become readers?

Reading and becoming a reader

The teaching of reading has consistently been at the top of many national and international educational political agendas and is a feature of international comparison and research. Reading is an understandable priority. Castles, Rastle and Nation (2018, p. 5) identify reading as 'the basis for the acquisition of knowledge, for cultural engagement, for democracy, and for success in the workplace. Illiteracy costs the global economy more than $1 trillion (U.S. dollars) annually in direct costs alone.' Being a reader is of course even more than purely a means of functioning well in society, it is a gateway to new worlds, the past, present and future, to different countries, cultures and to a myriad of adventures and experiences of countless characters both real and imagined. Oakhill, Cain and Elbro (2014, p. i) helpfully remind us that 'The ultimate aim of reading is not the process of reading the words but understanding what we read' and it is in this "understanding" that we are enabled to access the many benefits of reading.

It is clear that teaching reading is perhaps the most important and impactful job that any teacher will do. For this reason, successive governments have grappled with the best approach to teach reading. Sir Jim Rose was commissioned by the English government to review the way that reading was taught in English primary schools and in 2006 the 'Independent Review of the Teaching of Early Reading' was published. The review concluded that the most effective way to teach early reading was by using a systematic approach to the teaching of phonics which needed to be set 'within a broad and rich language curriculum that takes full account of developing the four interdependent strands of language: speaking, listening, reading and writing and enlarging children's stock of words.' (p. 70). The review also promoted the use of the 'Simple View of Reading' model developed by Gough and Tunmer some years before in 1986. Whilst the report highlighted the importance of a wide range of reading practices and approaches, the identification of the Simple View of Reading model and systematic phonics (and later synthetic phonics) were the two aspects that dominated subsequent policy and curricular. The Simple View (Gough and Tunmer, 1986) states that reading is made up of two components: language comprehension and word reading, and that the combination of these, enables reading comprehension. It is useful to remember that this model describes how we read rather than the teaching of reading, but the current curricular design (Department of Education, 2013) identified these two components and set out objectives for teaching in relation to both distinct areas. To understand more of the background to how this review came about, and the antecedence to its inception, you may want to read Moss and Huxford's (2007) 'Exploring literacy policy-making from the inside out' and Moss (2009) 'The politics of literacy in the context of large-scale education reform.' It is also useful to note that England was not alone in its quest to improve reading outcomes for children. In the United States of America, a similar review had been commissioned and the National Reading Panel reported in 2000, and this report had some similarities with Rose. In relation to the word reading element of the Simple View, systematic phonics is foregrounded and promoted as the prime approach to the teaching of early reading.

Following Rose's 2006 Independent review, the focus of policy narrowed, policy detailed the teaching of early reading using phonics (rather than the development of reading for all ages and stages). Whilst there is agreement amongst most researchers that phonics has an essential role to play in the teaching of reading (Torgerson, Brooks, and Hall, 2006) and "the relationship between letters and sounds is a non-negotiable" when learning to read (Castles, Rastle and Nation, 2018), it is also recognised that phonics is only one essential element, and on its own is not sufficient (Breadmore et al., 2019; Torgerson et al., 2019). Chapter 3 will explore some of the issues that this raises in relation to reading for pleasure and also in relation to the impact on diverse groups of children. It is also important to note that this framing of reading is culturally and socially situated and that reading is not confined to the ideas outlined in government policy, reports and curricular. Reading will mean something quite different to a child with special needs, for example, the child who learns to read the Qur'an, or the early years child who "reads" their favourite story to their teddy bear. These ideas will be explored in Chapter 2 when "what counts as reading" will be considered.

More than phonics

The Simple View has dominated many constructions of reading and there have also been many expanded models, such as Scarborough's Reading Rope (Scarborough, 2001) which begins to "unpick" the two elements of Language Comprehension and Word Reading. Duke and Cartwright (2021) recognise the "undeniable importance" of the two elements of the Simple View but propose a new and updated model, the "active view of reading" that recognises additional components to reading. The interrelationship between the two elements of the Simple View is highlighted in this "active view." They identify a bridging process between the two elements and these processes include reading fluency and vocabulary knowledge. In addition, they highlight the wider factor of active self-regulation including motivation and engagement as well as strategy use and executive function skills. They situate their model in the "text, task and socio-cultural" context in which the teaching and learning takes place. The highlighting of these additional processes will have some direct links to reading for pleasure and the benefits of reading for pleasure and this will be explored later in this chapter.

These models tend to focus on the cognitive or proximal elements of reading, but any primary school teacher will instantly be able to identify an entire range of factors that impact a child beyond those cognitive processes. Ellis and Smith (2017) propose a "Three Knowledge Domains" model which recognises that cognitive processes are just one element of the complex process of learning to read. Their model recognises that learning to read is socially and culturally situated and so the learning process is informed and impacted by a child's social and cultural capital (thinking about what the child brings to the learning process from their particular community and home experiences) and also the child's personal and social identity (including how they view themselves as a reader). Every encounter with a book will be different for each child as they all bring their unique perspectives and experiences to bear on their thinking and interpretation of the text. The Ellis and Smith (2017) article makes excellent further reading and will be explored in Chapters 4 and 7, as well as being referenced in many of the chapters in this book.

The wider social context of reading

These wider models acknowledge that reading is not merely a set of skills to master and knowledge to learn. The wider distal factors that impact reading have their foundations laid down before the start of formal education: the home literacy environment, in its widest sense, impacts early attitudes to reading and future reading attainment (Fletcher and Reese, 2005). There have been a number of seminal studies that locate reading as a social and cultural construct (Brice-Heath, 1983; Street, 1984) and more recently the work of Levy (2011) and Levy and Hall (2021) and that this requires the teacher to understand the community literacy experiences of the child and value all of these experiences, whether they are similar to the construct of literacy found in the school or not. These ideas will be further explored and developed in Chapter 7 in relation to what it means to read for pleasure and how it can be developed and promoted.

Why is reading for pleasure important?

The paragraphs above have attempted to set out the big picture of what we know about learning to read and how this has informed our approach to teaching. Whilst policy has largely focused on standards and attainment in reading, more recently there has been recognition that a focus on the cognitive processes alone can leave children able but unwilling to read. In the recent Progress in International Reading Literacy Survey (PIRLS, 2021), England has risen to fourth in the "league tables" of the fifty participating countries. However, despite being able to read, children in England report they do not enjoy reading or choose to read: only 29% of English children agreed with the statement they "very much like" reading, compared to 42% internationally. Of course, such league tables are highly contested in relation to how they are constructed, what they really show and what they mask. For example, in the 2021 study, despite rising in the table, England did not have a higher overall reading attainment score. The Covid-19 pandemic impacted both the way the study was conducted and also on how different countries were able to support their education systems during this period. It would be particularly useful to drill down into the data in the PIRLS study to find out how the children we are foregrounding in this book did. How much did the children from socio-economically disadvantaged communities; children with Special Educational Needs and children from historically vulnerable and minoritised groups, contribute to the rise in the international league table?

Perhaps it is also a reasonable question to ask as to whether it matters if children are reading for pleasure if they can read. Why does reading for pleasure matter so much for the children we are focusing on in this book? Using an extensive research evidence base, the Book Trust (2023) has grouped the benefits of reading into four core themes. They found that reading is shown to overcome disadvantages caused by inequalities and that children who read were found to be healthier and happier children with better mental wellbeing and self-esteem. This mirrors the findings of the 2002, Organisation for Economic Cooperation and Development (OECD) report which stated that 'Finding ways to engage students in reading may be one of the most effective ways to leverage social change' (p. 3). Children who read made more progress across the curriculum and were demonstrated to be developing creativity and empathy. Sullivan and Brown (2013, p. 37) found a 'positive link between leisure reading and cognitive outcomes' and they noted that this was 'not purely due to more able children being more likely to read a lot, but that reading is actually linked to increased cognitive progress over time'.

What is reading for pleasure?

We have detailed some of the benefits of reading for pleasure but what is reading for pleasure and how can we distinguish it from other engaging and motivating reading activities. Reading for pleasure is quite distinct. Cremin et al. (2014) in their seminal work in this area, define reading for pleasure as reading that is volitional, reading that is done because the reader wants to read and has the agency to choose what, when and how to read. Readers who read for pleasure do this "in anticipation of the satisfaction gained" and for many, the "satisfaction afterwards in interaction with others" (p. 5). Cremin et al. (2014) make clear that reading for pleasure can "involve any kind of text: novel- mag-comic-non-fiction, social media etc. in electronic or printed form." Reading for pleasure can "take place anywhere: at home, school-in the community, an office, bus, park etc." and that reading for pleasure can "be solitary or social and interactive."

Agency is at the heart of some of these definitions of reading for pleasure, and as you read this book, try to reflect on this idea and whether, in our current education system and curricular, the construct of agency we create in our classrooms is really agency. This struck me when listening to a teacher talk about her guided reading carousel, where one group was "reading for pleasure." Can you read for pleasure on demand, in this case, between 1.15 pm and 1.45 pm? As teachers, are we in danger of framing "reading for pleasure" as a curriculum subject? For the child who is an avid reader but cannot, "reading for pleasure" on demand in the designated timeslot, or the child who is struggling to read, who finds reading incredibly difficult and taxing, what does a timeslot in which to "read for pleasure" mean in relation to ideas of agency? What about the child who has no books or other text at home, who feels "unwelcome" or out of place in a library (if one even exists close to their home) or does not want to "sit" with a book (even in a bean bag surrounded by fairy lights) because they want to flick and flit with text on screen, do these children really have agency or the potential for agency in relation to reading for pleasure? Agency is a verb, agency is an action, but in relation to reading for pleasure, perhaps it is we as teachers who control the actions or what are considered to be acceptable actions in relation to our constructs of reading for pleasure. Do we as teachers, confine, define and frame what children should, could and might do in relation to reading and reading for pleasure. Is this really agency?

In Chapter 3, the focus will be not only on what reading for pleasure is but also what it is not and the chapter will propose the idea of "purposefully positive" reading and how this too can support the readers we are focusing on in this book and widen our thinking in relation to the reading culture we develop in relation to every encounter with text.

Other chapters will explore in more detail how classrooms can promote reading for pleasure and each will expand on the pedagogies of reading for pleasure. It is really helpful at this point to visit the Open University Reading for Pleasure website (https://ourfp.org/) which outlines in a clear and detailed way the pedagogies of reading for pleasure. It is a treasure trove of evidence based and tried and tested ideas and practices that support teachers in developing a reading-for-pleasure classroom. The key areas for exploration on the website and here in this book are

- How we create communities of readers in our schools, classrooms and community and how we can ensure that this community is inclusive and recognises the diversity of readers in them;
- How teachers can expand their knowledge of children's literature to support their communities of readers with special regard for minoritised groups and so developing "teachers who read and readers who teach";
- How teachers can create classrooms and schools that could be considered to be social reading environments that enable "book talk" that values the voices of all children;
- How teachers can read aloud for pleasure and purpose, both collaborating with children on book choices but also able to identify something new to tempt and enthral the reader;
- How teachers can support children in their independent reading as active, volitional readers.

Thinking about diversity and inclusion

This book aims to take a holistic view of reading for pleasure and inclusion. In today's increasingly interconnected world, and at times a world that is also fragmented and polarised, the importance of fostering a culture of diversity and inclusion cannot be overstated. In this book, the term "diversity" refers to the presence and inclusion of a wide range of different elements or characteristics within a group, organisation or society. It encompasses various dimensions, including but not limited to race, ethnicity, gender, sexual orientation, age, disability, socioeconomic status, religion, nationality, and educational background. The term "inclusive" will be used to discuss reading practices in the classroom that have been developed to equally and/or equitably provide children with opportunities to fully participate in and access the curriculum (specifically referring to reading practices and reading for pleasure), so that reading for pleasure is seen as inclusive by being aware of the diversity within and beyond our classrooms.

Diversity across the United Kingdom (and in the case studies we will be exploring, specifically in the city of Bristol) is naturally reflected in the classrooms across the country and its cities. However, there is extensive research (Ramdarshan Bold, 2022; Centre for Literacy in Primary Education, 2022) which highlights that children's literature does not echo the multiplicity of experiences, needs and backgrounds of many of the pupils who make up our school communities.

In 1990, Bishop authored a paper that has gone on to become a seminal text in the topic of diversity in children's literature and how they can reflect the "multicultural nature of the world" and how since then, while it has been amended and adapted by multiple authors, the metaphor she provided still holds value. Bishop suggested that the books can be windows, mirrors or sliding doors. When children encounter characters and stories that reflect their own experiences and encounter those different from their own, they develop a broader perspective, enhance their literacy skills, and form a deep appreciation for literature. We will return to and explore further this work in many of the chapters in this book where this work and the research and literature that followed have been employed. Enriquez (2021), for example, delves deeper still, cautioning that close approximations of readers are not enough. To use books as mirrors, books need to accurately reflect readers' multifaceted identities. The windows we provide pupils, through the books we read, should allow children to access multicultural learning within the curriculum, integrating diverse books throughout the school curriculum and school day. Finally, when we step through the doors, we should consider how we are experiencing the perspectives of others by rethinking viewpoints, positions of privilege and going beyond the story provided. Moreover, these texts should be used regularly as vehicles for learning on a daily basis, rather than simply being available to read (Heineke, Papola-Ellis and Elliott, 2022).

Research conducted by the Centre for Literacy in Primary Education (CLPE) from 2017 onwards, has reported a slow but steady rise in books featuring characters from minority ethnic backgrounds as well as increased visibility of authors, poets and illustrators of colour. While this is a welcome change, 'it does not necessarily guarantee quality in representation' (Centre for Literacy in Primary Education, 2022, p. 3). There is a growing recognition from teachers, writers and now publishers around this lack of diversity in children's literature and a slow growth in books that are beginning to reflect the pupils in our classrooms. However, due to this slow growth, teachers are responsible for making deliberate decisions about the books that they expose children to within the classroom (Leahy and Foley, 2018). When exploring representations in terms of ethnicity compared to real world and UK populations, however, some groups are represented even less than others, the Roma Gypsy community for example (see Chapter 7). As teachers, it is up to us to make mindful choices in the books we select for our classrooms. The aim is not to simply be conscious of the books that are out there but for these books to have a meaningful presence in our classrooms. Both of these considerations will be explored in many of the chapters of this book.

Moreover, exposure to diverse literature expands children's cultural horizons and broadens their understanding of the world. The opportunities to encounter characters from unfamiliar cultures and backgrounds allow children to gain insights into diverse perspectives, customs, and traditions. This exposure fosters respect and aims to break stereotypes and promote acceptance of all people and the rich experiences they carry with them. Reading about characters who may have different abilities or life experiences helps children develop compassion and inclusivity, enhancing their social and emotional growth.

Since the Salamanca statement was published in 1994 (a UNESCO document representing worldwide consensus on the direction of SEND) there has been a growth of literature exploring and addressing the topic of inclusive education. However, Nilholm (2020) shares that there is still a lack of progress and knowledge. This also holds true when we look at the texts and literature available to children. In recent years there has been increased research conducted, raising awareness of ethnic representation. However, in comparison to this, there is a lesser focus on disability representation as well as the intersectionality of disability and representations of identity e.g., ethnicity, gender, SEND. (Chan, 2023).

Inclusion is not a strategy. It is a sense of belonging and of community. As our school populations continue to become increasingly diverse – be that by race, socioeconomic status, ability, gender or sexuality, educators must also continue to evolve, ensuring that provision of education reflects the experiences of our pupils. In UNESCO's guide to inclusive education (2017) it shares the following definition: 'A process that helps to overcome barriers limiting the presence, participation and achievement of learners.' (p. 12). Some explore the view that unintentional exclusion may take place due to curricula, texts or activities which limit the full participation or accessibility of pupils (Milton and Forlin, 2017; Munns, Sawyer and Cole, 2013). Ainscow (2017) explores the development of inclusion on an international scale. She identifies that in some countries, inclusion is still thought of as an approach whereby children (with disabilities) are supported in accessing education within a general or mainstream setting. Internationally, however, Ainscow (2017, p. 9) writes:

> It is increasingly seen more broadly as a principle that supports and welcomes diversity amongst all learners. It presumes that the aim is to eliminate social exclusion that is a consequence of attitudes and responses to diversity in race, social class, ethnicity, religion, gender and ability.

According to Hague (2020, p. 3), there is a "hunger for change" among educators. A belief that more steps can be taken to celebrate the cultures of the UK people and the diverse experiences with the school landscape.

Why feeling included matters

Imagine walking into a room full of people and not feeling as though you belong there. You see no one that looks like you, no one with whom you may have something in common. It is like you are in the wrong place. Now let us mirror that in the curriculum we teach our pupils and extend that to books we provide for the young people we work with. Imagine being encouraged to read but none of the books relate to you. You don't see yourself or someone like you as a character in the books. If you do, they are not a main character – instead, they are a stereotype or caricature of you or a character that is barely part of the story. How likely is it that you are going to want to read? How invalidated would you feel? Chapter 4 will explore this further. The aim is not to simply provide you with teaching strategies for children but to create a classroom that is inherently inclusive. One which makes all children feel like they belong.

Inclusion also intersects with ideas of agency. To feel included, to feel part of a community, our worries, concerns, interests and passions need to be valued by that community. Representation in the literature certainly goes a long way to addressing this but we also need to consider our class of children as individuals, each bringing their own ideas, thoughts, feeling and humanity. There are particular issues that can galvanise children – the environment, sustainability and climate change are such issues. These issues have social justice at their core and for this reason, this book contains a chapter (Chapter 5) that reflects on this. In the same way, children's experience of social media, TikTok, YouTube and other online content is ubiquitous and inevitable. One chapter (Chapter 9) in this book considers how inclusion can be supported through critical literacy approaches.

Reader identity

Reading for pleasure, according to Parry and Taylor (2018) is not a separate issue, but one that is a fundamental part of children's emerging identities and their outlook on literacy. Cliff Hodges (2015) observed that children talked about their parents', grandparents' or family members' influence on their reading. While Kucirkova and Cremin (2020, p. 6) acknowledge the influence of family members as important, they argue that to nurture positive reader identities in pupils, there should be an understanding of the "shared social space that exists between children's, parents' and teachers' reading lives." This helps bridge the dialogue between school, home and pupil as well as the possibility of recognising diversity and commonality between the reading practices. From this, the reader identity can continue to be shaped over time.

Knowing our pupils' views in more detail can help teachers consider their practices and the needs of their pupils more effectively, possibly leading to reading-for-pleasure practices within all classrooms.

According to Wagner (2020), children, through interaction and talk about texts, construct ideas about what reading is and who they are as readers. These concepts of who they are as readers are reading identities, constructed by meaning and experiences through their reading (Wagner, 2018). Collier (2010) cites multiple authors to surmise that identity and literacy are intimately linked and that it is through this practice (reading, writing, use of multi-model texts) that children can draw on their own identity, developing and reshaping it.

The challenge

There is now a plethora of research papers and initiatives that have explored the benefits of all children having equitable access to practices and resources that can support reading for pleasure. However, teachers are very much aware of the barriers they face to both implementing initiatives and ensuring funding for the regular updating of children's literature. Perhaps the most significant tension that teachers identify is the pressure of internal and external accountability regimes (Carter, 2020; Moss, 2017) and the relentless nature of the testing and standards agenda. Whilst we know there is a clear link between reading for pleasure and raised academic achievement (Organisation for Economic Co-operation and Development, 2016), this link is not always immediate. The "quick fix" around reading standards is often the first to be reached rather than considering a culture change across a school.

Hempel-Jorgensen et al. (2018) outline the tension between instructional practices and reading-for-pleasure practices, and this will be explored further in Chapter 3. In addition, it has also been found that having the knowledge of effective pedagogies does not always ensure they are implemented in a way that all children can benefit from. Hempel-Jorgensen et al. (2018) found that in the classrooms they studied, children who entered the class as readers, who read for pleasure and purpose, left the class at the end of the academic year, having benefited from the reading-for-pleasure practices but for children who entered the class not seeing themselves as readers and who did not meet the expected standards for reading, left the classroom, at the end of the academic year with similar attitudes to reading than when had entered it: the reading for pleasure practices had not impacted on them in the same way for a number of reasons. This was observed in classrooms in areas of high socio-economic deprivation but it is a useful study by which to reflect on exactly how reading for pleasure pedagogies impact and acknowledge the different individual needs and circumstances of typically diverse classrooms. This will be explored further in subsequent chapters.

It is worth noting that the current National Curriculum for English (Department for Education 2013) states clearly in its introductory "Purpose of study" that "through reading in particular, pupils have a chance to develop culturally, emotionally, intellectually, socially and spiritually. Literature, especially, plays a key role in such development." In the aims, it states that pupils should "develop the habit of reading widely and often, for both pleasure and information" and so enshrined in law is the requirement for reading for pleasure to be a focus! In the attainment targets that follow, in each year group there is a statement about the importance of, and requirement to, develop children's "love" of reading.

The Ofsted Research Review Series (Office for Standards in Education, 2022) focused on English and made mention of reading for pleasure, although this came after it had set out the approach to the importance of phonics and early reading. It makes the claim that reading for pleasure is more likely to develop if children become "accomplished readers early" and so the thrust of the report is to ensure children master the skills and knowledge of reading. The report seems to miss that children can be readers for pleasure long before they master the skills of decoding. The Ofsted review views reading in one particular way and presents one ideological positioning of reading and whilst this is certainly valid, there are many other ways to understand reading. In Chapter 3 children with disabilities who may never "read" in the Ofsted sense of the word, are still able to read for pleasure, will be discussed and approaches explored. The report also touches on ideas of motivation for reading and the difficulties of "short term motivation" that do not lead to longer-term motivation for reading referencing studies by Toste et al. (2020) and Baker and Scher (2002). Chapter 6 will continue this discussion about the role of motivation and its connection to reading for pleasure. Interestingly, whilst the 2022 Ofsted report mentions children with Special Needs and/or Disabilities, it only does so in relation to ensuring these children have lots of repetition in their phonics learning. The needs of minoritised groups are not mentioned.

Children's voice

Most policy, government reports, curricular and guidance documents that direct primary education appear to see children as objects to be acted upon rather than unique individuals with their own agency and identities (Carter, 2019). This book deliberately aims to position the child as the expert of their own learning and therefore listening to the voice of the child becomes a key guiding principle of practice. The authors in this book are not suggesting that we ignore policy, research evidence and curricula, but that when we plan our approach to these, we also consider the "wisdom" of children. Each chapter will feature case studies which include children's ideas and points of view about the focus area of each chapter and these will be intertwined with the case study data from their teachers.

The case studies were informed by House and Howe (2005, p. 81) whose research focuses on evaluation. Whilst this book is not an evaluation of reading for pleasure practices, the case studies are very much in line with their view of evaluation as "democratic" and so "incorporat[ing] the views of insiders and outsiders [and] giv[ing] voice to the marginal and excluded." Greene (1997, p. 541) proposes that such research can give voice to "the normally silenced and can poignantly illuminate what is typically masked." Valuing the voice of the child is, according to Rinaldi (2006, p. 156) "a way of being, of thinking of oneself in relation to others and the world, a fundamental educational value and form of educational activity." Harris (2015, p. 27) notes that children are the most affected by reading policy but the least consulted. She highlights that the voice of the child is capable of "provoking educators to question their own assumptions" and in particular, in revealing "unintended consequences of instructional choice" and this highlights why we deliberately worked alongside children in the development of this book. There are many precedents in reading research where children have had their voices heard through their participation. In Carter's (2019) study about the phonics screening check, the views of children about how they learnt to read were explored, finding many of the children did not make the link between their phonics learning and reading. In Levy's (2009) study, she found how the introduction of graded readers narrowed children's definitions of reading and in Hanke's (2014, p. 143) study of children's views of guided reading, it was found that "pupils could misinterpret teachers' intentions" and so reduce the benefits of the approach.

Methodology for the case studies used throughout the book

The case studies in this book focus on children's ideas and views about reading, children's literature and reading for pleasure. The case studies also highlight the practises of their teachers and, in one case study, of the school librarian (see Chapter 4). The studies are drawn from a range of schools, each serving different communities ensuring a wide diversity of children, parents and teachers. Teachers were asked to select children for focus groups using Gemma Moss' (2000) categorisations: children who can read and do; children who can read but don't; children who can't read but do and children who can't read and don't read. Teachers were also asked to ensure the focus groups reflected the diversity within their school. Children from early years, lower and upper primary classes were included in the case study focus groups. Children's ideas and thoughts were gathered by adapting the "book blanket" reading for pleasure pedagogic approach (you can find more on this both in later chapters and also on the Open University Reading for Pleasure website https://ourfp.org/eop/book-blankets/), alongside a range of discussion prompts that aimed to elicit conversations about reading and books.

How to use this book

The authors of this book, teachers and researchers, hope this book, *Putting Social Justice and Equity at the Heart of Reading for Pleasure: Tools, tips and research to support professionals in primary classrooms.as a practical guide for teachers* serves as a starting point resource focused on fostering reading for pleasure, enhancing representation, and promoting social justice within the classroom. Throughout the book, you will be encouraged to reflect on your current school practices in ensuring that all students see themselves as readers who read for pleasure and purpose. You do not have to start on page one and read until you finish! You are encouraged to dip in and out of each chapter. Start with the chapter title that most interests you – ignore the chapters you feel you already know a lot about. You can perhaps return to these for some "skim reading" to check whether there is anything new in the chapter that might be useful in your context. You are encouraged to critically reflect on your own practices and then make intentional choices that promote equity and inclusivity. Whether you are a novice teacher or a seasoned educator, this book offers some valuable tools and actionable steps to transform your classroom into a vibrant community of readers and critical thinkers, who are socially aware and culturally competent.

Final thoughts

We hope you will enjoy reading this book – and hope you have picked it up because you want to read it, or because it has been recommended as a "good read" or because someone has read a part of it aloud to you and you want to read a bit more for yourself. We also hope that there is something in this book that you can take away and take into your classroom. This may be an idea, a piece of research you have not heard of before, a strategy or approach or a quote from a child or teacher. We hope you will be both affirmed and challenged.

References

Ainscow, M. (2017) 'Promoting inclusion and equity in education: Lessons from international experiences', *Nordic Journal of Studies in Educational Policy*, 6(1), pp. 7–16. [Accessed 01 June 2023].

Baker, L. and Scher, D. (2002) 'Beginning readers' motivation for reading in relation to parental beliefs and home reading experiences', *Reading Psychology*, 23(4), pp. 239–269.

Bishop, R.S. (1990) 'Mirrors, windows, and sliding glass doors', *Perspectives*, 6(3), pp. ix–xi.

Book Trust (2023) The Benefits of Reading. Available from: https://www.booktrust.org.uk/globalassets/resources/research/benefits-of-reading-booktrust-2023.pdf?

Breadmore, H., Vardy, E., Cunningham, A., Kwok, R. and Carroll, J. (2019) *Literacy development: Evidence review*. London: Education Endowment Foundation.

Brice-Heath, S. (1983) *Ways with words*. Cambridge, UK: Cambridge University Press.

Carter, J. (2019) 'Listening to the voices of children: An illuminative evaluation of the teaching of early reading in the light of the phonics screening check', *Literacy*, 53(1), pp. 49–57.

Carter, J. (2020) 'The assessment has become the curriculum: Teachers' views on the phonics screening check in England', *British Educational Research Journal*, 46(3), pp. 593–609.

Castles, A., Rastle, K. and Nation, K. (2018) 'Ending the reading wars: Reading acquisition from novice to expert', *Psychological Science in the Public Interest*, 19(1), pp. 5–51.

Centre for Literacy in Primary Education (2022) *Reflecting realities: Survey of ethnic representation within UK children's literature 2017-2021*. Available from: https://clpe.org.uk/system/files/2022-11/CLPE%20Reflecting%20Reality%202022%20WEB_0.pdf [Accessed on 21 November 2024].

Chan, M. (2023) Picturebooks and children's understanding of disability: Incorporating the perspectives of primary school teachers, BERA. Available from: https://www.bera.ac.uk/blog/picturebooks-and-childrens-understanding-of-disability-incorporating-the-perspectives-of-primary-school-teachers [Accessed 08 May 24].

Cliff Hodges, G. (2015) *Researching and teaching reading developing pedagogy through critical enquiry*. London: Routledge. [Accessed 17 August 23].

Collier, D.R. (2010) 'Journey to becoming a writer: Review of research about children's identities as writers', *Language and Literacy: An e-Journal*, 12(1), pp. 1-18. [Accessed 04 September 23].

Cremin, T., Mottram, M., Powell, S., Collins, R. and Safford K. (2014) *Building communities of engaged readers: Reading for pleasure*. London and NY: Routledge.

Department for Education (2013) *National curriculum in England: Primary curriculum*. London: DfE.

Department for Education (2024) PIRLS 2021: National Report for England Research report. Available from: PIRLS 2021: National Report for England (publishing.service.gov.uk). [Accessed 29 July 2023].

Duke, N.K. and Cartwright, K.B. (2021) 'The science of reading progresses: Communicating advances beyond the simple view of reading', *Reading Research Quarterly*, 56(S1), pp. 25-44. https://doi.org/10.1002/rrq.411

Ellis, S. and Smith, V. (2017) 'Assessment, teacher education and the emergence of professional expertise', *Literacy*, 51(2), pp. 84-93.

Enriquez, G. (2021) 'Foggy mirrors, tiny windows, and heavy doors: Beyond diverse books toward meaningful literacy instruction', *The Reading Teacher* [online], 75(1), pp. 103-106. [Accessed 24 October 23].

Fletcher, K.L. and Reese, E. (2005) 'Picture book reading with young children: A conceptual framework', *Developmental Review*, 25(1), pp. 64-103.

Gough, P.B. and Tunmer, W.E. (1986) 'Decoding, reading and reading disability', *Remedial and Special Education* 7, pp. 6-10.

Greene, J. (1997) 'Stakeholder participation and utilization in program evaluation', *Evaluation Review*, 12, pp. 91-116.

Hague, S. (2020) *Diversity and inclusion in schools*. Pearson Schools.

Hanke, V. (2014) 'Guided reading: Young pupils' perspectives on classroom practice', *Literacy*, 48(3), pp. 136-143.

Harris, P. (2015) 'Words and stuff': Exploring children's perspectives of classroom reading in the early school years', *Australian Journal of Language and Literacy*, 28(1), pp. 27-37.

Heineke, A.J., Papola-Ellis, A. and Elliott, J. (2022) 'Using texts as mirrors: The power of readers seeing themselves', *The Reading Teacher* [online], 76(3), pp. 277-284. [Accessed 24 April 24].

Hempel-Jorgensen, A., Cremin, T., Harris, D. and Chamberlain, L. (2018) 'Pedagogy for reading for pleasure in low socio-economic primary schools: Beyond 'pedagogy of poverty'?', *Literacy*, 52(2), pp. 86-94.

House, E. and Howe, K. (2005) Deliberative democratic evaluation in practice. In: Sage benchmarks in social research, *evaluation research methods*. Vol. 2. London: Sage, pp. 80-97.

Kucirkova, N. and Cremin, T. (2020) *Children Reading for pleasure in the digital age: Mapping reader engagement*. London: SAGE Publications Ltd. [Accessed 04 September 2023].

Leahy, M.A. and Foley, B.C. (2018) 'Diversity in children's literature', *World Journal of Educational Research* [online], 5(2). pp. 172-183 [Accessed 01 June 2023].

Levy, R. (2009) 'Children's perceptions of reading and the use of reading scheme texts', *Cambridge Journal of Education*, 39(3), pp. 361-377.

Levy, R. (2011) *Young children reading at home and at school*. London: Sage.

Levy, R. and Hall, M. (2021) *Family literacies: Reading with young children*. London: Routledge.

Milton, M. and Forlin, C. (2017). *Inclusive principles and practices in literacy education*. Leeds: Emerald Group Publishing.

Moss, G. (2000) 'Raising boys' attainment in literacy: Some principles for intervention', *Reading*, 34(3), pp. 101-106.

Moss, G. (2009) 'The politics of literacy in the context of large-scale education reform', *Research Papers in Education*, 24(2), pp. 155-174.

Moss, G. (2017) 'Reimagining the future in the light of the past', *Literacy*, 51(2), pp. 56-64.

Moss, G. and Huxford, L. (2007) 'Exploring literacy policy-making from the inside out', in *Education policy making*. London: Routledge Falmer.

Moxnes, A.R. and Osgood, J. (2018) 'Sticky stories from the classroom: From reflection to diffraction in early childhood teacher education', *Contemporary Issues in Early Childhood*, 19(3), pp. 297-309.

Munns, G., Sawyer, W. and Cole, B. (eds.). (2013). *Exemplary teachers of students in poverty* (1st ed.). Routledge. https://doi.org/10.4324/9780203076408

Nilholm, C. (2020). 'Research about inclusive education in 2020 - How can we improve our theories in order to change practice?', *European Journal of Special Needs Education*, 36, pp. 1-13.

Office for Standards in Education (2022) *Research review series: English*. Available from: https://www.gov.uk/government/publications/curriculum-research-review-series-english/curriculum-research-review-series-english [Accessed 20 November 2024]

Organisation for Economic Co-operation and Development. (2016). *PISA 2015 results (volume I): Excellence and equity in education*. Paris: OECD Publishing.

Parry, B. and Taylor, L. (2018) 'Readers in the round: Children's holistic engagements with texts', *Literacy*, 52(2), pp. 103-110.

Ramdarshan Bold, M. (2022) Representation of people of colour among children's book creators in the UK (2020-2021). Available from: https://www.booktrust.org.uk/globalassets/resources/booktrust-represents/2022/research-reports/booktrust-represents-representation-of-people-of-colour-among-childrens-book-creators-in-the-uk.pdf [Accessed on 21 November, 2024].

Rinaldi, C. (2006) *In dialogue with Reggio Emilia: Listening, researching and learning*. London: Routledge, Taylor and Francis.

Rose, J. (2006) *The independent review of the teaching of early reading*. London: DCSF.

Scarborough, H.S. (2001). 'Connecting early language and literacy to later reading (dis)abilities: Evidence, theory, and practice', in Neuman, S.B. and Dickinson, D.K. (eds.) *Handbook of early literacy research*. Guilford Press: New York, Vol. 1, pp. 97-110.

Street, B. (1984) *Literacy in theory and practice. Street*. New York: Cambridge University Press.

Sullivan, A. and Brown, M. (2013) *Social inequalities in cognitive scores at age 16: The role of reading. (CLS working papers '13/10)*. London, UK: Centre for Longitudinal Studies, Institute of Education, University College London.

Torgerson, C.J., Brookes, G. and Hall, J. (2006) *A systematic review of the literature on the use of phonics in the teaching of reading and spelling*. London: DFES.

Torgerson, C., Brooks, G, Gascoine, L. and Higgins, S. (2019) Phonics: Reading policy and the evidence of effectiveness from a systematic 'tertiary' review.†*Research Papers in Education*, 34 (2), pp. 208-238.

Toste, J.R., Didion, L., Peng, P., Filderman, M.J. and McClelland, A.M. (2020) 'A meta-analytic review of the relations between motivation and reading achievement for K-12 students, *Review of Educational Research*, 90(3), pp. 420-456.

UNESCO (2017) A Guide for ensuring inclusion and equity in education. Available from: https://policytoolbox.iiep.unesco.org/library/QEGJ5RNC [Accessed 01 June 2024].

Wagner, C. (2018) 'Being bilingual, being a reader: Prekindergarten dual language learners' reading identities', *Journal of Early Childhood Literacy*, 18(1), pp. 5-37.

Wagner, C. (2020) 'Seeing and nurturing young children's reading identities', *Journal of Language & Literacy Education*, 16, pp. 1-14.

2 What counts as reading?

Dan Northover

Introduction

'If as teachers we hold the reading reins too tightly and don't ensure that our reading for pleasure pedagogy is reader-led, reader-directed and reader-owned, we will never create communities of engaged readers. Honouring children's choice of texts is key, as is allowing them to exercise their rights as readers.'

(Cremin, 2019, p. 6)

This chapter seeks to explore some key aspects of children's volitional reading by first considering *why* children might choose to read. This first section explores what reading for pleasure might be, and why some children may think this might not be for them, before going on to consider how reading might be viewed as reading for purpose, as well as for pleasure. There is also a further exploration of why some children might not view reading for pleasure or for purpose as something that is for them by considering the work of the Centre for Literacy in Primary Education's research *Reflecting Realities* (2023). Following on from this, and framed by this discussion, the chapter will then move on to explore *what* children might choose to read, taking a deliberately broad stance to consider all of the different texts that children may choose to engage with. The chapter will conclude with a consideration of how children may be supported to engage with texts to read for pleasure or for purpose as part of 'reader-led, reader-directed and reader-owned' (Cremin, 2019, p. 6) reading.

Why might children choose to read?: Reading for pleasure or purpose?

It may be useful here to explore what can constitute the idea of "reading for pleasure." We can, of course, use academic definitions but what might be more useful here is to reflect on what it means to *you* in reality. So ... if you were asked to stop reading for a moment and imagine someone "reading for pleasure," what would that look like to you? Just hold that picture in your head – what are they doing? Where are they? Are they inside or outside? What is the temperature like? Are they standing up, sitting at a table, leisurely reclining, or even lying down? What are they reading?

There might have been a number of different scenarios that different people may have pictured; however, when I have asked this question a number of times to teachers and pre-service teachers, the answers are often variations on the following examples:

- Someone lying on a sunbed by a swimming pool in the blazing sunshine sipping a nice cool drink and reading a novel;
- Someone wrapped up warm and reclining on a comfy chair or sofa (perhaps in front of a warming fire) and reading a novel;
- Someone cocooned in a duvet in bed with soft lighting (main lights off and curtains drawn) and reading a novel.

While these are all perfectly valid examples of someone "reading for pleasure," they are perhaps presenting a certain stereotypical viewpoint of what "reading for pleasure" can look like, and with what sort of text it can take place with. The issue here is that this can often mean that if an individual does not undertake any of the scenarios above, then they may assume that they don't in fact "read for pleasure" themselves. This may well be the case with children in the classroom as well. Those children who don't consider themselves children who "read for pleasure" may well be those children whose ideas about what "reading for pleasure" looks like do not match with what they themselves do in reality. Perhaps then, it might be useful to begin to try and tease apart what we consider to be the "pleasure" part in reading for pleasure.

When do you read?

Before exploring where *pleasure* can be found in reading, it might first be useful to consider what reading is done across a day, whether for pleasure or not. Rather than pleasure here, the first step might be to consider the wide range of reading that is engaged with. One of the ways to do this is to complete a "Reading River" (Cremin, 2019), which is a tool to consider all the reading that you might do on a typical day from when you wake up in the morning to when you go to sleep at night - there's a great example from Jon Biddle that is available on the Open University's Reading for Pleasure website (https://ourfp.org/eop/reading-rivers/). This can be a particularly helpful activity to conceptualise "reading" and what "reading" can be in a broader sense than just "reading for pleasure" at this stage.

Why do you read?

It is helpful to engage in another exercise that is borrowed from the excellent Centre for Literacy in Primary Education's (CLPE) workshop 'The Power of a Rich Reading Classroom - Reflecting Realities, Nurturing Reader Identity' (https://clpe.org.uk/training) by considering and finishing the following statement:

I read because ...

When first completing this exercise, it may be tempting to use read as a synonym for "read for pleasure," and while that may be useful for some to reflect on, those who don't read for pleasure may well see this as a clear "opt out" moment and think *'well I don't read for pleasure, so this isn't for me'*. This exercise really is aimed not to ask about reading for pleasure, but more about what reading you actually do and why. You may read for comfort, or for exhilaration, or for the pure unadulterated joy of written prose, or you may read because you are told that you have to, within a work or school context. You may read because you are *'addicted to your socials'* or have various emails to reply to on a daily basis, or because you are currently interested in new healthy recipes to help improve your fitness levels.

Try asking children in your class to complete this same statement: I read because …

Look carefully at the responses, bearing in mind children are very adept at *'telling you what they think you want to hear'*!

You may well have tried finishing the first statement by saying that "it depends …" because you read different things for different reasons across a day, a week or a year, and so now have a go at the following activity by filling in the blank and completing the sentence a number of times:

I read _____ because …

This seems like a really simple exercise to complete, but when completing it, try to think of every single example of when you read something and why you were reading it. Here's a personal example of me as a reader and my many reading selves:

- I read children's fiction because it is entertaining and wise and teaches us about the world around us and because it is part of my job to be able to recommend texts to others.
- I read children's literature because it has been recommended to me by someone else and I want to discuss the book with them once I have finished reading it.
- I read academic literature about literacy because I find it interesting and because it is part of my job and supports my teaching and research.
- I read fiction literature in general because I enjoy exploring the worlds of the characters and reading interesting stories.
- I read education policy literature because it is part of my job and supports my teaching and research.
- I read sports news articles because I am interested in one particular football club but also because it helps me to relax to read about other things I don't particularly care about (like golf for example!).
- I read crime thriller novels because I particularly like really wanting to know what happens next and not being particularly invested in the characters.
- I read online current newspaper articles as I am interested in finding out what is happening across the UK and the rest of the world.
- I read regular update emails and messages from my children's school because they tell about what they are getting up to and give me useful information.
- I read online articles about technology because my brother is interested in technology and so my new knowledge can form part of our conversations together.
- I read social media through my professional account because I like to connect with, and learn from, other education professionals working in schools and universities.
- I read online education blog posts because I like to and learn from other education professionals working in schools and universities.

- I read stories aloud because this can help share stories with other people, either to help develop others' knowledge of texts at work, or to help my children to go to sleep at night!
- I read information signs and timetables because they help me navigate the world around me.
- I read cookery books with my wife because we like to discuss the recipes that we could (but rarely actually do!) make.
- I read emails through my work account because this allows me to communicate with other people about important parts of my job.
- I read online reviews of products because it helps me to make a decision when I am buying something new.
- I read the backs of cereal packets when I am eating my breakfast because I find it relaxing to allow my brain to switch off and concentrate on reading.
- I read text messages from friends and family to allow me to communicate regularly with them.

Try asking the children in your class to complete the following statement:

I read _____ because ...

You may like to provide some examples from your own list so children are clear about what can be included.

Reading for pleasure or reading for purpose?

After undertaking the activity above, it might be helpful to think about what some of the different purposes of reading are – why might we choose to read? In my example, part of the reading is undertaken for professional reasons – staying abreast of current developments in relation to a role, communicating with others and personal development. Another reason for some of the reading might include aspects relating to enjoyment and/or interests – reading about things that the reader is interested in. A further reason for some of the reading may be around necessity – helping to inform the reader about the world around them in an immediate sense. Finally, some of the reading seems to be linked to connections with others – either reading to support communication (either directly or indirectly) or in fact shared reading together. It therefore seems that there may be a number of different purposes for reading, and drawing on his experiences as a primary headteacher when considering his school's reading offer, Simon Smith (Smith, 2018; Smith, 2019) outlines seven potential purposes for reading:

1. Read to learn something new
2. Read to make us think
3. Read to be entertained
4. Read to be inspired
5. Read to inform
6. Read to help us understand others better (from Anne Thompson on X @ALibraryLady)
7. Read to help us understand ourselves (courtesy of Teresa Cremin).

While this may not be a definitive list and it could be argued that there could be overlap between the different purposes, this is an excellent starting point to generate discussion about *why* we might choose to read. This will be different for different teachers, and we might also expect children to come up with a different number of reasons why they might choose to read.

Looking back at your list from the previous exercise, try now to categorise some of the reading that you do into different purposes to come up with your own purposes for a reading list. You might then like to share that list with children in your class and ask them to do their own lists, or even work together as a class to explore your list and work together to create a class list.

This idea of "reading for purpose" can be seen in children's book publisher Farshore's recent research report entitled 'Reading for Pleasure and Purpose', where they suggest that "for many parents," "reading for purpose" may resonate more strongly than "reading for pleasure" (Farshore, 2022, p. 1). They go on to suggest that "messaging that recognises both may be a more inclusive way to encourage reading to children" (Farshore, 2022, p. 1) (see Chapter 7 for more discussion on reading for pleasure and families). I think this is a fundamental point that can be considered in relation to the way that we position reading and what reading can encompass when we are thinking about reading with the children in our classroom.

When exploring children's reading in the classroom, Moss (2000, p. 102) found that children may fall into three categories of readers: children who *'can't yet and don't'* read, children who *'can and do'* read and children who *'can and don't'* read. This may prove a useful exercise to undertake when thinking about the children in your class, although as we are focusing on reading for pleasure here, as opposed to reading instruction, I would also suggest adding in another category, children who *'can't yet and do'* read, which may be useful to consider if we think of those children who may choose to look at books that they may not be able to read all or even any of the words in. I think this is an important distinction when thinking about reading for pleasure; otherwise, we may conflate some potentially relevant principles of reading instruction, such as careful text selection matched to the attainment level of the reader, with reading for pleasure which should be "reader-led, informal, social and with texts that tempt" (Cremin, 2019, p. 6). The importance of children's agency within reading for pleasure is well-established (Cremin and Scholes, 2024; Guthrie et al., 2007; Lockwood, 2008; McGeown and Wilkinson, 2021; Oxley and McGeown, 2023; Reedy and De Carvalho, 2021) and having a real and respected choice is a crucial part of tempting children into reading. As teachers encouraging children to read, we should aim to facilitate *any* engagement with *any* text in *any* way, and we should aim to become a "noticing teacher" when children are reading and explicitly positively reinforce their choices. If this is not our default position, we may end up with growing numbers of children who *'can't yet and don't'* and *'can and don't'* choose to read, and who may definitively decide that reading is not an activity that is for them and is something to pretend to do only when asked. There is an example of this in Beth Bacon's book, *I Hate Reading: How to Read When You'd Rather Not*, which explores reading through the words of her two sons who discuss not liking reading and what to do about it in a humorous exploration of how to "read" when you don't really want to, which they sum up with the following advice, "Eyes on book. Bum on chair. Eyes side to side, side to side, side to side. (Repeat for 20 mins)" (Bacon, 2020).

This portrayal of reading in the classroom may well chime with some of you as reflective of children who either *'can't yet and don't'* read, or those who *'can and don't'* read, and we certainly may not expect these children to choose to read or even particularly enjoy reading during independent reading time in school. However, one of Beth Bacon's sons also recounts a time when he "got caught NOT reading" by his teacher in Year One when he was looking at the pictures:

> *'Then the teacher, Miss González, asked, 'Henry, are you just looking at the pictures?' And I was. The pictures were so good. I looked up at Miss González, then turned to a page with lots of words and I put my eyeballs back on the book. She left me alone'.*

(Bacon, 2020)

This is an interesting recount as I would argue that Henry *was* reading here – he was reading for pleasure. He was engaging with a text and gaining enjoyment from looking at the pictures which is a perfectly valid way to explore a book. The distinction here again between reading instruction and reading for pleasure may be an important one to consider (see Chapter 3 for a fuller discussion of this distinction).

How do you make the distinction between reading instruction and reading for pleasure in your classroom? What would you say is the difference between the two? Have you asked your children what they think the difference between reading instruction and reading for pleasure is?

When considering the example of Henry's reading discussed above, it might be useful to consider Pennac's (2006) suggestion that children should be in control of their own reading. In his book *The Rights of the Reader*, Daniel Pennac (2006) suggests that, as adults, *'when it comes to reading, we grant ourselves every right in the book, including those we withhold from the young people we claim to be teaching'*, and goes on to argue for ten rights for our young readers, and I have included my favourites from his list as an example below:

1   The right not to read.
2   The right to skip.
3   The right not to finish a book.
4   The right to read it again.
5   The right to read anything.

All ten rights have been put into a poster that has illustrations from Quentin Blake and is available to download from the National Literacy Trust (https://cdn.literacytrust.org.uk/media/documents/HO4_Rights_of_the_reader.pdf). This resource could be an excellent starting point to discuss what rights children should have in relation to their own reading for pleasure as part of a staff meeting and might also be a great starting point for teachers to work with their children to create their own class set of the rights that their children have. Pennac (2006) ends his list of rights with a call to action by arguing that *'if we want our sons, our daughters, all young people to read, we must grant them the same rights we grant ourselves'*.

Reading reflecting realities

One possible reason why "reading for pleasure" or "reading for purpose" might be viewed as something that some children do not identify with could be in part due to the fact that some children may not see themselves reflected in the books that they are reading, with Crisp et al.

(2016, p. 29) arguing that "the world depicted in children's books is overwhelmingly white [and shows] a world that is predominantly upper middle class, heterosexual, non-disabled, English-speaking, and male." As explored in Chapters 1 and 4, this is an issue as Rudine Sims Bishop (1990, pp. ix–x) explains in her seminal article: 'when children cannot find themselves reflected in the books they read, or when the images they see are distorted, negative or laughable, they learn a powerful lesson about how they are devalued in the society of which they are a part.' Bishop (1990, p. ix) goes on to explain how 'books can be windows, offering views of worlds that may be real or imagined, familiar or strange.' As well as windows, she suggests that books can also be "sliding glass doors, and readers have only to walk through in imagination to become part of whatever world has been created and recreated by the author" (Bishop, 1990, p. ix). Finally, she suggests that "when lighting conditions are just right, however, a window can also be a mirror … and readers often seek their mirrors in books" (Bishop, 1990, p. ix).

In February 2018, the Centre for Literacy in Primary Education (CLPE) launched their "Reflecting Realities" initiative, which aimed to "quantify and evaluate the extent and quality of ethnic representation in children's publishing in the UK" (CLPE, 2018, p. 4) for the first time. When considering the publishing data from 2017, they found that while 32% of school-age pupils were from racially minoritised backgrounds, only 1% of the children's books published had a racially minoritised main character, and only 4% of the children's books published featured any racially minoritised characters at all (CLPE, 2018). This disparity between the make-up of the UK population and the books that were being produced for its young readers led CLPE (2018, p. 10) to call for future books being published to better reflect the UK population, "not as a tick box exercise but as a meaningful and accurate representation of the interconnected, diverse society within which our children are growing up." CLPE have continued to conduct annual Reflecting Realties reports, and the latest report surveying the children's literature published across a year suggests that "30% of the children's picture books, fiction and non-fiction titles published in 2022 featured racially minoritised characters, compared to 20% in 2021, 15% in 2020, 10% in 2019, 7% in 2018 and 4% in 2017" (CLPE, 2023, p. 6), while children's books that featured a "main character from a racially minoritised background has increased to 14%, compared to 9% in 2021, 8% in 2020, 5% in 2019, 4% in 2018 and 1% in 2017" (CLPE, 2023, p. 8). When reflecting on the impact that the Reflecting Realities reports have had on the children's books being published, CLPE (2023, p. 7) state that:

> A greater volume of books in principle should equate to the possibility for young readers to encounter a greater breadth of titles that showcase presence across genres, convey different story worlds, explore a variation of themes, and depict wide ranging portrayals. A greater volume of books should create the opportunity for varied and nuanced representations of racially minoritised individuals and communities. It should enable representations that normalise and make mainstream characters that, in the past, have typically either been problematically portrayed, marginalised or were never even brought to life at all within the pages of the books.

And yet CLPE's (2018; 2019; 2020; 2021; 2022; 2023) current and previous reports have shown that there is still work to be done to ensure that we can answer the following question: "Do the portrayals we encounter in the literature we consume meaningfully and appropriately reflect the realities of all readers?" (CLPE, 2023, p. 7), with an increase in representation perhaps meaning that there is a "surplus production of generic representations that lack depth at best or are poorly rendered or problematic portrayals at worst" (CLPE, 2023, p. 7). Building on the ideas of Rudine Sims Bishop (1990, p. ix) assertion that "when lighting conditions are just right, however, a window can also be a mirror ... and readers often seek their mirrors in books," Enriquez (2021) argues that if we are aiming to consider books as mirrors for the children who read them, this means that the books should align with their identities and lived experiences. However, she cautions that if the only way that a book reflects a child is through physical appearance, this may be creating a "foggy mirror" that only reflects "vague contours of the identities and lived experiences that comprise a child's reality," and therefore "if we present [children] with foggy mirrors, we might also be stereotyping them and their families" (Enriquez, 2021, p. 104). There's an excellent illustrated example of this phenomenon in action within the pages of Jerry Craft's (2019) fantastic and award-winning graphic novel, "*New Kid.*" Within the book, the librarian offers a recommended book to one of the few Black children at a prestigious private school, Maury, commenting that it has *'won all the major awards for African American literature'* and saying to him that *'You're really going to identify with DaQuell, the protagonist. He's suffered so much, growing up in poverty without a father'*, to which Maury replies, while handing the book back, *Ummm ... thanks Miss Brickner, but my dad is the CEO of a Fortune 500 company*. The main character, Jordan Banks, reflects on this episode with his mini summary on the next few pages, which he titles *Judging Kids by the Covers of their Books!*, suggesting that what he calls *'Mainstream books'* have covers that have *'cool, colourful illustrations full of magic and hope'* and are filled with plots that can be summarised as *'a thrilling, magical tale that is sure to inspire readers of all ages to never give up until they have found the treasure they seek'*, as opposed to African American books which have covers that have *'a depressing photograph full of realism and hopelessness'* and have plots that are *'a gritty, urban reminder of the grit of today's urban grittiness'*.

The CLPE reports (2018; 2019; 2020; 2021; 2022; 2023) do show us though that things are beginning to change, and inspired by the character Jordan Banks (and of course his creator Jerry Craft!), here's a quick list of ten recently published children's fantasy books/series that contain a Black main character:

1 Tọlá Okogwu – Onyeka and the Academy of the Sun; Onyeka and the Rise of the Rebels; Onyeka and the Heroes of the Dawn; Onyeka and the Secret Superhero: World Book Day 2024
2 Kara West and Leeza Hernandez (illustrator) – Mia Mayhem Is a Superhero!; Mia Mayhem Learns to Fly!; Mia Mayhem vs. the Super Bully; Mia Mayhem Breaks Down Walls; Mia Mayhem Stops Time!; Mia Mayhem vs. the Mighty Robot; Mia Mayhem Gets X-Ray Specs; Mia Mayhem Steals the Show!; Mia Mayhem and the Super Family Field Day; Mia Mayhem and the Super Switcheroo; Mia Mayhem Rides the Waves; Mia Mayhem and the Cat Burglar; Mia Mayhem and the Wild Garden
3 Dhonielle Clayton – The Marvellers; The Memory Thieves; The Deadly Fates (expected 2025)
4 Kalynn Bayron – The Vanquishers; The Vanquishers: Secret of the Reaping; Rise of the Wrecking Crew (expected 2024)

What counts as reading? 23

5   Angie Thomas – Nic Blake and the Remarkables: The Manifestor Prophecy; The Book of Anansi
6   B.B. Alston – Amari and the Night Brothers; Amari and the Great Game; Amari and the Despicable Wonders
7   Jason A. Reynolds and Pablo Leon (illustrator) – Miles Morales: Shock Waves (A Spider-man Graphic Novel); Miles Morales: Stranger Tides (A Spiderman Graphic Novel)
8   Kwame Mbalia – Tristan Strong Punches a Hole in the Sky (Rick Riordan Presents); Tristan Strong Destroys the World (Rick Riordan Presents); Tristan Strong Keeps on Punching (Rick Riordan Presents)
9   Lamar Giles and Dapo Adeola (illustrator) – The Last Last-Day-of-Summer; The Last Mirror on the Left; The Last Chance for Logan County
10 Jason Reynolds and Raúl the Third (illustrator) – Stuntboy, In the Meantime; Stuntboy, In-between Time

As well as building our own knowledge of children's literature to be able to make recommendations like the list above, Enriquez (2021, p. 104) suggests that in order to allow children to use books as mirrors, we need to do two things:

- Get to know the rich, multi-faceted identities of each of our [children] and the topics, issues, and interests that are meaningful to them.
- Include [children] in the process of diversifying the classroom library. Ask them what characters … and what cultures and languages they would like to see reflected in those texts.

Perhaps if the fictional librarian from Jerry Craft's *"New Kid"* had taken Enriquez's (2021) advice, she would have been able to offer Jordan a list of fantasy books featuring African American main characters that he simply didn't believe existed.

As well as acting as mirrors, Bishop (1990, p. ix) reminds us that "books can be windows, offering views of worlds that may be real or imagined, familiar or strange." When considering this notion, Enriquez (2021, p. 104) suggests that if the windows are "tiny windows … limited in scope and size," how much of a view do they actually provide? She goes on to argue that when ethnically diverse books are only brought into the classroom for specific units of work (such as Black History month in the UK, for example) 'the window into other worlds shrinks to a tiny size, giving [children] only a peek, diminishing complex identities to stereotypes, diminishing rich experiences to broad generalizations, and significantly limiting possibilities for [children's] learning' (Enriquez, 2021, p. 104). As well as being a window, Bishop (1990, p. ix) suggests for a book to become a sliding glass door, "readers have only to walk through in imagination to become part of whatever world has been created and recreated by the author." However, Enriquez (2021, p. 105) argues that 'sometimes, though, those doors are heavy and [children] need our help to push them open far enough to walk through.' In order to try and avoid these "tiny windows" and "heavy doors," Enriquez (2021, pp. 104–5) argues that it is not simply enough to have a range of ethnically diverse books within our classroom, although I would argue that this *does* need to be the starting point. What is needed is to ensure that a wide range of books with racially minoritised people form a "constituent part of our work, making sure they are integrated meaningfully in our curriculum and instructional practices, and done so throughout the year" (Enriquez, 2021, p. 104). These books are vital, both to act as mirrors, but also to ensure that, within our reading for pleasure practices, and beyond (see Chapter 3 for a discussion of purposefully positive teaching of reading as distinct from reading for pleasure), we are supporting our children to 'push open doors and ... to fully explore worlds and lives unlike theirs ... [emphasising] the benefits of stepping through those doors, taking on the perspective of someone different from us, and communicating that diverse perspectives and experiences are truly valued and valuable' (Enriquez, 2021, p. 105).

Choosing texts that reflect realities

The next part of this chapter moves on to focus on exploring a broad range of types of texts that children may choose to read, and in light of the preceding discussion, it may be useful to consider the following questions from CLPE (2023, p. 28) across this range of text types, and in relation to your own collections of texts within your classrooms, libraries and schools:

Questions to guide considerations

Determining meaningful presence

- Do the racially minoritised characters featured in the books we stock reflect the UK population and the world at large, not as a tick box exercise but as a meaningful and accurate representation of the interconnected, diverse society within which our children are growing up?
- Are racially minoritised characters central to a broad range of narratives?
- Do racially minoritised characters exist across a range of genres and within both fiction and non-fiction?
- Are there a variation and balance of themes explored in the titles in which racially minoritised characters feature?
- Have you been attentive to the position that a racially minoritised character holds in the narrative? What position does the character hold? What is the dynamic within the cast? What is the extent of their agency and contribution to the plot?
- Have careful research and consideration been exercised to ensure respectful, nuanced and layered portrayals of racially minoritised characters?
- Are racially minoritised characters well-developed and authentically portrayed?
- How effectively is their being and personality conveyed?

Ensuring breadth and balance

- Are readers able to encounter varied portrayals of racially minoritised characters, depicted with a range of personalities and represented as experiencing a full spectrum of emotions in the books you stock?
- Is the content of our titles balanced, allowing for cultural specificity without reducing characterisations to derogatory stereotypes or one-dimensional shorthand?
- Have we assessed the balance of our stock to ensure that characters of colour are not predominantly defined by their struggle, suffering, exceptionalism or "otherness"?

Valuing the creatives

- Is there a sustained investment in both established and new authors from a range of backgrounds who are able to paint characters and worlds with the integrity that the subject matter deserves? Does your stock reflect this diversity of talent?

What might children choose to read?: Exploring a range of "texts that might tempt" children into reading

Cremin (2019, p. 6) suggests that for reading for pleasure practices and pedagogies to be successful, they must be

- Reader-led,
- Informal,
- Social, and with
- Texts that tempt

There is a key thought here with the phrase "texts that tempt," as this is all we can hope to do – tempt children into choosing to read. We cannot *make* children read for pleasure. What we can do is aim to show children that there are many ways to *be a reader*, many activities that *count as reading for pleasure* and many, many different texts that children can choose to engage with in whatever way they choose as part of their reader-led reading for pleasure.

It is vital for teachers to value children's choices about what texts *they* would like to read, even if these aren't necessarily choices that the teachers would choose for them. It is also the responsibility of teachers to try and encourage children to consider and explore the wide range of texts that are available for them to choose to read, which may involve broadening children's horizons. I often think about a Year 6 child I spoke with, as part of a reading for pleasure CPD project I was doing with a school, who was adamant that he was not a reader. He was very clear that he didn't like reading, and there was no kind of reading or text that he would be interested in reading, in or out of school. His eyes lit up, however, when another child mentioned Marvel comics, and he then said that if the school had them in the library, he would definitely want to read them! I would argue that it is part of our professional responsibility to showcase and share the wide range of reading material that is available with the children that we teach, in an attempt to support each and every child to find something that they can choose to read for pleasure, purpose or any other reason!

When considering what texts children might choose to read, the latest annual research from the National Literacy Trust (Clark et al., 2023, p. 36) shows that children are choosing to read a wide range of texts (both on paper and on screen), including

- Fiction
- Non-fiction
- Comics/graphic novels
- Magazines
- Poems
- News
- Song lyrics

As well as a variety of potential purposes for reading (as has been explored earlier in this chapter), there are also a number of potential pleasures of reading, and these pleasures may present similarly or differently across different texts, and therefore, the following section will consider what are some of the potential texts we can offer children and why these may prove pleasurable in different ways.

Narrative fiction

Narrative fiction can encompass any text that mainly uses words (some will also contain illustrations that are subservient to the text) to tell a fictional story. Therefore, this can include "early readers" or phonically decodable texts, early chapter books, novels or collections of short stories. When writing about the particular power of narrative fiction, children's author Katherine Rundell suggests that "above all, children's fiction spoke to me, and still speaks to me, of hope. The books say: look, this is what bravery looks like. Children's books say: the world is huge … They say: hope counts for something, bravery will matter, wit, empathy, love will matter" (Rundell, 2019, p. 48), and she goes on to argue that because "children's fiction necessitates distillation: at its best, it renders in their purest, most archetypal forms hope, hunger, joy, fear" (Rundell, 2019, p. 12). These compelling reasons for reading fiction may be reflected in the fact that fiction remains the most popular reading choice for children aged 8-18 in 2023 (Clark et al., 2023), and when considering narrative children's literature, Nodelman and Reimer (2003) explore some of the potential pleasures that reading stories can bring:

- Evoking emotions, whether positive or negative
- Visualising new familiar or unfamiliar people, characters or places
- Identifying with characters
- Being able to empathise with other people's different ideas, thoughts and experiences
- Enjoying a range of the different elements of stories, from familiar language patterns and plot devices, to the new and unfamiliar.
- Finding connections between different stories and also making connections with our own experiences.
- Sharing our reading with others, whether through reading aloud, or sharing our responses by talking with others about what we have read.

(see Nodelman and Reimer (2003, pp. 25-26) for a full unabridged list)

Consider the children that you know and what might be some of the "pleasures" that they would say they take from reading narrative fiction. This might be a useful activity for you to do first and then to ask the children in your class and compare your lists!

However, there will also be a number of ways that "pleasure" can be manifested in relation to all of the other reading that we engage in, and this will be something to consider as we think about the variety of other texts that children may choose to read.

Where might you find recommendations for narrative fiction?

- Inclusive Books for Children has a great website that offers categories and lists of recommended books, and they also run an annual book award: https://www.inclusivebooksforchildren.org/

What counts as reading? 27

- Reading charity BookTrust offers a whole section of their website dedicated to recommendations: https://www.booktrust.org.uk/books-and-reading/our-recommendations/, as well as an interactive book finder tool that allows for specific searches based on age and interests: https://www.booktrust.org.uk/books-and-reading/bookfinder/
- Books for Keeps is an online children's book magazine that offers recommendations and reviews, as well as articles and interviews with and by children's authors: https://booksforkeeps.co.uk/
- The Jhalak Children's and YA Prize accepts books for children, teens and young adults including picture books, chapter books, graphic novels, poetry, non-fiction and all other genres by writers of colour and aimed at young readers: https://www.jhalakprize.com/childrens-ya
- Love Reading 4 Kids offers reviews of a wide range of fiction books and includes search functions, book of the month recommendations as well as sample extracts of a number of the books: https://www.lovereading4kids.co.uk/.
- Books for Topics offer some useful "Branching Out" resources which might provide some guidance for readers to find similar books to ones that they have already read and enjoyed: https://www.booksfortopics.com/booklists/branching-out/
- Teacher Dean Boddington also has a number of useful resources that can be used in the classroom: https://misterbodd.wordpress.com/favourites/; https://misterbodd.wordpress.com/2024/07/26/read-like-your-teacher/; as well as a monthly newsletter of recommendations: https://misterbodd.wordpress.com/no-shelf-control/
- Barrington Stoke offers a great range of dyslexia-friendly books that are pitched high not only in terms of themes and content but also with simplified language for those readers who may not quite be ready for more challenging written text https://collins.co.uk/pages/barrington-stoke.
- The Open University website is an absolute treasure trove of all things reading for pleasure and in terms of book recommendations it has a texts and authors section: https://ourfp.org/texts-authors/ and an awards section that might prove particularly useful: https://ourfp.org/awards/.

Picture books

When defining a picture book, Wolfenbarger and Sipe (2007, p. 273) argue that it is "the inextricable connection of words and pictures and the unique qualities of the form, always rejecting the notion that a [picture book] is not simply a book that happens to have pictures." A book that happens to have pictures may be described as an "illustrated story: the pictures are subordinated to the words" (Nikolajeva and Scott, 2006, p. 8), and in contrast to this narrative fiction which may contain images, wordless picture books are picture books where "the written text is subservient to the visually rendered narrative" (Serafini, 2014, p. 25), and although they are called "wordless," "most wordless picture books contain a title and the author-illustrator's name" (Serafini, 2014, p. 24). Serafini (2014, p. 25) suggests that "all readers can enjoy wordless picture books and should be exposed to them whether or not they can read words proficiently." This assertion brings to mind Henry, who was discussed earlier in the chapter as "just looking at the pictures" (Bacon, 2020), and his clear enjoyment of looking at the pictures might mean that these books could provide an engaging resource for children who are self-professed "haters" of reading. However, Serafini (2014, p. 25) goes on to argue that wordless picture books should be available for all readers to access, contending that "as wordless picture books grow more complex, older readers will find challenges and enjoyment in these texts, which are too often relegated to younger readers."

When considering "the inextricable connection of words and pictures" (Wolfenbarger and Sipe, 2007, p. 273) in picture books, Nikolajeva and Scott (2006, p. 1) suggest it is the "combination of two levels of communication, the visual and the verbal" that make picture books unique. They go on to explain that there are five ways that words and pictures can be connected:

1. Symmetry: the words and pictures provide exactly the same information
2. Complementary: the words and pictures provide slightly different but complementary information
3. Enhancement: the words and pictures provide additional information to extend the meaning of each other
4. Counterpoint: the words and pictures tell different stories
5. Contradiction: the words and pictures provide opposite information.

(Nikolajeva and Scott, 2006)

Picture books are often ubiquitous among primary classrooms and are often found concentrated within the Early Years Foundation Stage and Key Stage 1 classrooms in particular. However, there are a large number of picture books available for older children to engage with and Bintz and Ciecierski-Madara (2022), Booker (2012), and Ghosh and Laird (2011) all argue that picture books should be available for children to read in Key Stage 2 and beyond.

Where might you find recommendations for picture books?

A number of the resources that were listed in the narrative fiction section above will also be useful for picture books by using some of the filtering options available on the different websites.

- The excellent and incredibly knowledgeable CLPE are huge advocates for the use of picture books within the primary classroom, and a number of high-quality picture books, suitable for a range of ages, can be found on the website: https://clpe.org.uk/books
- Initial Teacher Education lecturer Mat Tobin has an excellent resource that contains a large number of high-quality picture books: https://padlet.com/p0077346/high-quality-picture-books-for-cross-curricular-planning-eaf5llgdy71d
- The United Kingdom Literacy Association Book Awards offer a category for ages 3–6+ that contains a wide variety of recently published high-quality picture books: https://ukla.org/awards/ukla-book-award/
- Picture book enthusiast and primary headteacher Simon Smith's blog also has some excellent recommendations for picture books for each year group: https://smithsmm.wordpress.com/2020/08/23/year-1-year-6-picturebook-lists-so-far-links/

Comics and graphic novels

The National Literacy Trust (Clark et al., 2024, p. 1) suggests that comics "span diverse genres and include graphic novels, one-off comic strips, weekly magazines, webcomics, non-fiction and manga titles for children, young people and adults." While containing similarities to picture books, Stafford (2011, p. 48) argues a key feature of comics and graphic novels (which are often defined as storybook-length comics) are panels, which "are to comics what prose is to the novel. They are the fundamental building blocks of the text, the static images which tell the story through their sequencing. They usually take the form of vertical or horizontal rectangles but can also be square, circular or any shape imaginable." He also suggests that other key aspects of comics and graphic novels that may be recognisable are *speech balloons*, which show when characters are talking, *thought balloons*, which reveal character's thoughts, *narrative boxes*, which can help advance the narrative often using adverbials of time, and *sound effects*, which can help the reader to picture the scene more clearly (Stafford, 2011). When considering children's reading, in 2023, book sales figures suggest that middle-grade graphic novels are generally performing better than more straightforward fiction for the same age (Nielsen BookData, 2024a), while the latest data suggest that there has been a growing "interest in graphic novels and comic strip fiction" the "top fiction author this year is Dav Pilkey, creator of *Dog Man*, followed by *Bunny vs Monkey* writer and illustrator Jamie Smart at third … Also rising up the ranks is John Patrick Green and his *Investigators*" (Nielsen BookData, 2024b).

This growing interest is supported by Clark et al. (2024, p. 1) who suggest that "comics are a considerable part of the reading diet of many children and young people" with the latest annual reading research data from the National Literacy Trust suggesting that 40% of the children surveyed read comics or graphic novels (Clark et al., 2023). Clark et al. (2024, p. 10) suggest that it may be "the unique combination of genres, visuals and texts that comics offer, which can make reading more immersive and enjoyable" and they go on to state that "in their own words, children and young people have told us that they read comics because they are fun, cool and relatable." If we are aiming to move beyond Worthy et al.'s (1999, p. 23) assertion that "there is an ever-increasing gap between [children's] preferences and materials that schools provide and recommend," perhaps we would benefit from considering how we can provide, read and recommend comics and graphic novels to the children in our classes. Richardson (2017, p. 28) provides a useful closing thought about supporting children's choice in relation to their reading when considering a child's request at a school book fair to buy a graphic novel, and his parent loudly protested that he had to buy a "real book." She goes on to argue that "this parent and many others are stifling their child's ability to choose what to read and thus perhaps having the child choose not to read at all" (Richardson, 2017, p. 29). Of course, graphic novels are "real" books and maybe the text that offers the child the "gateway" into a love of reading. Richardson (2017, p. 27) argues that "they may help a student to look forward to reading – clearly a teacher's and parent's ultimate goal!" which I think is a sentiment that is easy to agree with.

Where might you find recommendations for comics and graphic novels?

Teacher Richard Ruddick has an excellent and continually updated resource that provides recommended graphic novels for KS2 readers: https://padlet.com/rruddick9zra/graphic-novels-73uh2srzpbia

The Beano is a long-running but ever-popular weekly comic featuring short comics with returning characters: https://www.beano.com/posts/beano-comic-online

The Phoenix Comic has a variety of different comics in each edition, some standalone and others serial parts of a longer story: https://thephoenixcomic.co.uk/

The National Literacy Trust has a number of useful resources on using comics and graphic novels but this is a good starting point: https://literacytrust.org.uk/blog/library-lifeline-part-18-i-want-to-build-my-schools-graphic-novel-library-but-where-do-i-start/

Lucy Starbuck Braidley hosts an excellent podcast discussing using comics in education: https://comicboom.buzzsprout.com/

Audiobooks

While audiobooks may not be considered "reading," it may be beneficial to explore them as a way for children to be exposed to narrative fiction, perhaps in a similar way to how we might be aiming to read aloud to children to show them the engagement with narratives and the possibilities that reading can afford. Therefore, it might be useful to consider how children might be supported to engage with audiobooks, both in and out of the classroom, as part of reading for pleasure practices.

Gaming

It may be a stretch too far to suggest that children can bring in devices and games during independent reading time, although that probably depends on individual teachers' and schools' policies! This is more a call to consider text-based computer games that children engage in as an example of them choosing to read for pleasure. There are a number of games that require the gamer to do lots of reading (e.g. Animal Crossing and Pokèmon games are well-known examples), and this is often either narrative text to advance the plot of the game, or character dialogue as part of the overall narrative plot of the game. It is important to encourage children to understand that this is a form of reading, and by playing these games, they are choosing to engage in reading, and this can and should form part of children's conceptualisation of a reader. This could also be said for paper or card-based games, such as Top Trumps or Pokèmon cards, which also involve lots of reading!

Going beyond narrative fiction

While children suggest that they read a wide range of texts (Clark et al., 2023), when asked to conceptualise what makes a reader, McGeown et al. (2020, p. 221) found that "[fiction] books were unanimously the kind of text mentioned, with far fewer references to other reading matter" and went on to state that children "often had to be prompted to discuss other kinds of texts, suggesting their concept of a reader was still synonymous with someone who reads books rather than other reading matter." This is important to consider as it tells us that we may still have work to do as teachers to support children's understanding of what it means to be a reader, what it means to read for pleasure (or purpose) and what reading can count as reading. If we want to encourage children to view *any* reading as potentially reading for pleasure (or purpose), then we need to make this explicit again and again with children and offer them the opportunity to read what they want to read within the classroom.

Non-Fiction

Clark et al. (2023) suggest that nearly 60% of children choose to read non-fiction, and when reflecting on his own childhood reading, headteacher Simon Smith (2018) recalls how a non-fiction book he was gifted was where he found his "reading for pleasure." He comments that it was "endlessly re-readable, [with] loads and loads to learn about. It was also glorious to look at, sumptuous in the detail and fantastically illustrated. It was the total package. I can't even begin to count the hours I spent laying on my bed reading it, lost in its pages, savouring its detail" (Smith, 2018). There are multiple pleasures that can be gained from reading non-fiction. This can be a simple delight in the book in itself or a pleasure that is *efferent*, where finding the acquisition of new knowledge and understanding is pleasurable or it may be an *aesthetic* pleasure where awe, wonder and curiosity may be the pleasurable experiences from reading the book (Alexander and Jarman, 2018).

Where might you find recommendations for non-fiction books?

The United Kingdom Literacy Association Book Awards offer a specific category for information books that contains a variety of recently published high-quality non-fiction books: https://ukla.org/awards/ukla-book-award/

Books for Topics offer some general recommendations for non-fiction: https://www.books-fortopics.com/booklists/top-notch-non-fiction/ as well as recommendations of book lists for specific interests or topics: https://www.booksfortopics.com/

There are also a number of publishers who are particularly interested in producing excellent non-fiction books for children:

- Flying Eye Books: https://flyingeyebooks.com/books/genre/non-fiction/
- Big Picture Press: https://www.bonnierbooks.co.uk/books/?_sfm_book_audience=childrens-non-fiction
- Wide Eyed Editions: https://www.quarto.com/ourbooks/default.aspx?booktype=BY_IMPRINTS&ourimprintid=10&imprintid=2072&webtitleimprint=Wide+Eyed+Editions&browsebyimprintscriteria=
- Little People, Big Dreams by Maria Isabel S·nchez Vegara are good introductions to biographies for a variety of notable people, both historical and current.

Reading non-fiction more widely on paper or on screen

Smith (2019) also suggests that we should consider our non-fiction offer more widely and asks whether we offer any of the following options for children to read:

- Encyclopaedias
- True-life stories
- Newspapers
- Diaries
- Biographies
- Magazines
- Leaflets
- Theatre and football programmes

- Recipe books/cards
- Posters
- Travel brochures
- Maps
- Timetables
- Food packaging
- Catalogues
- Letters and postcards
- Advertisements

There is a whole range of different reading opportunities contained in the list above (to which I'd also suggest adding joke books), but I'd like to just focus briefly on magazines. There is a huge range of magazines available that can focus on pretty much any interest that children may have. Magazines can provide reading material that is linked to:

- Other media that children enjoy, such as TV programmes like Peppa Pig or Paw Patrol,
- Toys or games that children like to play with, such as a variety of Lego-themed magazines or Pokèmon magazines
- Interests that children have, such as football magazines or fashion magazines
- Even magazines that aren't specifically designed for children can be linked to their interests, such as cooking, cars, gardening or fishing.

A key thought here is if there are texts such as magazines that are available for children to read that are linked to their interests, then this may be a useful consideration to have as part of our reading offer within our classrooms.

When thinking about the interests of the children in your class, try taking a look at the magazine aisle in a large supermarket and consider whether any of the magazines would interest your children.

Poetry

For some children, poetry can be "the thing" that awakens an interest in reading. CLPE's (2023) *Poetry in Primary Schools* report found that 88% of children enjoyed engaging with poetry, despite 79% of classroom book corners being found to have fewer than ten poetry books. However, because poems are often short, children may not always identify these as something that "counts." Poetry is a unique writing form and can succinctly connect with the lives and experiences of children. Initially, this brevity can be the main appeal of poetry (in the same way as the "quick facts" books or the joke book) to children, as well as children's widening knowledge of online performance poets, often delivering powerful renditions of their work. The rhythmic refrains and repetition can make the mechanics of reading easier for some children which gives confidence and agency. Poetry can be playful and creative, breaking the "rules" that children see that other writing is confined by. Reading poetry aloud regularly and offering children the chance to perform favourite poems can make the act of reading both a more physically active experience and enable an emotional connection to the words, engaging children in a community of readers. Poetry's musicality can draw children to poetry, and this underlines the need for poetry to be read aloud, to be taken off the page and into the world of the listener. Reading opportunities that are not "silent" are particularly important when thinking about poetry and reading for pleasure. When thinking about the offer in your classroom, consider the diversity of poets and poems available to the children, while aiming to provide a range of forms and subject matter, from the humorous to the powerfully serious.

Where might you find recommendations for poetry?

Here are some useful places to find such a range as well as ways to enable children to explore not just what they read, but how they read it as well:

- CLPE have a superb selection of poetry suggestions: https://clpe.org.uk/poetry along with their annual poetry awards: https://clpe.org.uk/poetry/CLiPPA and linked resources.
- The National Poetry Day has excellent poetry suggestions: https://forwardartsfoundation.org/national-poetry-day/
- Poetry By Heart is an excellent organisation that seeks to engage children in the performance of poetry. The yearly competition is quite an inspiration: https://poetrybyheart.org.uk/
- Nikki Gamble at Just Imagine https://justimagine.co.uk/2023/04/26/poetry-for-primary-schools/ offers really helpful approaches to "spring cleaning" poetry collections and her suggestions always foreground diverse poets and subject matter.

Song lyrics

Clark, Picton and Galway (2023) suggest that nearly 70% of children aged 8-18 read song lyrics, making them "the most popular material read on screen," and so it might be useful to consider how children might be supported to engage with reading song lyrics within the school classroom. Song lyrics could be considered as a form of poetry, or they could be seen as a different and unique text. Either way, engaging with song lyrics may provide a useful way to support children to engage with reading and to further broaden the definition of what reading is. Here is a useful lyric website that can be used to search for a variety of songs: https://www.musixmatch.com/search

Whose reading is it anyway?: Moving to "reader-led, reader-directed and reader-owned" reading

If our goal as teachers is to support children to choose to read, we need to ensure that we are providing breadth in everything that we do in relation to reading for pleasure. We need to ensure that children understand that there are a broad range of reasons for wanting to read, from pleasures to purposes and that there are a broad range of activities and texts that count as reading. We need to ensure that we walk the walk as well as talk the talk to ensure that we are sharing these broad ranges of reasons for reading and broad range of texts for reading with children as part of our practices. Finally, we need to understand that if we want children to want to read, we need to ensure that their reading is "reader-led, reader-directed and reader-owned" by them (Cremin, 2019, p. 6).

Conclusion and call to action!

Within this chapter, I have aimed to consider *why* children might or might not choose to read. I have encouraged you to think about your own reading practices and to extend your thinking to children to consider whether they might be motivated to read for pleasure or for purpose. I have aimed to encourage you to work alongside the children you work with to try and conceptualise reading as a broad activity that can take many different forms and that reading for pleasure or purpose must be framed with children's agency at the heart of all of our reading practices. I have then encouraged you to think carefully about the broad range of reading materials that could be made available for children to read and have challenged you to think about how you are ensuring that children know that all of this reading is accepted and encouraged.

Call to action

- Reflect on what "reading for pleasure" means for you? Try to capture your own definition in a drawing or a few sentences.
- Reflect on why you read. Think carefully about why you choose to read by completing the following sentence: I read because …
- What do you read and why do you read it? Try to come up with a list of all the different reading that you do and consider why you do it.
- Get to know the rich, multi-faceted identities of each of the children in your class and the topics, issues, and interests that are meaningful to them (Enriquez, 2021), and then consider how these are reflected in the text choices that you have available for your children.
- Ask the children in your class what characters they would like to meet and what cultures and languages they would like to see reflected in those texts that you have in your classroom (Enriquez, 2021).
- Use CLPE's (2023) Questions to Guide Considerations when choosing books for your classroom.
- Ensure that you are sharing a broad range of reasons for reading and broad range of texts for reading with children as part of your reading for pleasure practices.
- Ensure that the children in your class know that their reading for pleasure (or purpose) is "reader-led, reader-directed and reader-owned" by them (Cremin, 2019, p. 6).

References

Alexander, J. and Jarman, R. (2018) 'The pleasures of reading non-fiction', *Literacy*, 52(2), pp. 78-85.
Bacon, B. (2020) *I hate reading: How to read when you'd rather not*. London: Pushkin Press.
Bintz, W.P. and Ciecierski-Madara, L.M. (2022) 'Middle grades readings: Where are the picturebooks?', *Middle School Journal*, 53(3), pp. 22-30.
Bishop, R.S. (1990) 'Mirrors, windows and sliding glass doors', *Perspectives*, 6(3), pp. ix-xi.
Booker, K. (2012) 'Practical strategies: Using picturebooks to empower and inspire readers and writers in the upper primary classroom', *Literacy Learning: the Middle Years*, 20(2), pp. i-xiv.
Centre for Literacy in Primary Education (2018) *Reflecting realities - survey of ethnic representation within UK children's literature 2017* [Online]. London: CLPE. Available from: https://clpe.org.uk/research/reflecting-realities

Centre for Literacy in Primary Education (2019) *Reflecting realities - survey of ethnic representation within UK children's literature 2018* [Online]. London: CLPE. Available from: https://clpe.org.uk/research/reflecting-realities

Centre for Literacy in Primary Education (2020) *Reflecting realities - survey of ethnic representation within UK children's literature 2019* [Online]. London: CLPE. Available from: https://clpe.org.uk/research/reflecting-realities

Centre for Literacy in Primary Education (2021) *Reflecting realities - survey of ethnic representation within UK children's literature 2020* [Online]. London: CLPE. Available from: https://clpe.org.uk/research/reflecting-realities

Centre for Literacy in Primary Education (2022) *Reflecting realities - survey of ethnic representation within UK children's literature 2017-2021* [Online]. London: CLPE. Available from: https://clpe.org.uk/research/reflecting-realities

Centre for Literacy in Primary Education (2023) *Reflecting realities - survey of ethnic representation within UK children's literature 2022* [Online]. London: CLPE. Available from: https://clpe.org.uk/research/reflecting-realities

Centre for Literacy in Primary Education (2023) *Poetry in primary schools report*. London: CLPE Available from: https://clpe.org.uk/research/poetry-primary-schools-2023

Clark, C., Picton, I. and Galway, M. (2023) *Children and young people's reading in 2023* [Online]. London: National Literacy Trust. Available from: https://literacytrust.org.uk/research-services/research-reports/children-and-young-peoples-reading-in-2023/

Clark, C., Starbuck Braidley, L., Cole, A. and Chamberlain, E. (2024) *Children and young people's engagement with comics in 2023* [Online]. London: National Literacy Trust. Available from: https://literacytrust.org.uk/research-services/research-reports/children-and-young-peoples-engagement-with-comics-in-2023/

Craft, J. (2019) *New kid*. New York, NY: HarperCollins.

Cremin, T. (2019) 'Reading communities: Why, what and how?', *NATE Primary Matters*, pp. 4-8.

Cremin, T. and Scholes, L. (2024) 'Reading for pleasure: Scrutinising the evidence base–benefits, tensions and recommendations', *Language and Education*, 38(4), pp. 537-559.

Crisp, T., Knezek, S.M., Quinn, M., Bingham, G.E., Girardeau, K. and Starks, F. (2016) 'What's on our bookshelves? The diversity of children's literature in early childhood classroom libraries', *Journal of Children's Literature*, 42(2), pp. 29-42.

Enriquez, G. (2021) 'Foggy mirrors, tiny windows, and heavy doors: Beyond diverse books toward meaningful literacy instruction', *The Reading Teacher*, 75(1), pp. 103-106.

Farshore (2022) *Reading for pleasure and purpose* [Online]. Glasgow: Farshore. Available from: https://www.farshore.co.uk/wp-content/uploads/sites/46/2022/03/Reading-for-Pleasure-and-Purpose-Report-Farshore.pdf

Ghosh, K. and Laird, S. (2011) 'Creative uses of picture books with KS2 children', *English Four to Eleven*, 43, pp. 3-8.

Guthrie, J.T., Hoa, A.L.W., Wigfield, A., Tonks, S.M., Humenick, N.M. and Littles, E. (2007) 'Reading motivation and reading comprehension growth in the later elementary years', *Contemporary Educational Psychology*, 32(3), pp. 282-313.

Lockwood, M. (2008) *Promoting Reading for pleasure in the primary school*. London: SAGE.

McGeown, S., Bonsall, J., Andries, V., Howarth, D., Wilkinson, K. and Sabeti, S. (2020) 'Growing up a reader: Exploring children's and adolescents' perceptions of 'a reader', *Educational Research*, 62(2), pp. 216-228.

McGeown, S. and Wilkinson, K. (2021) *Inspiring and sustaining reading for pleasure in children and young people: A guide for teachers and school leaders*. Leicester: UKLA.

Moss, G. (2000) 'Raising boys' attainment in reading: Some principles for intervention', *Reading*, 34(3), pp. 101-106.

Nielsen BookData (2024a) *Looking back at 2023 in the UK and Ireland* [Online]. Available from: https://nielsenbook.co.uk/looking-back-at-2023-in-the-uk-and-ireland/

Nielsen BookData (2024b) *Reading adventures in children's fiction & graphic novels* [Online]. Available from: https://nielsenbook.co.uk/reading-adventures-in-childrens-fiction-graphic-novels/

Nikolajeva, M. and Scott, C. (2006) *How picturebooks work*. Abingdon: Routledge.

Nodelman, P. and Reimer, M. (2003) *The pleasures of Children's literature*. 3rd edn. Boston, MA: Allyn and Bacon.

Oxley, E. and McGeown, S. (2023) 'Reading for pleasure practices in school: children's perspectives and experiences', *Educational Research*, 65(3), pp. 375-391.

Pennac, D. (2006) *The rights of the reader (illustrated by Quentin Blake)*. Translated from the French by Sarah Ardizzone. London: Walker Books.

Reedy, A. and De Carvalho, R. (2021) 'Children's perspectives on reading, agency and their environment: What can we learn about reading for pleasure from an East London primary school?', *Education 3-13*, 49(2), pp. 134-147.

Richardson, E.M. (2017) 'Graphic novels are real books": Comparing graphic novels to traditional text novels', *Delta Kappa Gamma Bulletin*, 83(5), pp. 24-31.

Rundell, K. (2019) *Why you should read children's books, even though you are so old and wise*. London: Bloomsbury Press.

Serafini, F. (2014) 'Exploring wordless picture books', *The Reading Teacher*, 68(1), pp. 24-26.

Smith, S. (2018) *The reading offer…What choices are you giving children?* [Online] Available from: https://smithsmm.wordpress.com/2018/01/07/the-reading-offer-what-choices-are-you-giving-children/

Smith, S. (2019) *The purpose of reading…What is your reading offer part 2*. [Online] Available from: https://smithsmm.wordpress.com/2019/06/16/the-purpose-of-reading-what-is-your-reading-offer-part-2/

Stafford, T. (2011) *Teaching visual literacy in the primary classroom: Comic books, film, television and picture narratives*. Abingdon: Routledge.

Wolfenbarger, C.D. and Sipe, L.R. (2007) 'A unique visual and literary art form: Recent research on Picturebooks', *Language Arts*, 84(3), pp. 273-280.

Worthy, Moorman and Turner (1999) 'What Johnny likes to read is Hard to find in school', *Reading Research Quarterly*, 34(1), pp. 12-27.

3 Not reading for pleasure but "purposefully positive"

Understanding the difference between reading for pleasure and using great texts for teaching

Jane Carter

Introduction

In Chapter 1 of this book, the tension between reading for pleasure and reading instruction was introduced. We know that teachers across the country are made constantly aware of attainment expectations, and whilst reading for pleasure has continued to have a raised profile, this has often been in relation to its impact on attainment, rather than for any of the other benefits it might bring. This chapter will first provide some context to the possible tensions between pedagogies for the instruction of reading and reading for pleasure pedagogies. It will consider the often-stated dichotomies between skills and enjoyment; standardised testing and individualised needs and interests, and teacher-directed and child-led reading. The chapter will consider the role of the accountability agenda in relation to reading attainment standards and its consequences for the approaches to teaching adopted. It will also reflect on the time constraints that teachers are constantly mindful of and how this can impact on time dedicated to reading for pleasure in the classroom setting. The chapter will then introduce what I am calling, "purposefully positive" practice. This is not a reading-for-pleasure pedagogy but is a way of acknowledging the many varied and engaging approaches used when teaching English curriculum objectives using children's literature. The chapter will explore the differences between reading engagement and reading motivation and how this links to a "purposefully positive approach." From the first sharing of books in the home and nursery to sharing a challenging Year 6 read, this "purposefully positive" approach will be explained and exemplified. In one sense, this chapter is not strictly about reading for pleasure, but it is about how a school can create a climate or culture that enables the pedagogies of reading instruction to support, rather than undermine the pedagogies of reading for pleasure.

The context for possible tensions between reading instruction and reading for pleasure

As Applegate et al. (2014, p. 189) outline there is much agreement about "the vision of the ideal reader." This ideal reader is one who is "avid, engaged and enthusiastic, immersed in the joy of reading" and one who reads because they have some intrinsic pleasure or purpose to their reading. This frequent, engaged practice of the "ideal reader" supports their continual improvement as identified in Stanovich's (2008) 'Matthew Effect.' The 'Matthew Effect' is a reference to a Bible passage in the book of Matthew that states that, "to those who already have, more will be given." In relation to reading, this means that the child who reads, who can read, and who has access to books to read, will reap the benefits of being a reader, which in turn, enables the child to want to read more and this reading will further develop the skills and knowledge of the reader. Put simply, the more reading a child does, the better they become at reading and so the more they will read. At each step, learners accrue the multiple benefits of being a reader and become the "ideal reader" as envisioned by Applegate et al. (2014). This book, with its focus on inclusion, has at its heart the child who, for a variety of reasons, does not begin this virtuous circle – so may not have access to texts when young, is faced with barriers when making the transition to school, or who does not "fit" the expected model of attainment progress. This child, according to Simpson and Cremin (2022, p. 3) is in a "sealed cycle of disadvantage" exacerbated by what is called the "pedagogy of poverty" which will be explored later in this chapter.

It is worth pausing at this point and reflecting on the challenges that you as a teacher or pre-service teacher face. How does your school manage the "standards agenda"? How is reading conceptualised in your school in relation to both reading attainment and reading for pleasure? How are these two potentially conflicting goals managed in terms of the curriculum, time and reading culture?

Teachers from across the case study schools in this book had clear views on this and these may resonate with your thoughts and ideas. Here are some of their thoughts:

"There isn't time to have more than 10 minutes of reading time after lunch as we have other curriculum areas to cover."

"They need to read their reading book which may be in another class because they are a low attaining reader. They need to get better at reading first."

"We are expected to maximise the time we are actually teaching reading directly."

Interestingly, this also transferred to children's view of reading. In one case study school, it appears that children conflate learning to read (and so attainment and standards) and reading for pleasure. When asked about reading for pleasure, these were their responses:

Rob:	We do reading skills, so after lunch we get a certain amount of time to read.
Sarah:	Not a certain amount. It's usually like 5 or 10 minutes because we have science or something straight after.
Ahmed:	Because if we didn't, because if we don't. Because if we don't have a limited amount of time....we wouldn't be able to do our other work so.

With these challenges in mind, knowing how to enable children to develop as Applegate etal's (2014, p. 189) "ideal reader" who not only can read at an attainment level expected for their age but who are also "avid, engaged and enthusiastic, immersed in the joy of reading" continues to be a source of debate and discussion amongst researchers.

Since the Independent Review of the Teaching of Reading (Rose, 2006), successive governments have introduced a raft of policy and guidance about reading. Policy has focused largely on one aspect of reading: teaching early reading and systematic synthetic phonics, in particular. The approach to early reading has concentrated on the cognitive aspects of reading, in line with a preference for scientific research approaches (Moss, 2016). The National Curriculum (DfE, 2013) replicated the Simple View of Reading model (Gough and Tunmer, 1986) in the programmes of study, separating word reading and comprehension. The curriculum also made use of systematic synthetic phonics (rather than any other phonics approaches), alongside the requirement to use phonically decodable text, a key feature of the approach to early reading. Whilst reference is made to children's enjoyment and engagement with reading, the emphasis is on "getting children reading" and this was evident in the Ofsted report *Getting them reading early* (2014). You may be familiar with the phrase "learn to read and then read to learn" which seems to suggest that children need to learn to read first, before being able to read for purpose and pleasure. The Ofsted research review of English (2023) is very clear that whilst reading for pleasure and having a love of reading is important, it can only happen when and if a child can read. It aligns engagement with reading, first and foremost with success in reading. It states:

> If children struggle with reading early on, they may not be persuaded to read more. The findings [of studies] emphasise the overriding importance of children getting off to a successful start with reading, as this is the strongest predictor of later motivation.

The English Curriculum, perhaps not unreasonably, positions the reader as someone who can decode and make meaning from texts in English. It is apparent that a child who struggles with reading will not have access to the widest range of texts; however, this construction of reading as only being about decoding words, is just one view of what it means to be a reader.

As you read this, coming to mind may be a range of children you know, or teach, who do not quite fit with the "official" construction of reading. Robinson, Moore and Harris (2018, p. 91) make a strong case for "recognising the unrecognised cohort" of children who have learning disabilities and particularly those with "severe and profound learning disabilities" who will never be able to read in the conventional sense as set out in the National Curriculum. They argue, however, that this minoritised group of children can and do read for pleasure. The "reading" of text may look different from how most other children may read. Lawson et al. (2012, p. 101) make the point that viewing literacy as a set of skills that focus on written text, necessarily excludes and positions as "other" or "deficit," children with severe or profound learning difficulties that mean they will rarely, if ever, be able to access this "one view" of being literate. They argue that children with learning difficulties regularly engage in pleasurable social, interactive and multimodal literate activity with text. Flewitt, Nind and Payler (2009) introduces the idea of "inclusive literacy" which views text beyond the written to include the visual, spatial and spoken, and therefore encompasses a version of a text that can be inclusive of the sensory engagement by children with learning difficulties.

The framing of reading for pleasure in the Ofsted review (2022) seems to focus on "future" benefits i.e. teach the skills early in order to reap the benefits of engagement later. Whilst the report recognises the many benefits of reading for pleasure, it also challenges schools and settings to reflect on which activities support the goal of engaged reading, and which they suggest could be a distraction, taking time and energy away from reading itself. Again, this is a very narrow view of reading and engaged reading. In the early years, the pleasurable sharing of books is at the heart of effective early years practice, recognising not only the foundation that this lays but also, perhaps more importantly, the "in the moment" benefits of engaging with the text in a variety of ways. The sustained concentration of children in the early years as they browse, drink in a story from the pictures, re-run and often re-tell a story that has been previously shared, are all evidence of the "here and now" benefits of reading – where reading is not confined to the decoding of the words in a text.

Of course, the future benefits are also well documented. Grover et al. (2020) highlight how early shared reading with children who have English as an additional language, develops language skills, including English vocabulary, range and depth and more complex syntactical structures; cognitive skills; socio-cognitive skills and extends knowledge of the world. Sun et al. (2023) identified a highly positive correlation between early reading for pleasure (between the ages of birth and two and a half) with later performance in cognitive tests. They demonstrated how this early reading for pleasure impacted the way the brain developed. They also showed that these children had fewer mental health problems as young adolescents (aged 10-12) and had less screen time than those children that did not have these early experiences. Reading for pleasure is therefore not just about the independent act of decoding words on the page for personal gratification but is also a shared and social experience that encompasses a wide range of activity that has both "in the moment" and longer-term impacts.

Targets and standards

Simpson and Cremin (2022) argue that much of the drive to continually raise attainment (whilst at the same time, continuing to change what is considered to be "expected" in relation to attainment) can be located in governments globally, focusing on international comparison using the Progress in International Reading Literacy Study (PIRLS) and the Programme for International Student Assessment (PISA) as a test and ranking measure of their country's policy success in reading. This, they argue, reduces literacy and reading specifically to a "set of self-contained and transferrable skills and competences and fails to take account of differences and of the influence of text and context on the learner" (Simpson and Cremin, 2022, p. 2). In England, The White Paper: Reading: the next steps (DfE, 2015) deals specifically with the need to raise standards of achievement in reading, and in a later paper, Education Excellence Everywhere (DfE, 2016), there is a foregrounding of the success of initiatives such as the Phonics Screening Check in raising standards in reading. This document also claims the government is interested in "outcomes and not methods" (DfE, 2016, p. 12). For practising teachers, this statement perhaps feels a little surprising as the curriculum clearly *does* state "how" and which "methods" to use, for example in the approach to teaching early reading and phonics. This is further embedded in the most recent Ofsted inspection criteria. Gemma Moss (2017) gives a comprehensive overview of how the standards agenda, with a focus on outcomes, has framed recent literacy policy. The National Literacy Strategy introduced in 1998 heralded a new age of "deliverable" outcomes that the then Labour government established as a way of holding the policy to account. Targets, testing and data tracking became the approach promoted to secure a standardised set of outcomes and "raised" attainment. When the National Literacy Strategy was in place, it was accompanied by regular and comprehensive training and support.

Such an interventionist approach by the government therefore inevitably holds that government accountable for the outcomes. Over the past ten years, there has been a shift towards removing support and training in favour of giving schools the "autonomy" to meet the standards and holding the individual teacher accountable for each child's progress, and so distance the hand of government from responsibility. If children do not learn to read and do not meet the standards set, then the "blame" lies with schools and teachers. Moss (2017 p. 59) points out what is obvious to most teachers but perhaps not to policy makers: that children enter school with very different early experiences and so:

> Without paying attention to the levels of disadvantage reflected in school catchments, a list of the best schools produces a list in which schools with more socially advantaged pupils dominate, rather than schools that genuinely represent the best in teaching and learning.

However, targets and standards comparisons are a key driver to how schools and individual teachers make decisions about whether to adopt a new initiative or change practice, based on the projected impact on attainment. Not surprisingly, teachers talk about how best to ensure children reach the required standard in the required assessment. Whether it is the assessment of early skills of reading in the Phonics Screening Check (Carter, 2020), or the assessment of reading comprehension in Key Stage 2 (Tennent, 2020), teachers report the narrowing of the curriculum that is taught in order to focus on the elements that are tested. This was seen very starkly in Carter's (2020) study of the unintended consequences of the Phonics Screening Check where teachers reported that they had to "hold back higher attaining readers" in order for them to pass the screening check and that they asked parents of high attaining readers to stop encouraging their children to "make sense" of what they read but to focus only on decoding. Teachers reported "teaching non-words" (rather than using them as a way of assessing which phonics skills and knowledge children had) because they were a feature of the assessment. Moss (2017, p. 62) suggests that "the assessment tools themselves simply become the curriculum." Finding the time and space therefore to develop the distinctive pedagogies of reading for pleasure becomes more of a challenge. Whilst the links between reading for pleasure and attainment are clear, they do not present themselves as a neat "input and output" equation and require a longer-term shift in culture and approach than some schools feel they have the time, tenacity and bravery to pursue. The case studies for this book have shown regularly the commitment of teachers to reading for pleasure pedagogies but the children in the case studies often give a slightly different view from the perspective of the young reader.

Pedagogy of poverty

This tension between reading for pleasure and reading instruction and the pressure of the accountability agenda is often felt most forcefully in schools in areas of low socio-economic status. The research is clear that children in areas of poverty have lower outcomes in reading attainment: it is essential to note however, that it is structural inequalities that influence the complexity of factors that impact families and so attainment, rather than locating "blame" with a deficit few of families in poverty (see Chapter 5 for more on this area).

Roberts-Holmes and Bradbury (2016) found that this focus on performance data meant teachers felt constrained because the expectation to close attainment gaps steered their pedagogical choices and so marginalised how to engage children with reading through a more child-centred approach. Hempel-Jorgensen et al. (2018) argued that when children were from low socio-economic status homes and/or they were considered to be "struggling readers," teachers tended to frame reading for that child as purely an issue of technical proficiency. Thadani et al. (2010) argue that these children are more likely to be given skills-based exercises, compounding the child's view of reading as something more limiting and certainly not something that is linked with pleasure, engagement or enjoyment. Haberman (1991) identified this as the "pedagogy of poverty" when he was describing children in America in low socio-economic contexts. It was found these children experienced teaching as a transmission of knowledge where they were expected to be passive and compliant. Clearly, this is diametrically opposed to reading for pleasure where children need to be active, volitional and engaged.

Think about the children in your class who you are aware are from lower socio-economic home environments and reflect on how each child experiences reading in your class? You may want to reflect on whether children from this group who are not attaining at expected levels have a different experience of reading to those children who are finding learning to read more challenging. Can you also think more widely about your school: what does the data tell you about different groups of children as they move through the year groups in your school?

Engagement and motivation

What good teachers do

Ellis (2007) argues that teachers need to apply their knowledge of the reading process to their experience in practice of teaching reading. This then enables an understanding of the variations and contradictions that application of research in practice illuminates. Many teachers and pre-service teachers will be familiar with the uncomfortable realisation that the research literature they have read, and which seemed so clear in the setting of a teacher education classroom, often only gives a generalised view of a process. It does not account for the individual nuances needed in teaching to meet the needs, interests and idiosyncrasies of each child in the class. One size does not fit all!

The Ellis and Smith (2017) Three Domains of Knowledge model is mentioned regularly in this book as it is at the heart of understanding inclusive practice. It identifies that in order to support reading development, the teacher needs to understand the cognitive skills and knowledge of the child but alongside the personal-social identity of the reader and their cultural and social capital. These three domains are key to a teacher being able to form a comprehensive picture of each child as a reader and so approach their assessment and subsequent teaching appropriately. What this requires teachers to be is, what Ellis, Anderson and Rowe (2017) call, the "noticing" teacher who is not only aware of which of the cognitive skills are needed at any time but also aware of how best to approach the teaching in relation to understanding the child's cultural and social context. Considering the impact of each teaching approach adopted in the classroom on both motivation and cognitive processes – the two being related – is an important focus for good teachers of reading (Wigfield et al., 2014). What is required is the need to weave together the multidimensional layers of reading, bringing together "pedagogical form and content" (Alexander, 2005, p. 46). The 2016 Organisation for Economic Cooperation and Development (OECD) recognised that "Changes in our concept of reading since 2000 have led to an expanded definition of reading literacy, which recognises motivational and behavioural characteristics of reading alongside cognitive characteristics."

These are, of course, fine sentiments but how can a teacher do this and manage the considerable diversity of individual needs, and the demands of the standards agenda and continually ensure engagement and motivation?

As a contribution to this discussion, what is proposed in this chapter is "purposefully positive" teaching. This is *not* the pedagogies of reading for pleasure but a recognition that much of teachers' time and energy is taken by the teaching of the cognitive aspects of reading and how this can be approached in a way that enhances engagement and motivation, and so laying the foundations for, and providing a seamless connection with, reading for pleasure. McGeown et al. (2015) drew attention to the need to be aware of children's enjoyment (or not) of *learning to read* as this impacts on future engagement and motivation.

Are children enjoying the phonics lessons and the comprehension or reading lessons in your school? Do children maintain this enjoyment of the learning process as they move from the early years to Key Stage 1 and into Key Stage 2? There are many reports that highlight gender differences in reading attitudes (Clark, Picton and Galway, 2023; Lindorff, Stiff and Kayton, 2024) and so it is particularly relevant to think about the genders in your class – do they equally enjoy the *process* of learning to read?

Purposefully positive

Purposefully positive practice is a combination of a number of different elements:

1. Creating a whole school ethos or climate that celebrates all aspects of reading.
2. Ensuring every encounter with text from the first decodable text to a more complex novel in year 6, is approached first from the aspect of engagement with meaning, providing an opportunity to make connections, invite discussion and critical thinking and foregrounding children's views, preferences and opinions.
3. Recognising that children have different preferences for approaches to teaching and learning – at a very basic level, some children like to have an embodied, active learning experience and others prefer independent, quiet and reflective learning opportunities.
4. Knowing and using children's interests and cultural and social contexts to make choices about the books that will be used in whole class or guided teaching, even when the focus is the development of cognitive skills, goes hand in hand with developing a relationship with text.

It is important to be clear here, **this is not reading for pleasure**. The teacher is very definitely taking control of the learning (and so the child's agency is not at the forefront) in order to address curriculum requirements or school guidance and policy. The teacher here makes the choice of the text used (even if this is in consultation with children) and the teacher is prescribing the "when" and the "what" of reading. If we reflect back on what reading for pleasure is - in relation to volitional reading - it is clear, the "purposefully positive" approach is not that. The "purposefully positive" approach does however support and create a culture for reading for pleasure. It aims to engage and motivate a child in the act of learning to read so that children see reading as something they would want to do of their own volition when they are not being taught to read. We feel it is important, however, when we teach, to be really clear about this distinction. It was common in the case study schools in this book, for teachers to talk about reading for pleasure when in fact, they were talking about their *teaching of reading*. For example, one case study teacher said, when asked about effective reading for pleasure approaches: '*I found guided reading works because they are all pulled into a story together and experience that conversation; they pull it apart and put it back together again*'. This is not reading for pleasure but would be a good example of the "purposefully positive approach" that can have the potential to create a reading ethos that encourages reading for pleasure. The intention here is significant, the teacher goes on to say how her approach supports the scaffolding of book choice, how it can be the "hook" that gets children reading and how it emphasises the social element of reading through conversation and discussion - she is laying the foundations for reading for pleasure.

Purposefully positive phonics teaching

There is no more important time in a child's reading journey for this purposefully positive approach to be embedded than in the early stages of learning to read, the stage that is now dominated by phonics. The Ofsted Research Review (2023) identified the significance of children learning to read early in their school careers as this impacted their later motivation to read and so likeliness of becoming readers who read for pleasure and purpose. In the curriculum, there is a prescribed use of systematic synthetic phonics as the prime approach to achieving this goal. There can be unintended consequences to a phonics first, fast and only approach (Carter, 2020) if the purpose of reading, to make meaning, is not an equal focus to the teaching of letter-sound correspondences. Beard, Brooks and Ampaw-Farr (2019) warn that teachers, in their use of phonics programmes, have lost sight of why we teach phonics - it is not a subject in its own right, it is a means to an end and so explicit application in reading is essential. If we understand reading as a meaning-making process that requires engagement with text for pleasure and purpose, then a purposefully positive approach is essential.

The usual sequence of a phonics lesson is revised, teach, practise, apply - although this varies a little across phonics schemes and programmes. Typically, a lesson begins with the revision and review of previously taught skills and knowledge, then a new grapheme is taught. This is followed by the practising of reading and writing the new grapheme, often in single words. The final part of the lesson involves the application of the new learning to continuous sentence or text reading and writing, integrating through application of the new learning with previous learning.

Teachers are skilled at appearing excited by children revising known sounds, interspersing at pace, praise and prompts as children do this. With the increase in the number of online resources, it is essential to remember that "purposefully positive" teaching is about the development of the relationship between the teacher and the child. Online materials can be engaging but they cannot replace the teacher's embodiment and modelling of the enthusiasm and excitement for developing these skills as a reader, making explicit that this development of skills is part of the journey of readers.

As the phonics lessons follow a set pattern, there is a danger that they become a little stale and can feel teacher-manual or flipchart-driven. It is important to avoid just going through the motions. In John Hattie's seminal work, *Visible Learning* (2009, p. 23) he says,

> We rarely talk about passion in education as if doing so makes the work of the teacher less serious….Passion reflects the thrills as well as the frustrations of learning – it can be infectious, it can be taught, it can be modelled and it can be learnt.

There is no more important lesson than early reading lessons for this passion for reading to be visible to our children. There are some fabulous examples of lessons available online that demonstrate this passion for teaching reading.

Even at the "practise" part of the lesson, when children are reading a single decodable word, the link to meaning needs to be made clear – a simple definition, a picture or the insertion of the word into a sentence, the asking of a linked question, is enough to make explicit to children that the point of the sounding and blending of the word is to be able to read a word that carries meaning – meaning that is purposeful.

However, it is the application part of the lesson that offers the real opportunity to bring reading alive, to enable children to truly grasp the point of the effort of decoding. This part of the lesson should never be missed – it is the culmination of the teaching sequence. The National Curriculum (Department of Education, 2013) made the use of phonically decodable text a requirement and this was further exemplified and explained in the Ofsted Research Review (2023). Cheatham and Allor (2012) reviewed the evidence for the use of decodable text and concluded that decodability was only one of many useful criteria to "grade" books and so ensure children developed their reading skills. It was found, however, to be a "critical characteristic" of text for early readers and enabled greater success with decoding. Ofsted (2023) drew the conclusion that enabling successful decoding was enough to motivate children. This may certainly be enough to motivate a child who is focused on and incentivised by a success that is based on powering through the decodable book levels; however, this narrow view of "reading" is less likely to support reading for pleasure and purpose. This is not to say that for all children, the extrinsic motivation of the book level is detrimental but where children compare themselves with their peers only in relation to book levels and where meaning, purpose and engagement become secondary, the culture created is not one conducive to reading for pleasure. In the case study schools, many children talked about reading in terms of wanting to *'rise through the book levels'*, to *'become a free reader'* and *'I just want to get to gold'* – reading for some children was first and foremost about achievement as measured through the reading scheme. Levy's (2009, p. 361) research found:

> The reading scheme shaped the children's perceptions of themselves as readers as well as defined constructions of 'reading'…the dominant use of the reading scheme was also seen to discourage some children from attempting to read any book, including those existing outside of the scheme.

To avoid this, it is the "apply" part of the phonics lesson that can shift the focus to meaning. Even when the decodable text is used, and maybe especially when a decodable text is used, the book needs to be read as if it has the potential to be an engaging read, or at least one that deserves thought, attention and effort and one that we can't wait to hear its meaning and message.

Think about how the books used for learning to read are talked about in your school. Is it likely that children will see these as the only important books in the school? Do we talk about "reading books" in our school as something distinct from all other books? After all, are not all books "reading books"?

Purposefully positive approaches with decodable books – and all books!

It is quite possible teachers and pre-service teachers are now sighing heavily – making meaning from text that uses the first graphemes taught (often SATPIN) are rarely texts that seem, on the surface, to be texts that invite discussion and cause strong reactions and opinions. If you think of some of the titles of these texts: 'Sid's Nits'; 'Tip It'; 'Not a Pot'; 'Pat It'; 'Sit In', you can get a flavour of the possible 'underwhelming' nature of these 'narratives'! But this must not deter us from the purposively positive engagement we need to plan for children for this text. Storylines may be rather weak and contrived in these early reading books, but where possible children's choice and agency can still feature a little. There are often a number of books at each level – children can be given the choice as to which book they want to begin with. Encourage children to give their reasons for this choice. Think about representation in these books. Are there high-quality representations, are children of colour in main roles? Pay attention to "wall-papering" – where a publisher has tried to squeeze into every book a range of diverse character representations, sometimes using stereotypes and tropes in the illustrations, rather than providing authentic representations. Having said this, such illustrations still provide the opportunity to "notice" representation. Ask children to scan illustrations and encourage them to think and talk about the illustration e.g.

1 What is going on in the picture?
2 What might those in the picture be doing and why? Encourage and be open to answers that are drawn from children's experiences, e.g. *'That girl is going to the mosque; 'That boy is on his way to his Taekwondo class'; 'She looks like she is good at football'. 'He is in a wheelchair and looks like he is enjoying playing with his friends'.*
3 Do you think the children in the story are all friends?

Sometimes, such "book talk" opens quite important conversations and provides opportunities to address topics such as racism, stereotypical views of people with disabilities or from particular community backgrounds. These conversations can be rather uncomfortable for the teacher but providing the youngest children (and in fact all children) with the avenues to share ideas and opinions, can enable myths and inaccuracies and prejudices to be challenged in a safe and supportive environment.

Having chosen a book, the text needs to be introduced with some verve, passion and interest. If the teacher does not appear curious as to what may be in between the covers of the book, why should children! Use the front cover to wonder about characters, plot and language. Prompt discussion around predictions, make connections with other books read and, in particular, connections with non-scheme books that have been read aloud or shared. Scheme books in the early stages are short and so take little time to read and plan for. When we think about diversity and inclusion recognise that the same approach to a book introduction will rarely ensure all children are motivated and engaged and so try out different approaches. Here are some ideas:

1. **Bring in a range of objects that feature in the book.** In the earliest of books, these could be objects that reflect the pictures rather than the text in the book. Before reading the title of the book show children the objects. Tell children that all of these objects can be found in the story. Can children predict what the story might be about? Can children predict what the title of the book might be? Reveal the title, and ask if children would like to change their predictions now they know the title.
2. **Use the "see and wonder" approach.** Ask children to look at the front cover, ask children what they can see (literally what can they see and name on the cover) and then what does this make children wonder about what the book will be about. Make a note of any predictions on post-it notes and make sure you return to them when you have read the book. Did the book match children's predictions?
3. **Wrap the text and pass the parcel.** As the music stops, a child can take off a layer which can reveal a clue about the book. This sort of activity is often used for read-aloud books or books that are the focus of a unit of work, but if we want children to be motivated by *learning* to read, then this sort of approach is particularly valuable.
4. **Wrap the text and tear** a little bit of the paper to reveal first a corner, and then another corner, or the side of a book or the bottom of the book. Each time, encourage children to think about what the book might be about, how they know and why they think this, making connections to their lives, homes, other books and experiences.
5. **With non-fiction early decodable texts, you can still use the KWL grid.** What do you **K**now about the subject; what do you **W**ant to know and then when you have read the book, what have you **L**earnt. Inevitably there will be a lot of unanswered questions – the early decodable text is unlikely to answer all (if any) of children's questions about a subject area. This opens the opportunity for pursuing children's interests beyond the phonics lesson, providing books that are beyond the child's current reading level that can be selected and taken home for someone to read to them at home or for many children in an inclusive classroom, this may be asking a teaching assistant to read it to them, or during a book buddying opportunity with children from an older year group, asking the older child to help them find the answers to their questions.
6. **More simply, walk through the book with verve and passion.** Summarise what the book is about and what happens as you flick through the pages, sharing your excitement about the book. Pause on certain pages, explaining what is going on and encouraging children to make connections – connections with other books they have read; other books you have read to them; and their own experiences, likes, dislikes and preferences. Be mindful that children have a diversity of experiences. Where a child or group of children are not as likely to have had the experiences outlined in the book,

bring in additional pictures or short film clips that help exemplify and explain what is meant. Validate the experiences children do bring, to avoid the compounding of the divide between different cultural experiences.

You may be thinking that these approaches take too long and there is a time constraint to a phonics lesson. If this is the case, think about when else you introduce early reading books to children – small group activities; guided reading; as part of the continuous provision, and reflect on how the books are introduced to children. Does it make them hungry to read them?

Having introduced the book, it is useful to "debug" the book. This means identifying the bits that might be tricky for the class. This is often particular words that are more difficult to decode or contain the new graphemes that have been more recently introduced. Once again, the connection to meaning needs to be a focus alongside the necessary decoding and word recognition skills. In a time-constrained phonics lesson, this may be as simple as giving the meaning of a word, sharing a picture that helps with the word's meaning, putting the word into a sentence, or asking children to put the word in a sentence. There are lots of approaches to vocabulary instruction that may work more effectively in reading beyond the phonics lesson and here are just a few.

1. **Focus on shades of meaning**. This is when you take one word from the text you are reading e.g. "bad," and generate as many other words that mean the same thing e.g. terrible, evil, nasty, wicked. For children, this can be a whole class oral activity, with the teacher acting as a scribe. Of course, this just tells us what children already know and the teacher may want to add in more words that they think children do not know but mean the same as the starting, known word e.g. dreadful, vile. The next step is to ask children to rank the words into their shades of meaning, from the word that means "about as bad as you can be" to the words that means "bad but not so bad"! Working from what is known and building from here, is a useful principle to use.
2. **Colour chart words**. Most DIY shops have displays of paint colour charts with each card having different shades of the same colour. These work really well when used with the shades of meaning activity. One colour chart could have all the words synonymous with the word "bad" – with a different word on each colour shade. These make great reference points for children's writing as well.
3. **Use a zone of relevance board**. Create a target board on the whiteboard and select a character or event in the story. Using the shades of meaning words, or others you have created for this activity, ask children to place words on the board. Words that most effectively match the selected character or event, place right at the centre of the target board, words that are useful but not essential for describing the character or event, place on one of the outer rings of the target board. Any words that are not relevant, place beyond the target. The discussion between children and where needed, facilitated by the teacher is where the learning happens.
4. **Give children a list of words to search for in a text** and once found children can work out the meaning from the rest of the words in the sentence. Agree on the meaning and then play with the words: draw it; act it out; create a glossary for the book; include it in a silly sentence; find which word is the longest and which word has the most consonants etc.

5. **Play pairs**. Give children words in pairs and ask children to evaluate the meaning of the words:
   - Is similar or a synonym, if it is, ask children to add another synonym.
   - Are opposites or antonyms and if they are, ask children to add another antonym.
   - Are related in some way in relation to meaning or features, and if they are, can children add another related word.
   - Are the words unrelated and if they are, can children add two words that are related to each of the words.
6. **Play would you rather?** In this activity the teacher selects two focus words that are challenging for the age and stage of the children but linked to the text being read, e.g. in year 5, I might use the words "audacious" and "subversive" when describing Sophie and Miss Eliot, in Katherine Rundell's "Rooftoppers." We then play the "would you rather" game by asking children a series of questions – would you rather be described as audacious or subversive in the local newspaper if you had managed to persuade the head teacher to give everyone an extra day of holiday. Would you rather be described as audacious or subversive if you tripped up the race leader on school sports day when no one was looking so your friend could win? What if the race leader was a bit of a bully?

Once the book has been introduced and "debugged," the next step is for children to read the book! We know that reading a book more than once has many benefits. Some schemes, such are Read Write Inc and some intervention programmes such as Boosting Reading @ Primary, use a three-reads approach, with a different focus for each time the text is read. We know that automatic and speedy decoding frees cognitive capacity to focus on comprehension. Perfetti's (1999) bottleneck analogy helps to explain this and this blogpost details the main points well https://littlemissdht.wordpress.com/2018/03/30/how-does-cognitive-load-theory-relate-to-the-teaching-of-reading/. The model makes clear that fluency in decoding – when decoding becomes an unconscious skill – enables the reader to understand what they are reading as they read, "in the moment." By reading a text more than once, children have the opportunity to develop decoding speed and accuracy as they read the text not just once, but two or three times. One of the three reads will focus, in the early stages of learning to read, on just being able to decode the words on the page, whilst the second read provides more opportunity to increase speed and accuracy and more importantly to dwell on meaning – for pleasure and purpose. The third read enables a child to read with greater fluency and expression and this too can provide children with a huge amount of pleasure by trying out different voices for characters, approaches to the emphasis of particular words in sentences and for slowing and increasing reading pace for effect. Of course, none of this "just happens" for every child and this needs to be modelled and taught.

Just because a book is from a reading scheme or decodable reading framework, it does not mean that it cannot be engaged with in ways that both develop comprehension (and the range of strategies needed to comprehend) and support motivation and engagement with reading. A purposefully positive approach would include using the following sorts of activities:

1. **Small world enactments of the story** by providing children with small world figures and/or Lego to encourage children to enact the story. This can be done in pairs,

groups or individually. This simple activity provides a window on children's literal comprehension.

2. **Sequencing** of the story. You can make a copy of the main pictures from the story and ask children to sequence these in order and to retell the story as they do this. Provide children with a word bank from the text and ask children to select one of the pictures in the sequence and to decide which of the words in the word bank match the picture. Make sure at least five words in the bank match each picture. Clearly, some words will match every picture and so this reduces the workload of making and cutting up the words! This activity involves a lot of reading as each of the words has to be read before being selected or not. Older children can be given a series of the pictures before reading the text. Children can predict the story, trying to decide the order of the pictures. They will be expected to pick up clues as to the likely sequence as they do this. Older children, after reading the text, can re-sequence their pictures if necessary and consider why they had thought there would be a different order. Children can select one picture and write over the picture their thoughts and feelings about characters or their description of the character or just words and phrases for this part of the story. Using a challenging wordless picture book with older children for an activity like this, provides a rich opportunity for discussion, critical engagement and a focus on meaning. A favourite of mine is *Professional Crocodile* by Giovanna Zoboli and Mariachara Di Giorgio, and more commonly used in schools, Aaron Becker's (author and illustrator) *Journey* trilogy, without forgetting the amazing works of Shaun Tan and David Weisner.

3. **Hot seating of the main character.** This often works more effectively with younger children when the teacher takes on the hot seated role and supports children to generate questions beforehand. Teacher in role never fails to excite children, although for some neurodiverse children, it can be helpful to explain what you are doing before this activity, and by wearing something that can be easily linked to the main character and so by taking this off at the end of the hot seating, children have an additional visual signal.

4. **Using the hearts, minds and voices strategy.** This approach encourages children to think about what a character might be feeling (the heart); what they might be thinking (minds) and what they are saying (voices). In very simple early reading books, there may be little complexity to the characters, but it gives children a chance to make meaning in a different way. It can be helpful to make a large heart and a thought and speech bubble to represent each. If these are laminated and so wipeable, they can be used in whole-class teaching and then children can "play" with these and try out different ideas in continuous provision activities. This sort of activity can be combined with freeze-framing.

5. **Freeze framing drama approach.** Identify a particular moment in the text where a number of characters appear – either in the pictures of the text, or for older children, in the extract that is the focus of the activity. A freeze frame is a frozen moment in time, or the scene if the book had been a film and the film had been stopped at this exact moment. Take each character in turn and select a child to take on this character. Ask the class to decide, where they should stand or sit, which direction they should be facing, how they should stand or sit, what expression should be on the face etc. At each

step ask children why they think this and encourage whole class engagement by asking them to try out some of the poses and expressions for themselves. The creation of the freeze frame is what is supporting comprehension. With younger children, there is no need to write anything, but it could be followed by photographing the scene or drawing the scene and adding speech bubbles – or even the hearts, minds and voices from above.

6   **Alternatives to questions**. Questions, written or oral, are often the main way of returning to a text to explore meaning and comprehension. However, there are lots of alternatives to questions that may provide variety for a class. You can give children a series of statements about a character or event they have just been reading about. Ask children to sort these into those they agree with and those they do not. You could ask them to sort them into those that are true, those that are false, and those that they are not sure about. Each time, children need to return to the text to talk about their choices.

These are just a very few ideas that could be used but the focus has been on ensuring the learning to read process can be meaningful and engaging, even with the simplest of reading scheme texts. Some of the ideas so far can be used for teaching reading beyond the phonics lesson and the remainder of the chapter will explore this further.

Spend a few minutes reflecting on your "purposefully positive" practice. Is every book encountered by children from reception to year 6 introduced with verve and passion? When you observe the teaching of your colleagues, do you feel an infectious enthusiasm for learning to read?

Using great texts for teaching

One of the ways children are introduced to new authors, genres, worlds and ideas is through the books their teachers share with them. Any choice of text for English teaching will usually be based on the needs and objectives of the literacy focus but this does not preclude other considerations. Chapters 2 and 8 are useful to identify new ways of increasing knowledge of children's literature and there are a few thoughts in relation to "purposefully positive" choices here in this section. A good place to start is always the work of the Centre for Literacy in Primary Education (CLPE). This charity has some fabulous units of work based around text, from their Power of Reading project, with a number of teaching sequences being offered for free on their website https://clpe.org.uk/teaching-resources/power-of-reading-teaching-sequences. These units do not provide specific teaching of skills or strategies necessarily, but they are excellent springboards for developing purposefully positive engagement with text. What is guaranteed with CLPE is the quality of the text as the experts at CLPE will have carefully considered the text in relation to quality, diversity and inclusion.

Text choice is also about the possibilities that can be opened for guided discussion and book talk (and so comprehension) that enables children to consider some of the bigger issues within society. In a "purposefully positive" approach, the "purposeful" element is as much about text choice that has these wider elements in mind, as much as the text's opportunity to explore grammatical features, vocabulary and character exploration. A book like *What Happened to You?* or *You're Amazing* by James Catchpole can provide an opportunity to talk about disability and the author has collaborated on designing lesson planning that can be used with the books https://thecatchpoles.net/2021/08/08/official-what-happened-to-you-lesson-plan-created-with-the-author/. Introducing an understanding of poverty can be quite controversial but using a book such as Kate Milner's *It's a No Money Day* can provide a springboard for children to either identify and/or empathise with the characters. Again, there are good ideas available on how to initiate these discussions sensitively: https://carnegiegreenaway.org.uk/wp-content/uploads/2021/04/CKG21-Shadowing-Resources-Its-A-No-Money-Day.pdf. Whilst it is important to know your classes' community heritages and stories, and so find texts that will enable children to identify and engage with characters that are "just like them," it is equally important to introduce children to communities and heritages that are not familiar to them. Perhaps consider using text like *Ossiri and the Bala Mengro* by Katharine Quarmby and Richard O'Neill that focuses on the traveller community with lesson plans from CLPE: https://www.hayfestival.com/schools/downloads/RR-ONeill-KS1-Ossiri-lesson-plan.pdf. Chapter 7 about engaging communities and families with reading for pleasure has more about this particular marginalised community.

A critical reading of text, or a "reading against" approach can also help us to identify texts to use or can help the teacher to plan using the text. Chapter 9 explores this in some depth and is helpful to read having read this chapter.

Reflect now on what considerations you currently make for text choice for literacy lessons? Do you consider the meaning and message of books, the world they are introducing children to and the opportunities they provide for exploring the bigger issues?

Conclusion and call to action!

In this chapter we have reflected on what is and what is not reading for pleasure. The idea of a "purposefully positive" approach to all encounters with books across the school day has been introduced.

1. Audit your approach to teaching – is every encounter with a text one that is approached with verve, passion and thoughtful critical engagement. If you can find a way to ask your class how they see you as a teacher of reading, this can be very informative!
2. Spend time planning the "apply" part of a phonics lesson. This part of the lesson is perhaps the most important. It demonstrates the point of reading, the culmination and purpose of phonics teaching. Consider how your school approaches this and what can be learnt from each other.
3. Reading schemes provide a helpful scaffold for young readers but if they are the sole focus of understanding what it means to be a reader, consider how this can be mitigated by the range of exposures to text that children see as part of learning to read.

References

Alexander, R. (2005) *Towards dialogic teaching: Rethinking classroom talk*. York: Dialogos.
Applegate, A., DeKonty, M., Applegate, M., Mercantini, A., McGeehan, C., Cobb, J., DeBoy, J., Modla, V. and Lewinski, K. (2014) 'The peter effect revisited: Reading habits and attitudes of college students', *Literacy Research and Instruction*, 53(3), pp. 188–204.

Beard, R., Brooks, G. and Ampaw-Farr, J. (2019) 'How linguistically-informed are phonics programmes?', *Literacy*, 53(2), pp. 86-94.

Carter, J. (2020) 'The assessment has become the curriculum: Teachers' views on the phonics screening check in England', *British Educational Research Journal*, 46(3), pp. 593-609. https://doi.org/10.1002/berj.3598

Cheatham, J. and Allor, J.H. (2012) 'The influence of decodability in early reading text on reading achievement: A review of the evidence', *Reading and Writing: An Interdisciplinary Journal*, 25(9), pp. 2223-2246.

Clark, C., Picton, I. and Galway, M. (2023) *Children and young people's reading in 2023*. London: National Literacy Trust.

Department for Education (2013) The national curriculum in England: Key stages 1 and 2 framework document. Available from https://www.gov.uk/government/publications/national-curriculum-in-england-primary-curriculum

Department for Education (2015) *Reading: The next steps*. London: DFE.

Department for Education (2016) *Education excellence everywhere*. London: DFE.

Department for Education and Schools (1998) National Literacy Strategy. London: DfES

Ellis, V. (2007) *Subject knowledge and teacher education: The development of beginning teachers thinking*. London: Continuum.

Ellis, S., Anderson, J. and Rowe, A. (2017) *Report on the renfrewshire literacy approach August 2015 – July 2017*. University of Strathclyde: Renfrewshire Council.

Ellis, S. and Smith, V. (2017) 'Assessment, teacher education and the emergence of professional expertise', *Literacy*, 51(2), pp. 84-93.

Flewitt, R., Nind, M. and Payler, J. (2009) 'If she's left with books she'll just eat them': Considering inclusive multimodal literacy practices', *Journal of Early Childhood Literacy*, 9(2), pp. 211-233. https://doi.org/10.1177/1468798409105587

Gough, P. and Tunmer, W. (1986) 'Decoding, reading and reading disability', *Remedial and Special Education*, 7(1), pp. 6-10.

Grover, V., Ryland, V., Gustafsson, J.-E. and Snow, C. (2020) 'Shared book reading in preschool supports bilingual children's second language learning: A cluster-randomised trial', *Children Development*, 91(6), pp. 2192-2210.

Haberman, M. (1991) 'Pedagogy of poverty versus good teaching', *Phi Delta Kappan*, 73(4), pp. 290-294.

Hattie, J. (2009) *Visible learning: A synthesis of over 800 meta-analyses relating to achievement*. London: Routledge.

Hempel-Jorgensen, A., Cremin, T., Harris, D. and Chamberlain, L. (2018) 'Pedagogy for reading for pleasure in low socio-economic primary schools: Beyond 'pedagogy of poverty'?', *Literacy*, 52: 86-94. http://doi.org/10.1111/lit.12157

Lawson, H., Layton, L., Goldbart, J., Lacey, P. and Miller, C. (2012). 'Conceptualisations of literacy and literacy practices for children with severe learning difficulties', *Literacy*, 46, 101-108. https://doi.org/10.1111/j.1741-4369.2011.00603.x

Levy, R. (2009) 'Children's perceptions of reading and the use of reading scheme texts', *Cambridge Journal of Education*, 39(3), pp. 361-377.

Lindorff, A., Stiff, J. and Kayton, H. (2024) *PIRLS 2021: National report for England*. London: Government Social Research.

McGeown, S., Johnson, R., Walker, J., Howatson, K., Stockburn, A. and Dufton, P. (2015) 'The relationship between young children's enjoyment of learning to read, reading attitudes, confidence and attainment', *Educational Research*, 57, pp. 389-402.

Moss, G. (2016) 'Knowledge, education and research: Making common cause across communities of practice', *British Education Research Journal*, 42(6), pp. 927-944.

Moss, G. (2017) 'Reimagining the future in the light of the past', *Literacy*, 51(2), pp. 56-64.

Office for Standards in Education (2023) *Research review series: English*. London: Ofsted Publications.

Office for Standards in Education (2014) *Getting them reading early*. London: Ofsted Publications.

Organisation for Economic Cooperation and Development (OECD) (2016) PISA 2018 draft analytical frameworks. Paris: OECD. https://www.oecd.org/pisa/data/PISA-2018-draft-frameworks.pdf

Perfetti, C.A. (1999). Comprehending written language: A blueprint of the reader. In Brown, C and Hagoort, P. (Eds.), *The neurocognition of language*. Oxford: Oxford University Press, pp. 167-208

Roberts-Holmes, G. and Bradbury, A. (2016) 'The datafication of early years education and its impact upon pedagogy', *Improving Schools*, 19(2), pp. 119-128. https://doi.org/10.1177/1365480216651519

Robinson, D., Moore, N. and Harris, C. (2018) 'The impact of books on social inclusion and development and well-being among children and young people with severe and profound learning disabilities: Recognising the unrecognised cohort', *The Reading Teacher*, 71(4), pp. 411-419.

Rose, J. (2006) *The independent review of the teaching of early reading*. London: DCSF.

Simpson, A. and Cremin, T.M. (2022) 'Responsible reading: Children's literature and social justice', *Education Science*. 12, p. 264. https://doi.org/10.3390/educsci12040264

Stanovich, K.E. (2008) 'Matthew effects in reading: Some consequences of individual differences in the acquisition of literacy', *The Journal of Education*, 189(1/2), pp. 23-55. http://www.jstor.org/stable/42748659

Sun, Y., Sahakian, B., Langley, C., Yang, A., Jiang, Y., Kang, J. and Feng, J. (2023). 'Early-initiated childhood reading for pleasure: Associations with better cognitive performance, mental well-being and brain structure in young adolescence', *Psychological Medicine*, 54(2), pp. 1-15.

Tennent, W. (2020) 'The assessment of reading comprehension in English primary schools: Investigating the validity of the key stage 2 reading standard assessment test (SAT)', *Education 3-13*, 49(4), pp. 481-494.

Thadani, V., Cook, M.S., Griffis, K., Wise, J.A. and Blakey, A. (2010) 'The possibilities and limitations of curriculum-based science inquiry interventions for challenging the "Pedagogy of poverty", *Equity Excellence Education*, 43, pp. 21-37.

Wigfield, A., Mason-Singh, A., Ho, A. and Guthrie, J. (2014) 'Intervening to improve children's reading motivation and comprehension: Concept-oriented reading instruction', in Karabenick, S. and Urdan, T. (eds.) *Advances in motivation and achievement*. Bingley: Emerald Group Publishing Limited, pp. 37-70.

4 Connecting people and planet through reading for pleasure

Verity Jones and Amanda D Webber

Introduction

"In France I found a leaf beetle... called it Norman... gave it some mint"

Year 5 primary school child

In this chapter, we seek to explore how children's enjoyment and engagement with reading can provoke a connection between people and the planet that has the potential to support well-being and enable active citizenship. We introduce this overlap between eco-pedagogy and reading for pleasure by considering how opportunities for children to enjoy reading experiences can encourage and enable social and environmental action. Through this lens, we reflect on who benefits from the pleasure of reading books with an environmental focus. We will present insights into how M.G Leonard's *Beetle Boy* – a short chapter book of fiction relating to insects – has been used with classes of 9- to 11-year-olds (Years 5 and 6). *Beetle Boy*, the first part of a "beetle-focused" trilogy, is a fictional story focusing on thirteen-year-old Darkus Cuttle as he tries to find out what has happened to his father (Bartholomew "Barty" Cuttle) an entomologist (beetle expert) who has gone missing from his workplace; the Natural History Museum in London. Throughout the story, Darkus is helped not only by friends and family but also by a host of amazing beetles.

Using *Beetle Boy* to reflect on reading for pleasure pedagogies, and teacher and children's responses to the text, we highlight how a personalized, supported and fun engagement with literature about, with and for social and environmental justice can reframe children's lives, from one which might otherwise be experienced as a static, fatalistic and pre-determined future, to one that is more hopeful. We suggest that reading for pleasure's pedagogy and practices can support the aims of eco-pedagogy and vice versa, and highlight transformational praxis.

Do we need to have issues of climate change and sustainability in our classrooms?

We are currently living in a time of climate and ecological emergency (IPCC, 2023) and environmental themes, including sustainability, are understandably prominent in public discourse, with children wanting to spend more time in Nature (National Trust, 2024), know what is happening in their environment, and understand what the responses and possible

DOI: 10.4324/9781003409939-4

actions are (Hickman et al., 2021). It is well documented that if children can have regular outdoor experiences, they are more likely to develop a connection and empathy with Nature (Barkham, 2020; Thompson, Aspinall and Montarzino, 2008). However, children's access to the environment and outdoors is often restricted. Over the last 50 years, children's physical activity and personal mobility have consistently reduced (Balmford et al., 2002; Witten et al., 2019), not helped by the COVID pandemic of 2019/2020. The lockdowns and enforced limited mobility resulted in even greater restrictions on children's movement and engagement with the environment which is slow to return. This situation builds on the public rhetoric that childhood is increasingly "de-naturalised" (Taylor, 2013).

What are the barriers for children to learn about climate change and sustainability?

If you are a pre-service teacher, you could be forgiven for making an assumption that climate change and sustainability would be explicit in the curriculum, perhaps in the subject areas of geography and science. As such, you may think children can rely on schools to provide them with the knowledge, understanding and skills to navigate these uncertain times. While this is the case in many curricula around the world, from Australia to Spain, India to Malta, Wales to Japan (UNESCO, 2021), there is no explicit reference to climate change or sustainability in England's Primary National Curriculum (Department for Education, 2013). Curricula in Scotland and Wales have explicit reference to sustainability, with the latter being designed in response to the United Nations Sustainable Development Goals (United Nations 2022). However, all of England's schools must have climate action plans in place by 2025. These action plans should increase practical knowledge, develop a sense of agency in the face of climate concerns, and inspire positive change through a whole-setting approach (Department of Education, 2024a).

It can be argued that sustainability is not a focus for many educational settings because of the approach to governance of schools – by which we refer to how UK schools are defined by academic performance and economic drivers to produce a population that is work-ready. This could be seen as a neo-liberal approach to governance. Within such a context, time and focus on being outside and/or learning about planetary welfare is not the priority (see Cudworth (2020) on how initiatives like Forest Schools may support this). In 2021 it was noted by Ofsted, that geography field trips, which do have an explicit mention in terms of outdoor learning in the primary curriculum, often go unfulfilled (Freeland, 2021).

While curriculum demands and governance may make including sustainability in learning a challenge, many schools in England do teach about these issues and you may be a teacher or pre-service teacher who has confidently embedded sustainability and climate change into children's learning experiences. Or, you may feel, like many other teachers, uncomfortable teaching these issues due to a lack of subject and/or pedagogical knowledge. As a result, you may, like many others as shown in the research, limit or avoid such topics (Howard-Jones et al., 2021). You may also have concerns about children's wellbeing, and worry that teaching about sustainability may cause more harm than good. In this chapter, we will try to explore some of these concerns, as well as consider how reading for pleasure can provide a vehicle to open discussion in a safe and sensitive way.

How do children feel about climate change and sustainability, and what is its impact?

Many children in our classrooms are aware of how our planet is experiencing extreme weather events, and how ongoing wars are claiming land and resources. As teachers and pre-service teachers, we often encourage our learners to watch BBC's children's news programme *Newsround* and read the children's newspaper *First News*. These media, along with the news updates children may overhear produced for older ears and eyes, can raise a multitude of emotional responses including fear, anxiety, guilt and anger (Jones and Podpadec, 2022). We have worked with classes of 6- and 7-year-olds who have told us how they are scared they will die because the world is going to flood as the icecaps melt and all the animals are going to die with them. These responses are impacting children's wellbeing and mental health (Clayton and Karazsia, 2020). Global concerns are not just the worry of older children and adults but are becoming increasingly common throughout our primary schools. While Scoffham (2021) argues that informing children about global issues is essential, pre-service teachers are often mindful that they do not want to make children feel worse and do not know how they would navigate distress.

How do you feel about teaching sustainability and climate change to children? Reflect on whether your feelings have impacted on what you have and haven't done in class, or what you might or might not plan to do in the future.

Research suggests that talking about how we feel in relation to sustainability and climate is positive for adults and children's wellbeing alike- acknowledging that the situation is scary supports children in recognising that they are not psychologically dysfunctional (Gimalova and Edgington, 2023; Hickman, 2020). Reading offers a safe space through which to explore and talk about difficult issues. Reading for pleasure pedagogies encourage supporting children's careful choice of books through recommendations, along with space and time for informal book talk. Mickenberg and Nel (2011) position literature as a space where children can challenge the current state of the world. By offering a range of books that explore different environments, different relationships with nature, and position people, plants and animals in interesting ways, we can encourage children to explore their feelings and responses to big issues. That said, it is pertinent to reflect on Ofsted's English subject review (Department of Education, 2024b) where it was noted that texts should be chosen first and foremost on literary merit. For children to make the most of their reading, they rely on their teachers to know and understand text quality. There are a number of chapters in this book that provide further details about the role of teacher knowledge.

How can I support children to access quality books?

To encourage reading for pleasure, the Teachers as Readers project (Cremin et al., 2009) found that having a wide and current knowledge about children's literature was essential, but it is also important for teachers to provide systems through which children can make their interest in books and their requisition known. In our two case study schools (which we have called Mayfly Primary and June Bug Juniors for the purposes of our research and this chapter) books were presented and available in both the library and classrooms. These areas were well stocked with a diverse range of books that the children were confident in how to search. In June Bug Junior School, when the children were told that *Beetle Boy* was just the first in a trilogy, children jumped from their seats and ran to the bookshelves and filing system. They then spoke to the librarian to request copies be purchased. Knowing how the school library system works is important and gives children agency in what is available to be read, encouraging child-led reading based on their interests.

The Teachers as Readers research has shown that having a physically engaging environment can tempt children into texts as well as offer spaces to relax, browse, and read for pleasure. Book talk is also important to promote books. At both Mayfly Primary and June Bug Juniors, teachers shared *Beetle Boy* by reading aloud. At June Bug Juniors, the teacher read the first few chapters aloud to the class, they posed questions and piqued their interest in a book that placed insects at the heart of a story and had the potential to inspire awe and wonder for nature. Those children who wished to continue to read on, independently, were provided with a copy of their own. Starting children off on their journey through the book was certainly successful with children commenting:

> "All I can say is I couldn't put it down. It's really good."

> "I was like, I'll just finish this chapter, then four chapters later ... I finished it in a `weekend"

At Mayfly Primary, the teacher read aloud the whole story to the class with children volunteering to contribute. One child remembered the desire to read aloud and the pleasure it gave them:

> "I begged her [the teacher] all of last week if I could read the book [out loud]. She finally said, yes. I could read a page and I read that page."

These responses resonate with the findings of the National Literacy Trust's 2023 survey, where 38% of 8-18-year-olds were found to be more likely to read books recommended to them and 32% were motivated to read when given a book of their own (Clark, Picton and Galway, 2023).

As with any pedagogies, the teacher must reflect on the benefits and challenges. In the school that promoted *Beetle Boy* through a shared class reading, some children who had English as an additional language found it difficult to follow the spoken word. This excluded some from the pleasure of the narrative and reduced the possibility of connection with nature. Children from Mayfly Primary commented:

> "I tried so hard to listen, but I keep forgetting what happens. I only remember the main bits. Yeah, it (Beetle Boy) is a bit more complex [to follow than other books that have been read aloud]. I feel like there's more stuff to understand".

Children spoke of how they found having their own copy of the class reader helpful when reading previous books. This allowed them to take turns to read out loud or flick back through if they wanted to re-read a section. These strategies are important when considering inclusion. Being included in accessing text such as *Beetle Boy* is not only important in the reading classroom but in the wider context of accessing nature. Dixon, Thomson and Fricke (2020) talk about the growing number of children learning English as an additional language (EAL) in schools and how these children tend to underperform in relation to their non-EAL peers. We would argue that reading pedagogies that do not allow children to explore issues relating to people and the planet also contribute to the ongoing feelings of exclusion that Black, Asian and other ethnic minorities experience in outdoor spaces.

Since 2009, Natural England has conducted an annual survey (see the People and Nature Surveys) to, among other aims, monitor the use of the natural environment amongst different demographic groups (Natural England, 2024). These, and other research in the UK, strongly indicate that minority ethnic groups use green space less frequently than those of a white heritage (Boyd et al., 2018; Carter et al., 2009; NatureScot 2020). Minority ethnic communities have also been identified as facing the highest number of barriers to the use of green space (Morris et al., 2011). Barriers that have been identified include a lack of knowledge, a lack of confidence and discrimination, (Boyd et al., 2018; Burdsey, 2013; Morris and O'Brien, 2011; Morris et al., 2011) – issues that could be explored through narratives around books such as *Beetle Boy* in the classroom. There is a critical need for these conversations.

Despite the UK's legal mandate, a large body of research and policy intended to reduce ethnic divides in access to Nature, The Landscape Review, commissioned by the Department for Environment, Food and Rural Affairs, identified how the British countryside is "an exclusive, mainly white, mainly middle-class club, with rules only members understand and much too little done to encourage first time visitors" (Glover, 2019, p. 15). The report suggests that there is still a long way to go before diversity objectives are met and calls for ambitious strategies to reduce these barriers and for greater levels of accountability to meet diversity and inclusion objectives. The authors warned that the UK "countryside will end up being irrelevant to the country that actually exists" (Glover, 2019, p. 70) should changes not be made. These changes, barriers and feelings of exclusion can be explored and discussed through our reading classrooms – with the appropriate texts and pedagogies.

Take a moment to think about how you support learners in accessing books at school. Who might find it challenging? Similarly, who might have limited access to nature outside of school and how might books (and which books) offer opportunities to become more familiar with these spaces?

Can books really change children's behaviour?

Through books we can help to signpost and plan how children can feel involved with solutions as active agents for change. This is where eco-pedagogy and reading for pleasure can collide in interesting and beneficial ways for people and the planet.

Eco-pedagogy is informed by the work of Paulo Freire, a teacher of literacy. Freire's teaching encouraged the reader not to merely read the word (decode) but to (re)read the world (comprehend) in context (Freire, 1997). Reading in this way is not passive but can be a critical determiner of and for action: reading can be transformational. As an eco-pedagogy, reading provides an opportunity for children to be supported in navigating transformative actions that ultimately have the aim to end socio-environmental injustices and human dominance over nature. Gadotti (2008) notes that an eco-pedagogical goal is to teach children when reading to identify connections between social injustices, and between social injustice and environmental violence. We add that reading-for-pleasure pedagogies have the ability to support this goal. In our case study, we focus particularly on applying these principles to the reading of the book *Beetle Boy*, exploring insects, nature and the environment. Children often have strong reactions to insects – often negative ones! Why do you think this might be the case and how would a change in attitude towards insects be beneficial?

Case study

This chapter focuses on research conducted in two primary schools in England: June Bug Juniors and May Fly Primary. May Fly Primary is a larger than average academy school in a diverse city location; approximately half of the pupils speak English as a second language. The school is in one of the 20% most deprived neighbourhoods in the UK, with over 36% of pupils eligible for free school meals (UK Ministry of Housing, Communities & Local Government, 2019). The proportion of children who have special educational needs (SEN) and/or disabilities is higher than the national average. By comparison, June Bug Primary is an average-sized primary school located in a residential area in one of the 10% least deprived neighbourhoods in the UK (UK Ministry of Housing, Communities & Local Government 2019). Most pupils are white British, and the proportion of disabled and SEN pupils is below average. A well below-average proportion of disadvantaged pupils is eligible for the pupil premium, and 9% are eligible for free school meals. Both schools have large outdoor spaces with woods and activity areas and highlight the importance of reading within their curriculum. Four focus groups were conducted with 26 year 5 and 6 children (9-11 year olds) across the two schools, and interviews were held with their teachers. In addition, an interview was held with M.G. Leonard, author of Beetle Boy, the children's book that formed the focus of this study.

Young readers of *Beetle Boy* recognized that one of the purposes of the book was to change people's minds about insects and M.G. Leonard, author of *Beetle Boy*, has been candid in her admission that this was her aim (Jones and Webber, 2024). Children reflected that people often dislike insects and many spoke about their own feelings towards these animals. Importantly, young people spoke about how, having read *Beetle Boy*, their feelings about insects had changed:

> "I want to be completely honest. I was a bit scared of beetles before I read the book, but now I know how like clever they are, and what's different stuff they've got about them. I think that if I found one, I'd be more interested by it instead of terrified".

As one young reader noted, reading the book made insects more familiar and "safer":

> "I think insects are a bit more safer now... If I see a beetle I'll be like, "Oh." But because I read the book I feel like it's okay."

Not only did children feel greater confidence around insects and feel they would not harm them but many also spoke about how they no longer wanted to harm, kill or "squish" them. Children talked about how having read the book, their opinions of beetles had changed to the extent that they acted differently around them. As one young reader commented:

> "[Before reading the book] I probably would have stepped on a beetle. But now I wouldn't touch it, I would just look at it. I would go to my garden and just look at it. I wouldn't stamp on it"

Others talked about "playing kind":

"Now I kind of feel comfortable, and little bugs or ladybugs I'll just put them on my hand. And they can just walk around my hand. And I play kind with them. I give them food or something. I put them on a leaf."

Through these conversations we can see that, a direct response to reading *Beetle Boy* has been to develop a greater respect and shift towards an awe and wonder for the insect kingdom. This is a testament to the power of reading for pleasure and its impact on environmental empathy - critical at a time of extinction crisis.

Of course, animals of the non-human kind have had an important role in children's literature for hundreds of years - many of them presented as talking beasts - a strategy used to directly assist the young reader in developing understanding and empathy for nature by authors as early as the eighteenth century. For example, Anna Sewell's *Black Beauty*, through the voice of a horse, amplified anti-cruelty messaging (Elick, 2015), while later titles such as Kenneth Grahame's *The Wind in the Willows* (1908) and John Lofting's *Doctor Dolittle* series of stories in the 1920s, implored the reader to be kind to, and look after, wild and domesticated creatures alike.

You may want to stop for a moment and consider which books you are familiar with that incorporate animals. How are they depicted and what is their role in the story? Is there an underlying moral? Is this moral about human behaviour toward each other, such as being kinder or caring, with the reader being asked to identify with the animal character, or is moral about the animals themselves, their environment or human attitude towards them?

In 1975, Margaret Blount wrote at length about the creatures to be found in children's fiction. She noted that by far the most prolific species was the rodent, either rat or mouse. Elick (2015) suggests that forty years on, this claim still holds with rodents - depicted as either vulnerable, misunderstood or undesirable - still being numerous in the pages of children's books, and often as a secondary character. Such depiction makes rats and mice ideal subjects where typical human power relations may be overthrown and subverted, to critique the status quo - which, in the context of climate change, could invite children (also the vulnerable or often overlooked in society) to recognize and identify with these characters and feel empowered for change.

While many tales (from *Aesop* to *Mickey Mouse*) have had rodent protagonists that help humans overcome various evils, to our knowledge there are no popular children's books (in the UK at least) with a sustainable theme, fighting climate change, or celebrating mitigation strategies, or developing an empathy for non-humans and love of biodiversity that draw on a cast of rodents - although perhaps Robert O'Brien's *Mrs Frisby and Rats of Nimh* could qualify here! However, there is a small, but growing shelf of books that include insects that are beginning to grab children's attention.

Insects, like rodents are often positioned as undesirable. They are, for many, harvest wreckers, biters and itch makers and disease spreaders. Yet insects are beginning to make themselves more known, both through their explicit presence as central characters (for example, in M.G. Leonard's *Beetle Boy*) or important support characters (in Nicola Davies *The Song That Sings Us*) or in their acknowledged absence (in Sita Brahmachari's *Where the River Runs Gold*) within children's narratives. In doing so, insects offer interesting ways for teachers to bring sustainability into reading-for-pleasure pedagogy and purposively positive encounters with text (see Chapter 3 for more on this).

Children often have a connection with insects before they even enter our classroom. Children can be enthralled by the sight and sound of insects that may buzz, wriggle or skuttle in the playground, the park or garden, conversely, they may feel uncomfortable in their presence. A negative association can inhibit children's enjoyment of outdoor spaces and impede the development of an ethics of care for the planet (Fisher and Lorenz-Reaves, 2018). Developing awe and interest in insects through reading could support a personal interest in a child's surroundings, as well as the development of environmental stewardship.

At this point it's useful to think about your own relationship with insects and how you feel about them. How might your feelings influence the children in your class and, if you are uncomfortable around certain creatures, how might you work to ensure negative messaging is not passed on.

Insects are important. They have the greatest diversity of all animals on the planet (Stork, 2018). Dwindling numbers have led to predictions of catastrophic consequences in relation to food production communicated in government reports (UK House of Commons, 2024) and children's online news platforms alike (e.g. CBBC's Newsround, 2022). Within our classrooms, minibeast hunts are often a much-loved aspect of science inquiry, while handprint butterflies and jolly busy bees can decorate an inviting reading corner. Whether it's Eric Carle's *Very Hungry Caterpillar* or Julia Donaldson's *Ladybird* that hears about a potential burglary at the farm, popular picture books with insects are frequently shared, read out loud, and brought to life in the classroom.

At this point we ask you to pause for a moment and think about what books are available in school that invite children to read about environmental issues and connect with nature. Are they fiction or non-fiction? What age/stage are they aimed at? What might be missing?

Texts that tempt: What might learner-led reading look like?

Reading for pleasure is successful when it is learner-led. In recent research, most children agreed that looking after the environment was important to them and they wanted to do and know more about it and how to protect it (Natural England, 2022). Children and young people are increasingly becoming more vocal in their demands for greater action to be taken by big businesses and governments in the face of climate change. Authors and publishers have responded to these demands, resulting in more titles being available within the genre. Youth climate activists, role models to many children, are beginning to be represented on bookshelves – for example, *"Flight"* and *"Birdgirl"* by Mya Rose Craig, Valentina Camerini's biography *"Greta's Story,"* Zoe Tucker's *"Greta and the Giants"* and Emma Reynolds *"Drawn to Change the World"* – a graphic novel collection highlighting the work of 16 youth activists from around the world. While these titles may begin to fulfil the reading desires of non-fiction fans, there is also a growing number of children's books about issues relating to sustainability and climate within the developing genre of climate fiction – or what is often referred to as cli-fi.

The cli-fi narrative is often framed around a dystopian context, drawing on the familiar trope of a nightmarish reality resulting from catastrophic climatic events: Elle Fountain's

"Melt" explores responses to melting ice sheets in the Arctic on indigenous communities; Marcus Sedgewick's "Floodland" is set in a futuristic Britain where climate change has turned cities into islands; Sita Brahmachari's "Where the River Runs Gold" explores themes of climate change, extinction and social justice. Through narratives of children's eco-literature, young readers can subvert scary eco-disaster tropes and rethink the state of the planet in terms of protagonists that can save us. They can be seen by some children as a way to make sense of a dystopian world where their worst fears have been realised. Children have a growing appetite for these cli-fi stories; however, not all children will be drawn to them.

Being able to identify the shift from reading because your teacher told you to, to reading for pleasure can sometimes be difficult to detect. However, one example of this shift is in the enthusiasm of children to find out more about a topic of interest. We saw this in abundance when children came to talk about their response to what they read in *Beetle Boy*:

"I went into more of it and I looked up some stuff about beetles, I realised that the thing I enjoyed most about the book was the fact that it had a large element of truth in it... so I actually kind of fact checked it".

"I wanted to look up and see what a Rhinoceros beetle looked like".

"I didn't know really about beetles and things. But now I kind of like them more, and I searched up interesting facts".

In reading *Beetle Boy* and becoming excited about the story, children were able to recognise that there was a whole world of beetle knowledge for them to discover. Three children shared their excitement about beetles in a conversation:

Child 1:	Once reading the book I realised that you don't actually know what special abilities they [insects] have and how many there are.
Child 2:	And how clever they are
Child 3:	Yea, after reading Beetle Boy, it's like, wow, they're really, actually really cool.

Being "really cool" helped the children enjoy the story. Having a topic in a reading book that is "really cool" is something that teachers may be able to tap into – supporting children to search for, identify and develop understanding on a specific topic. For example, teachers could suggest questions about the accuracy of a fact and suggest a fact to check. Teachers might invite children to share a fact about the book's topic and challenge readers to find out more facts independently to share. Such support and informal chat may encourage some children to extend their reading from fiction to non-fiction. In a study by Lewis, Edmunds and Carter (2024) it was found that children who were not usually interested in reading and who said they enjoyed science and maths much more, were more engaged in reading where the text used for their usual literacy learning had a scientific theme or included scientists as characters. This research "translated" high level research about micro-plastics into literary texts: poetry and stories, engaging the "scientist" in reading and the "book lover" in science! This research also wanted to challenge the idea that books with a science focus had to be non-fiction. It should be noted that the divide between those who read fiction and nonfiction has, for some time been stereotyped by gender. Previously it has been shown that boys may prefer non-fiction to girls, who prefer fiction (Hall and Coles, 1997; Millard, 1997; Topping, 2015). However, Merga (2017) has suggested that the disparity between boys and girls preferring non-fiction is not as wide as initially believed and that it is classroom culture that can dictate the borrowing habits of the children within it. Supporting all learners to explore non-fiction texts can support a greater understanding of people and planet. Asking readers to draw or find examples of what they think settings, plants and animal species from the book they are reading can develop understanding of a place. Such activities can also allow readers to explore why particular settings, plants and animals have been used, once they know what particular species look like or do. Through such activities, an inquisitiveness and greater appreciation of people and planet may develop.

Tempting talk: Does it matter if a book is not factually correct when we're talking about nature?

Through our geography and science lessons we may well share "facts," through our English we have the ability to take those facts and use them in creative and new ways, exploring and extending situations, characters and topics in new and exciting ways. As teachers, we need to be mindful of the line between imagination and fact. In saying that, we do not mean we must only teach fact, quite the contrary. We've found that children are more than capable of recognising what is and isn't fact and enjoy exploring these themes. *Beetle Boy* is an interesting case in point. M.G Leonard, the author of *Beetle Boy*, worked with an entomologist to fact check the abilities and habits of insects in the story. We have already commented on how a number of children enjoyed fact-checking about insects. However, with regard to the divide between fiction and non-fiction, the children recognised that an author does not need to have a total commitment to fact for a fictional work to be of interest and enjoyed. Children made the following comments:

> "Everything is kind of exaggerated a bit [in Beetle Boy]. Because, like the beetles are a lot more powerful even than normal ones are. [This representation] makes you more interested in them as well because it makes them seem more interesting".

> "In my opinion, I don't really mind if I found out that it wasn't exactly 100% fact. But I think that if there's a small element of truth, then it's still ok".

For those children who had fact-checked, we have seen that knowing what was true assisted with their enjoyment. However, for those who did not fact-check, some young readers were under the impression that the representation of beetles was all imagined:

> "No, it's fake, it's all fake"

> "And their [beetles] behaviour, they act like humans. That is not a real"

Identifying something as "fake" and "not real" is in many ways unproblematic to the enjoyment of a text. As teachers, we may wish to disrupt this understanding of what is fake or imagined and real, especially when the themes might support the understanding of underrepresented species at a time of climate and ecological emergency. Framing the beetles of *Beetle Boy* as "fake" is to undermine the diversity of species on the planet. We would therefore suggest that a teacher using *Beetle Boy* or other fictional texts relating to plants and animals should explore these themes through critical reading and fact-checking. Related classroom activities might include research projects, writing nonfiction fact files, or instructions on how to keep the plant or animal alive. Once secure in the adaptations of plants and animals to their habitat, learners could be invited to imagine their own species, re-writing extracts of stories to include their own creations and being able to discuss the real and imagined skills of each and where the inspiration for these came from.

The diversity and exoticness of beetle species are celebrated throughout the book with details given about their interesting morphology, physiology and behaviour. For example, we learn how the bombardier beetle can spray acid from its bum, a useful trick when wanting to melt through a metal lock to escape from capture. If children don't know that this is an accurate depiction of the bombardier beetle it's a missed opportunity of awe, wonder and an enjoyable session of bum talk in the classroom!

Are all animal books going to support reading for pleasure?

We have already commented on the long history of non-human animals in children's literature. In fact, before reading *Beetle Boy* in May Fly Primary the class had read S F Said's, *"Varjak Paw"* – a mentor story of cats, friendship and loyalty. The story has Varjak Paw – a Mesopotamian blue kitten – as its protagonist, surviving in a city full of dangerous dogs, cat gangs and mysterious "vanishings." Reflecting on the enjoyment of *Beetle Boy* it was notable that those children of Muslim faith began to reflect on their reading of Varjek Paw as a comparison and immediately shared their fear and dislike of dogs. For example, comments included:

> "I would never touch a dog".

> "All my family, nearly all the Somalians are scared of dogs".

Islam teaches that all forms of animal cruelty are forbidden, yet many Muslim scholars agree that dogs are unclean, and as such, contact with them is disliked and even feared by some. Some children spoke of this dislike – in relation to characterisation of Varjek Paw, and how *Beetle Boy* was more enjoyed because of the lack of dogs in the text. Informal talk about two books with an animal theme encouraged one child to recount a distressing experience:

> "I'd seen a man with two dogs and no leash. And the guys are shouting at us for no reason. And the dogs were barking".

This comment came with obvious fear and discomfort to the child, it came amongst a conversation about beetles and how children felt they had a new respect for them. Such conversations are a reminder that, as a teacher, it is important to be aware of the cultural importance of some animals and how a story with, for example a dog as protagonist, may be read by children from different cultural heritages, or who have negative experiences of dogs. When recommending and talking about books with children, knowing the child and recognising their funds of knowledge is always going to help support appropriate choice (see Chapter 7 for a discussion of funds of knowledge).

Conclusion and call to action!

In this chapter we have considered how reading *Beetle Boy* has supported children in reading for pleasure. In so doing it has identified how children may respond to different access strategies that teachers use to present books to children, and how some strategies may exclude certain readers. We have considered how the discussion of plants and animals from texts might support changes in behaviour and greater empathy towards the planet at a time of climate and ecological emergency. These changes in behaviour can not only relate to an awe, wonder and protection of a species but also a desire for knowledge. We have noted that fact-checking can be a route into wider reading for some children, while for others it is necessary to ensure that misconceptions around plants, animals and planetary processes are disrupted. Finally, we have considered how children's books can have the potential not only to support greater respect for the planet we share with other non-human animals, but also how we can support other humans in respecting this. Children's books about the climate and nature are powerful tools for teachers to use and we encourage you to be critical, fact-finding friends to the children in your class in order to encourage enjoyment, engagement and empathy with the world.

Take a moment to have a final reflection on what this chapter has discussed:

1. Who is in your class and what funds of knowledge and identity do they bring?
2. How might you prepare to have conversations about sustainability?
3. What texts will help you identify a range of species to develop a connection and curiosity with/about nature and wildlife?
4. What good news stories might you bring to sustainable book chat to support children in seeing the good work that's going on?
5. What Reading for Pleasure strategies might you use to develop a love for eco-literature and when are you going to do it?

References

Balmford, A., Clegg, L., Coulson, T. and Taylor, J. (2002) 'Why conservationists should heed pokemon', *Science, (American Association for the Advancement of Science*, 295(5564), p. 2367.

Barkham, P. (2020) *Wild child: Coming home to nature*. London: Granta Books.

Blount, M. (1975) *Animal land: Creatures of children's fiction*. New York: W. Morrow.

Boyd, F., White, M.P., Bell, S.L. and Burt, J. (2018) Who doesn't visit natural environments for recreation and why: A population representative analysis of spatial, individual and temporal factors among adults in England. *Landscape and Urban Planning* 175, pp. 102-113. https://doi.org/10.1016/j.landurbplan.2018.03.016

Brahmachari, S. (2019) *Where the river runs gold*. London: Orion Children's Books.

Burdsey, D. (2013) 'The foreignness is still quite visible in this town': Multiculture, marginality and prejudice at the English seaside', *Patterns of Prejudice*, 47(2), pp. 95-116.

Camerini, V. (2019) *Greta's story: The girl who went on strike to save The planet*. Simon & Schuster Ltd.

Carter C., Lawrence A., Lovell R. and O'Brien L. (2009) The Forestry Commission Public Forest Estate in England: Social use, value and expectations. Final Report Farnham: Forest Research. https://cdn.forestresearch.gov.uk/2022/02/pfe_social_study_final_report.pdf [Accessed 21 November 2024].

CBBC Newsround (2022) Insect Numbers Are Falling across the UK, According to New Survey. https://www.bbc.co.uk/newsround/61336166 [Accessed 17 June 2024].

Clark, C., Picton, I. and Galway, M. (2023) *Children and Young People's Reading in 2023*. National Literacy Trust. https://nlt.cdn.ngo/media/documents/Reading_trends_2023.pdf [Accessed 21 November 2024].

Clayton, S. and Karazsia, B.T. (2020) 'Development and validation of a measure of climate change anxiety', *Journal of Environmental Psychology*, 69, p. 101434.

Craig, M.R. (2023) *Flight*. US: Puffin Books.

Craig, M.R. (2023) *Birdgirl*. UK: Vintage.

Cremin, T., Mottram, M., Collins, F.M., Powell, S. and Safford, K. (2009) 'Teachers as readers: Building communities of readers', *Literacy*, 43(2009), pp. 11-19.

Cudworth, D. (2020) 'Promoting an emotional connection to nature and other animals via forest school: Disrupting the spaces of neoliberal performativity', *The International Journal of Sociology and Social Policy*, 41(3), pp. 506-521.

Davies, N. (2021) *The song that sings us*. Cardiff: Firefly Press.

Department of Education (2013) National curriculum in England: Primary curriculum. https://www.gov.uk/government/publications/national-curriculum-in-england-primary-curriculum [Accessed 21 November 2024].

Department of Education (2024a) Sustainability leadership and climate action plans in education. https://www.gov.uk/guidance/sustainability-leadership-and-climate-action-plans-in-education#climate-action-plans [Accessed 05 June 2024].

Department of Education (2024b) Telling the Story: the English education subject report. https://www.gov.uk/government/publications/subject-report-series-english/telling-the-story-the-english-education-subject-report [Accessed 05 June 2024].

Dixon, C., Thomson, J. and Fricke, S. (2020) 'Language and reading development in children learning English as an additional language in primary school in England', *Journal of Research in Reading*, 43(3), pp. 309-328.

Elick, C. (2015) *Talking animals in children's fiction*. Jefferson: McFarland & Company, Inc Publishers.

Fisher, N. and Lorenz-Reaves, A. (2018) 'Teaching with live insects', *Science and Children*, 56(4), pp. 32-39.

Fountain, E. (2021) *Melt*. London: Pushkin Children's Books.

Freeland, I. (2021) Geography in Outstanding primary schools. https://educationinspection.blog.gov.uk/2021/05/11/geography-in-outstanding-primary-schools/ [Accessed 19 September 2023].

Freire, P. (1997) *Pedagogy of the heart*. New York: Continuum.

Gadotti, M. (2008) *Education for sustainable development: What we need to learn to save the planet*. São Paulo: Instituto Paulo Freire.

Gimalova, M. and Edgington, L. (2023) Eco-anxiety in Children and Young People: what can we do to help? The British Psychological Society. https://www.bps.org.uk/blog/eco-anxiety-children-and-young-people-what-we-can-do-help [Accessed 17 June 2024].

Glover, J. (2019) *Landscapes Review*. https://assets.publishing.service.gov.uk/government/uploads/system/uploads/attachment_data/file/833726/landscapes-review-final-report.pdf [Accessed 14 June 2024].

Grahame, K. (1908) *The wind in the willows*. London: Methuen.

Hall, C. and Coles, M. (1997) 'Children's reading choices: Questions of quality', *Use of English*, 48, pp. 138-148.

Hickman, C. (2020) 'We need to (find a way to) talk about ... eco-anxiety', *Journal of Social Work Practice*, 34(4), pp. 411-424.

Hickman, C., Marks, E., Pihkala, P., Clayton, S., Lewandowski, R.E., Mayall, E.E., Wray, B., Mellor, C. and van Susteren, L. (2021) 'Climate anxiety in children and young people and their beliefs about government responses to climate change: A global survey', *Lancet Planet Health*, 5, pp. e863-e873.

Howard-Jones, P., Sands, D., Dillon, J. and Fenton-Jones, F. (2021) 'The views of teachers in England on an action-oriented climate change curriculum', *Environmental Education Research*, 27(11), pp. 1660-1680.

IPCC. (2023) Summary for policymakers, in: Core Writing Team, H. Lee and J. Romero (eds.) *Climate change 2023: Synthesis report. Contribution of working groups I, II and III to the sixth assessment report of the intergovernmental panel on climate change*. Geneva, Switzerland: IPCC, pp. 1-34. https://doi.org/10.59327/IPCC/AR6-9789291691647.001

Jones, V. and Podpadec, T. (2022) 'Young people, climate change and fast fashion futures', *Environmental Education Research*, 29(11), pp. 1692-1708.

Jones, V. and Webber, A.D. (2024) 'In conversation with.... M. G. Leonard', *Primary Science*, 181, pp. 4-5.

Leonard, M.G. (2016) *Beetle boy*. UK: Chicken House Books.

Lewis, F., Edmunds, J. and Carter, J. (2024) 'Using literary materials as a gateway to science', *Primary Science*, 182, pp. 23-25.

Lofting, H. (1920) *The story of doctor doolittle*. US: Frederick A Stokes.

Merga, M. (2017) ''Do males really prefer non-fiction, and why does it matter', *English in Australia*, 52(1), pp. 27-37.

Mickenberg, J. and Nel, P. (2011) Radical Children's literature now!. *Children's Literature Association Quarterly*, 36, pp. 445-473. https://doi.org/10.1353/chq.2011.0040.

Millard, E. (1997) *Differently literate: Boys, girls and the schooling of literacy*. London: Falmer Press.

Morris, J. and O'Brien, E. (2011) 'Encouraging healthy outdoor activity amongst underrepresented groups: An evaluation of the active England woodland projects', *Urban Forestry and Urban Greening*, 10(4), pp. 323-333.

Morris, J., O'Brien, E., Ambrose-Oji, B., Lawrence, A., Carter, C. and Peace, A. (2011) 'Access for all? Barriers to accessing woodlands and forests in Britain', *Local Environment*, 16(4), pp. 375-396.

National Trust (2024) Children's Urgent Call: More time in nature essential shows new survey by National Trust and First News. https://www.nationaltrust.org.uk/services/media/childrens-urgent-call-more-time-in-nature-essential [Accessed 17 June 2024].

Natural England (2022) The Children's People and Nature Survey for England: 2022 update. https://www.gov.uk/government/statistics/the-childrens-people-and-nature-survey-for-england-2022-update [Accessed 14 June 2024].

Natural England (2024) The People and Nature Surveys for England. https://www.gov.uk/government/collections/people-and-nature-survey-for-england [Accessed 05 June 2024].

NatureScot (2020) Scottish Nature Omnibus - summaries - The Black and Minority Ethnic (BME) community and nature. https://www.nature.scot/doc/scottish-nature-omnibus-summaries-black-and-minority-ethnic-bme-community-and-nature [Accessed 21 November 2024].

Reynolds, E. (2023) *Drawn to change the world*. London: HarperAlley.

Said, S.F. (2014) *Varjak paw*. London: Corgi Children's.

Scoffham, S. (2021) 'Finding Hope at a time of crisis', *Primary Geography Spring 2021*, 104, pp. 8-9.

Sedgewick, M. (2010) *Floodland*. London: Orion Children's Books.

Stork, N.E. (2018) 'How many species of insects and other terrestrial arthropods are there on earth?, *Annual Review of Entomology*, 63, pp. 31-45.

Taylor, A. (2013) *Reconfiguring the natures of childhood*. London: Routledge.

Thompson, C.W., Aspinall, P. and Montarzino, A. (2008) 'The childhood factor: Adult visits to green places and the significance of childhood experience', *Environment and Behavior*, 40(1), pp. 111-143.

Topping, K.J. (2015) 'Fiction and non-fiction Reading and comprehension in preferred books', *Reading Psychology*, 36, pp. 350-387.

Tucker, Z. (2019) *Greta and the giants*. London: Francis Lincoln Children's Books.

UK House of Commons (2024) Insect decline and UK food security. Second report of sessions 23-24. Science Innovation and Technology Committee, London.

UK Ministry of Housing, Communities & Local Government (2019) English Indices of Deprivation. https://www.gov.uk/government/statistics/english-indices-of-deprivation-2019 [Accessed 14 June 2024].

UNESCO (2021) Learn for our Planet. 377362eng.pdf (unesco.org) [Accessed 14 June 2024].

United Nations (2022) Sustainable Development Goals Report 2022. https://unstats.un.org/sdgs/report/2022/ [Accessed 21 November 2024].

Witten, K., Kearns, R., Carrol, P. and Asiasiga, L. (2019) 'Children's everyday encounters and affective relations with place', *Social and Cultural Geography*, 20(9), pp. 1233-1250.

5 Representation in children's literature

Karan Vickers-Hulse, Kalpa Ghelani, Emma Thomas and Nick Latham

Introduction

The purpose of this chapter is to consider the importance of representation through the careful curation of literature and practice in the classroom. It will build upon the influential reports published by the Centre for Literacy in Primary Education (CLPE, 2018, 2019, 2020, 2021, 2022) which have inspired positive changes in the publishing industries. This chapter aims to build on this positive change (CLPE, 2021) and look at the impact and implications for educators. We use the work of Bishop (1990) to explore how the concept of literature is compared to "windows, mirrors and sliding doors" and how this can be integrated into current classrooms and school life. We discuss the impact that texts and engagement with literature can have on the development of the secure social identity of children. This chapter will give practical strategies to teachers and other professionals in creating a classroom culture that fosters a sense of belonging and makes children feel valued and includes case studies to reflect the voice of the child and their teachers. We hope that this chapter will support teachers in becoming allies with the children in their classrooms, working *with* children to promote the joys of representation and diversity through a range of lenses such as class, gender, sexuality, ethnicity, neurodiversity, and disability (including invisible disabilities). The thread of representation will feed into subsequent chapters.

The importance of representation in children's literature

Representation of racial identities portrayed in children's books has improved with studies such as the CLPE's Reflecting Realities reports from 2017 onwards highlighting the significance of Black and ethnic representation in children's books and providing practical support for practitioners in how to move forward. In 2021, the percentage of children's books published that featured Black, Brown and minoritised groups rose to 20% however, true representation also requires a diversity of experience, stories and voices where children can learn about others as outlined in Bishop's (1990) research. Although representation in children's books has improved, this has largely focused on racial identity and not protected characteristics such as gender, sexuality, and disability (Equality Act, 2010) with data from the Cooperative Children's Book Centre (CCBC, 2023) demonstrating that no more than 5% of books include physical, cognitive, neurological, and psychiatric disabilities, LGBTQ and/or non-Christian characters. This indicates that there is a lack of representation of protected characteristics which means that there is still work to be done before we have an authentic representation of *all* protected characteristics in children's literature. Consideration also needs to be given to the type of representation demonstrated in children's books. Although representation may be present in books, this may not always be positive, with representation of protected characteristics sometimes stereotyped. Books may also feature a protected characteristic as being the main feature of a story or as an "issue" within the narrative rather than an incidental attribute of the character. For example, a historical perspective indicates from a study by Biklen and Bogdana (1977) that literature predominantly portrayed negative stereotypes of characters with disabilities which made it simple to ignore this group of people in this period. Representation of people with disabilities has improved since 1977 however, more recently, Saunders (2000) identified that subliminal or negative messages persist. Bishop (1990) highlighted the importance of children seeing themselves represented in literature to develop a sense of belonging and value. Her seminal work discussing the role of books as "Windows, Mirrors and Sliding Doors" represents how books allow children to learn about the diverse world around them, enabling them to understand others, understand themselves and develop empathy. This metaphor has been used widely among educators, librarians, and publishers to critique the lack of authentic diversity in children's literature (Reed, 2022). Authentic diversity is a key component of the Centre for Literacy in Primary Education's (CLPE) drive to explore the diversity of children's literature within classrooms in the United Kingdom (UK). The inclusion of diverse literature must be well considered, avoiding tokenistic inclusion.

Curating your literature collection

As we curate our classroom or library collections, we have a responsibility to include literature that features characters and authors which represent the identity of the children we teach, have taught, and will teach in the future – moving away from what has historically been one-sided. This identity might refer to racial identity, sexuality, gender, ability, disability and more as well as intersectionality across and within these groups. In the past, narratives presented by authors and publishers were often "windows" into a world of predominantly white characters – or even animals and inanimate objects. When occasionally white authors did write books that included children of colour, they often featured harmful stereotypes, tokenism, and inauthentic stories (Reed, 2022). Building a collection of children's literature needs to be embedded alongside classroom practice in a truly meaningful, purposeful, and carefully considered way. Building on Bishop's initial work, Enriquez (2021) embraces the metaphor and moves to show how we can best apply this in practice. She looks to rethink mirrors as "foggy mirrors" where "close approximations are not good enough" (Enriquez, 2021, p. 104). Though her paper refers to racially diverse literature, it can be applied across the protected characteristics. Knowing our children, their rich identities and interests and listening to their voices are key here. Windows are re-considered as "tiny windows." By this, Enriquez (2021) offers up the idea that one mirror or one window is not enough as it limits children's access to new or unfamiliar worlds. She asks if we can consider how many opportunities we have where we can incorporate diverse literature into our practice. Finally, she encourages teachers to look for opportunities to provide children with books where they need help to open doors; the aim being to rethink our own privilege, position and perspectives. In responding to these texts, as teachers, we need to reflect on how these books have been written and how language or context have an impact on young readers. Representation in texts supports children in identifying and learning about differences in the people around them (Botelho and Rudman, 2009) which is essential in developing social equity and understanding complex social relationships. Understanding difference and the significance of positive and authentic representation can also support children in developing a sense of self and "theory of mind" (Kidd and Castano, 2013). Theory of Mind (ToM) is the capacity to identify and understand others' subjective states and allows successful navigation of complex social relationships such as those that exist in educational settings where each person is unique with their own identity and personality. Literature and the use of diverse texts is one way that teachers can support children to grow their Theory of Mind and develop empathy and understanding for others whilst championing their own identity and sense of self.

Representation in the teacher workforce

Data demonstrates that 95.7% of the teacher workforce in England are white (UK Government 2023) however, the children in UK classrooms are much more diverse with regards to race as well as class, sexual orientation, and physical and cognitive abilities. Therefore, an understanding of teacher positionality is crucial (Johnson-Bailey, 2012) as our conceptions of diversity and identity have a direct impact on the way we approach and engage with literature and the texts we choose to use in our classrooms (Saleh, 2023). We, as teachers, have a responsibility to ensure that we make intentional choices with regard to the books we use and how they are thematically linked within and across the curriculum to avoid tokenism but also to confirm the importance of diverse texts, stories, and voices within the whole school curriculum (Scafe, 1989 cited in Saleh, 2023).

Teachers understand the importance of including diverse voices and texts as a way to ensure representation but there is often a lack of guidance and education for pre-service and in-service teachers on how to embed this into classroom practice (Elliott et al., 2021). Although, thankfully, this is changing for pre-service teachers, there is still little statutory training to support in-service teachers in understanding how to incorporate diversity and representation into their day-to-day classroom practice. We hope that this chapter will support you in embedding diverse literature in a meaningful way in your own classrooms.

You may like to pause and consider at this point what diversity looks like in your classroom and school. Think about the teachers and wider workforce in your school; think about where the positive images are around your classroom and school and also think about the books you have on offer.

A case study approach

To inform the writing of this chapter we took a case study approach. Our case study school was a large, diverse, city primary school which was in the relatively unique position of having a school librarian. We had the opportunity to work with the teachers, librarian and children. It is useful to bear in mind that this is a case study based in one school and the themes that were identified are from discussions with the children and staff of this school. Other case

Figure 5.1 Example of "book blanket" used in the research.

studies within this book will provide further windows into the views of children and teachers. We began the research with a book blanket followed by a semi-structured interview with the children, enabling us to have an open conversation about their choice of books, their interests and their views about reading.

Figure 5.1 shows an example of a "book blanket" used in the research.

Children were encouraged to articulate their responses as they browsed the selection, talking to their peers about what they liked or disliked and why. Once the children had sufficient time to browse, they selected a "favourite" book (or two) and were asked what the reasons were behind this choice. After the children had made their selection, researchers asked follow-up questions to better understand the children's choices. Questions were structured to allow for an open dialogue between researchers and children as opposed to a formal interview: tell us why you chose that book? What is the book about? Why does that book interest you? Is that the type of book you would normally read? How did you know this would be a good book for you? These discussions were recorded on a digital audio capture device and analysed afterwards with children's voices being used to identify themes for discussion and development. Although this work was conducted as a formal research project, this is a formula that could be adapted to enable you to conduct similar research within your own classroom or setting. You may choose to embed this within your normal classroom practice (e.g. during a reading lesson) or conduct a book blanket activity to kickstart a focus on reading for pleasure. How do you currently hear children's voices about what texts are on offer; what their preferences are and where you might identify gaps in their knowledge of communities beyond their own?

During research conversations, and an analysis of responses, representation was interpreted as that of race and ethnicity with some discussion of Pride and additional needs such as Special Educational Needs (SEND) and English as an Additional Language (EAL) for example. From the data collected, four themes were identified:

- Sense of belonging/feeling valued.
- Book choice.
- Prompts for discussions.
- Reading environment.

Whilst these themes mainly relate to the representation of (and participants' interpretation of) race and ethnicity, the outcomes of this study can be explored through the wider meaning of representation and consideration of other protected characteristics such as gender, sexuality, disability and neurodiversity.

Theme 1: Belonging

Schools can be viewed as a place for fostering a sense of belonging for the community it serves (Vincent, 2021). This theme of belonging was evident in the participant discussions. Children chose books with characters who "looked like me," whether that be the same afro hair, wearing a Hijab or parent book characters who shared the same race and ethnicity as theirs. One girl said: *"This is my story."* The stories these books told also held a sense of belonging for the children. This sense of belonging cultivated a sense of pride in children. Two children who had read a book about Mosques wrote a book review for a school display board and held an assembly to share and celebrate their Islamic faith. Their teachers said, *"One of the girls wanted to do a book on Ramadan which just shows her pride in her faith and wanting to share that with the rest of the school. It was beautiful."*

Cremin et al. (2014) discussed how creating reading communities can positively impact Reading for Pleasure (RfP). Fostering a sense of belonging for all children through children's literature supports RfP and offers children a powerful way of meeting their expectations of belonging at a time when they are figuring out who they are and will become (Traille, 2007). It was evident how the school's RfP practice had created a community of readers which offered children the opportunity to belong, as a reader, to a community of readers ranging from peers to teachers. This active community of engaged readers enabled children to discuss, recommend and share books together. It is evident that RfP is a particularly social process (Cremin et al., 2014) and the school's community of readers demonstrated how different children created their own range of reading communities. For example, higher attaining children shared books between them, and some lower attaining children deliberately sought each other out when new books had been purchased that appealed to not only their skills but also their preferences. The teachers had identified this group as one that did not regularly talk about their book choices with their peers. One teacher commented, *"So, when we came back after lockdown, it was obvious that reading stamina was low and nobody was challenging taking on a big book, so I quickly ordered a lot of Barrington Stoke books. Those books are so nice-slim books but really good authors."*

The knowledge of children's books and understanding of their readers shown by the teachers and the school's librarian, ensured that the range of children's books offered, meant readers of any attainment felt they belonged to this community of readers. This school has created a sense of belonging for children as readers *and* as readers at their individual attainment. One child said, "*she (school librarian) is definitely really helpful; she knows every book in every place...I don't know any books that are interesting, so I just have to go to her.*"

It was also evident, for children, that seeing their parents and teachers as readers was a powerful tool in both their developing reader identity *and* their sense of belonging to a community of readers. Children talked about what their parents or wider family read – often non-fiction or other texts, both on and offline, including community and religious texts. Sometimes as teachers, we unwittingly give children the impression that reading and RfP is just about stories and books. The teachers and librarian at our case study school tried hard to widen what is considered as "reading" to enable inclusion and acknowledgement of the range of reading practices. Knowing more about families' and parents' reading practices can support schools in developing reading relationships with families (Cremin et al., 2014). Many children we spoke to talked about a shared reading culture in their family and talking to their parents about their reading which was not necessarily in English. Therefore, it is important not to make assumptions about parental literacy and discover how to collaborate teachers', children's and parents' reading practices and lives (Cremin et al., 2014). The Strathclyde Three Domain model (Ellis and Smith, 2017) outlines three areas of knowledge for the teacher about each child in their class. The teacher needs to have a clear assessment of the child's cognitive skills and knowledge of reading and writing; their cultural and social capital (including their funds of knowledge, beliefs about reading and their experience of reading) and finally an understanding a child's reader identity and agency.

The combination of school's knowledge and understanding of the children's reader identities, funds of knowledge and reading skills creates a meaningful sense of belonging for the children as a reader, a powerful factor in reading for pleasure. Chapter 7 has a focus on the family and community and provides further exploration of this aspect of reading for pleasure as well as providing some useful strategies to support practice.

Pause and reflect on how your children would respond to questions about their sense of identity as a reader and, in particular how they see themselves as belonging to a community of readers within and beyond the classroom. Who are the children at the margins of your communities of readers? How can they be encouraged to be part of a community – is this about book choice and availability or finding a community of readers who are most like they are as a reader? Who are your children's role models as readers?

Theme 2: Book choice

To successfully cultivate Reading for Pleasure (RfP), the TaR (Teachers as Readers) research project by Cremin et al. (2009) found that teachers need a wide and current knowledge base of children's literature as well as knowledge of the children's reading habits and preferences. It was apparent that this was a key part of the RfP practice in the case study school. There is a clear drive from the school librarian, as well as teaching staff, when it comes to book choice and good practice. For many teachers, access to a school librarian may be limited or non-existent, but there will undoubtably be practices that we can apply in our own contexts. The school librarian had a system in place to support book choice for whole-class reads. The librarian said, *"the literacy lead and I get together quite regularly, we work together really closely and I think we've got a pretty strong [strategy], we kind of know the school books being used by now and we'll try and pick books that are representative; that we've got a good mix of male and female lead characters, or protagonists and different backgrounds. And if we know that there's been a trauma with one child and that might come up in a book that they're due to read, we'll swap that out for something else. If we've got something that's going to be a trigger. So that kind of changes year on year."*

The librarian reflected on how they had supported teachers in subsequently choosing books for class readers (specifically for RfP, not for integrating within English learning) and ensuring there was a diverse spread of authors and protagonists represented across year groups and classes with representation of the contextual factors of children in the school in mind.

For books that children choose in their classroom, she shared a different approach demonstrating the discussions or light conversations that can be had around book choice developing reader identity and an understanding of children's own book preferences. She explained, *"The reception and year one [children] come up [to the library] for story time, but they have book baskets in their classes that they can borrow from and then year 2 upwards come in and borrow a library book and we'll always start with a 'book chat'. So, I'll say what I've been reading this week and it's always a children's book. [The children] that want to talk about the book that they've read this week would talk about what they liked about the book if it reminded them of anything else. Would they recommend it? Who might they recommend it to? Would they want to go on and read others in the series, if it's part of the series. It's very, very relaxed 'book chat' and it is quite lovely, and I'll often ask the class teacher as well 'What have you been reading this week?' so that they see us as readers. I think it's important that they know that we're readers. We might be the only adults that they're seeing read.*

This opportunity to take an active role in recommending books to peers and discussing preferences, not only empowers the children and pupil voice but can further encourage independent book talk by having provided this scaffold or framework. This can, in turn, support children in making choices (National Literacy Trust, 2023). It is a powerful way to "teach" children how to make choices, how to frame choice preferences and then to make decisions about what might be chosen to read and what can be discarded.

There was also an emphasis on the knowledge of children's literature which underpinned these relaxed and informal "book chats." The librarian identified the ways she kept up with what was current in children's literature, *"I listen to, watch online or read so many book reviews. It's every night. I'm just doing that. There are different sites that I'd go to. There's the Nikki Gamble 'Book Blast' I listen to and watch online every month. The School Library Association has got one next Friday. I think it is about new books. I'm always looking at book bloggers, talking to them and the librarian community is supportive. And there are different Facebook forums (reading for pleasure in primary schools or libraries in primary school). Those sorts of things."*

Cremin et al's. (2009) TARs research highlights the importance of teachers' knowledge about their children, their interests, and their contexts and that this knowledge feeds into the development of RfP in schools. Speaking with the class teachers, their practices reflected this:

- Knowing what children are interested in and making recommendations based on their knowledge of their children.
- Modelling book talk and sharing recommendations so that children are taught how to do the same.
- Talking to and learning from more experienced or knowledgeable staff e.g. Reading lead, librarian so that books are representative and mindfully chosen so that they are meaningful within the classroom context or the intended learning taking place.

The conversations that took place with the class teachers, the children and the librarian all demonstrated that the children were confident in picking literature that they would enjoy reading and were able to share their choices with their peers and with researchers. Children were able to explain *why* they chose books and there was a strong sense of reader identity from all participants. One of the initial observations on arriving in the school library was how the books were displayed. This included promotions of particular books through vibrant displays which were changed regularly. When children were asked if they read books where the main character had any similarities with themselves, one child immediately shared their thoughts about this demonstrating how they could name a book in their library that represented them. She said, whilst pointing to the display hanging from the ceiling, *"The Proudest Blue...she wears a hijab when she's playing... like me. So yeah, she has a similar personality to me."* At the time of the study, there was a striking display of "The Proudest Blue" by Ibtihaj Muhammad as well as a display of books about Ramadan, highlighting books relevant to the time of year and the practices of observing Ramadan among the Muslim community. This display provided children with representation of religion and culture that was relevant to the school community and the identities of children. Each class was encouraged to create ideas for displays about a book of interest and meaning to them, enabling children to share their pride in their interests, choices and sometimes, their culture heritage and religion. This was one example of how books chosen as a focus for display enabled children to be aware of the books in the library. The shelving enabled many books to be "cover facing" and this enhanced children's awareness of what was available and in particular supported the multiple responses of children identifying and choosing books where they were able to relate to or identify with the characters. This was seen by the librarian who talked about another child, *"The first book she picked up had a character with an Afro haircut just took one look and said: 'She's got hair like me'! and I thought, well, that's quite a thing."*

This informed consideration of the types of books we, as teachers offer our children shows the impact of careful school curation with regard to text choice as well as how they are displayed in school spaces. The school library had a diverse selection of texts which included a range of authors; books about issues such as bereavement and trauma; and a separate section for 11+ readers. This was driven by the librarian's focus on developing a curated selection of children's books that represent not only ethnicity but also further carefully selected topics that can develop empathy and understanding of the wider world. This is something that could be replicated at a classroom as well as school level.

Consider how you can create this sort of reading culture in your school and classroom.

1. When in your school day/week are children encouraged to share their recommendations. It is worth remembering that not every child is comfortable sharing with the wider class. They can be encouraged to leave post it notes inside the front cover of a favourite book, or even on the page where their "best bit" can be found.
2. You could have an "empty" bookshelf in your room at the start of a term or fortnight. Give children the opportunity to add a book to the shelf, selecting one or two books that have been their favourite read over the previous few weeks. It is worth noting that not everyone's choice fits in a shelf – if that choice is an online article or post or is a comic or magazine. Your shelf may need to be accompanied by a magazine rack and web selection book, where children can jot down new websites or online links they have found. This can become your physical bookstagram!
3. You could have a small white board or chalk board for children to jot up their recommendations – these are easily wipeable and so adaptable and changeable.
4. Some teachers like to provide a theme every few weeks to further focus recommendations – for example, your best animal story, favourite non-fiction book or graphic novel, text that most represents you as a reader.
5. Many classes or year groups have their own class book blog – ensure you give the children who volunteer to create a blog, time to do this during the school day and that those children on the margins are encouraged to blog as well.
6. Early years classrooms are often the places you see most reading scrap books or floor books. These books offer children and teachers a creative way to respond to a book or any text they have read. They can be drawings or comments, photocopies of pages from the book with notes and jottings, they can be illustrations of the book as a whole or a focus on the themes and emotions evoked from reading the book. There are many examples of these online (look at anything by John Biddle here) as they are worth looking at but be careful not just to look at those that are stunning masterpieces, a floor book or scrap book does not have to be elaborate or the preserve of the talented artist!

Theme 3: Generating discussion

A key aspect in ensuring all children feel a sense of belonging and feel valued through text choices is through careful navigation of the discussions that are generated by the texts they are exposed to. When teachers are reviewing book choice, it is important to recognise that the books will inevitably generate discussion among the children – this will need to be carefully and sensitively managed by the school staff to ensure that negative stereotypes are not reinforced. In our case study school, the teacher recounted a time when a child expressed shock at a story where there was a White mum and a Black dad, assuming that this was unusual. The other children responded to the child and began to talk about their own families and that their parents were from different racialised groups. This conversation allowed misconceptions to be addressed and was peer generated. The teacher could also have followed up using other texts or contextually appropriate references to develop this understanding of difference. What was important here was ensuring all children felt included and comfortable in the class, able to share their thoughts without fear of being "told off" or "stigmatised" for having a view that was considered by others as incorrect or invalid. Children only have their own experiences to guide them and widening book selection is one way to vicariously widen those experiences. As outlined at the start of this chapter, Bishop (1990) reminds us that books are our "windows, mirrors and sliding doors" in addition, Koss' (2015) research found that children's books were one of the most effective mediators to communicate cultural and societal values. Having this knowledge of children in our class is a very powerful tool for the teacher in relation to guiding book choices as well as supporting peer friendships, developing a shared set of values and understanding how issues can arise between peers.

During discussions, the school librarian detailed a situation where a child had come into the library with her class to choose a book. The child was a Syrian refugee and selected the book "The Day War Came" by Nicola Davies, which is a highly emotive text, told in rhyme, detailing the flight from war and the misconceptions surrounding refugees. The book also contains wonderfully evocative illustrations by Rebecca Cobb. The librarian said that she watched the child flick through the text for a while before clutching the book to herself saying *"This is my story"*! In this situation, the adult did not need to engage, the power of the text was enough to allow the child to feel seen and represented. Clearly, the teacher and librarian kept a close eye on the child, aware that whilst identifying with the book the child may also have had past traumas inflamed. With this in mind, many schools have used the International Rescue Committee's educational resources, "Healing Classrooms" https://www.rescue.org/uk/irc-uks-healing-classrooms to support teachers in developing "inclusive and nurturing learning spaces where refugee and asylum-seeking students can gain the necessary academic, social and emotional skills to develop their full potential."

Mantei and Kervin (2014) state that picture books are an important and accessible form of visual art for children because they offer, among other things, opportunities for making connections to personal experiences and to the values and beliefs of families and communities. As discussed in theme two, there was a display celebrating the Islamic festival of Ramadan in the school library as well as a selection of books. This display and positive representation led to two children asking if they could do an assembly for the whole school to teach the rest of the children (and adults) about their festivals and beliefs. Following the assembly, the teachers were able to pick up discussions in their own classrooms and answer any questions that children may have. It also allowed for connections to be made across classes and year groups. Children in other classes, who were also Muslim, did not realise that the children who presented in the assembly shared the same beliefs until they did their assembly. This sharing of beliefs and values allows connections to be made and is an excellent starting point for generating discussions and addressing misconceptions. Findings from CLPE reports (2016) suggest that children benefit from frequent, regular, and sustained opportunities to talk together about the books that they are reading. The more experience they have of talking together and sharing their thoughts and opinions about what they have read, the better they get at unpicking the meanings in texts. This then allows them to make explicit what the text means for them and how this may differ for some of their peers. In the situation above, the children felt able to share their personal experiences with a wider group following interacting and engaging with displays and texts in the safe space of their school library. This then allowed the whole school to develop an understanding of ideas, issues, and values, regardless of their previous knowledge and understanding of the festival of Ramadan. Talking about books is supportive to all readers and allowing children to share and discuss in these sorts of ways is not only empowering but allows children who may find reading difficult to be able to engage with the content and develop their understanding through listening to others and asking questions. Embedding high-quality, diverse and well-selected texts into a school curriculum allows children to meaningfully engage, make personal connections and ask questions (CLPE, 2020). Allowing children to be exposed to discussions about texts that they may not have read themselves also supports the development of their own background knowledge, which Smith et al. (2021) state can support children in comprehending a wider range of texts by making links between text coherence, background knowledge and learning from texts.

Beyond discussion generated for reading comprehension purposes, where and when in the school day is there space made for more sensitive and thoughtful reflections? Which resources are shared with staff about how to manage such discussions such as the International Rescue resources mentioned above or sites such as the Empathy Lab https://www.empathylab.uk/empathy-day

Many of the teachers in the study talked about the role of empathy. The ability to empathise and to encounter the lives of others in the text can be a factor in a child's developing RfP – where a nuanced understanding of "pleasure" is needed. This is not pleasure in another's trauma but a desire to step into the shoes of another and to lose oneself entirely in someone else's experience and life story. The author Neil Gaiman (2014 at the 2013 Reading Agency Lecture) said of reading books, "You get to feel things, visit places you would never otherwise know. You get to learn that everyone else out there is a me, as well. You're being someone else, and when you return to your own world, you're going to be slightly changed." We can highly recommend watching this lecture – it is powerful and insightful and you can find it here: https://www.youtube.com/watch?v=yNIUWv9_ZHO. However, discussions that arise from this need to be handled carefully. Zakai (2019) argues it is the role of a teacher to help children make sense of events and issues they may find disturbing or frightening and that the teacher needs to equip children with the tools needed to navigate the complexities of the world around them. While books that introduce children to these wider issues can capture the imaginations of children and in turn enable the opportunity for insightful discussion, Schneider (2009) found that they were often used by teachers to promote simpler ideas and themes, such as "getting along" and "tolerating others." It was found teachers often shied away from the opportunities presented to discuss the more challenging issues reading such texts could have bought. McDonald (2018) goes further and suggests that many of the books we read to children about some of the bigger issues such as migration and refugees actually position the protagonists as "victims" who have to become "worthy" of being plucked from a refugee camp. In opening discussions with children, it can be useful to keep in mind Freire (1970) who says what is required is the "Critically reading [of] the word and the world" by asking children, why they think things are as they are? What is the change they want to see? What are the many perspectives and opinions? And how can we take action? This touches on ideas of critical literacy and this is further explored in Chapter 9.

Theme 4: Environment

The environment a school creates around reading, reading for pleasure and representation within literature can have a significant impact on its children. At the case study school, the school's library and librarian are a huge asset to the school and the environment, both physical and in creating an atmosphere for reading; Merga (2022) refers to these as "climates." Since their arrival in 2020, the librarian at the school has made it their goal to promote reading for pleasure by ensuring that every child in the school is represented in a book and has their life and experience reflected with a particular focus on diverse authors, characters, and voices. Upon arrival at the school, the librarian began by taking away any older literature that portrayed inappropriate stereotypes that could not be introduced or discussed in a productive way. We, as teachers, need to be mindful of the books in our reading corners and libraries, what stereotypes they may reinforce or challenge and what environments they represent and could create within our learning spaces (Shaddai Tembo in Thomas, 2022). One example the librarian gave was that of a book that represented Native Americans as "red Indians" and reinforced some of the negative stereotypical representations of this group. This book was one of many that were around 40-50 years old at the time and some therefore had dated conceptions of different groups in society. By checking, reflecting on and sorting the content within our school libraries and classroom book corners, we as teachers can begin to impact what environment we wish to create around reading within our schools and classrooms.

The librarian also found a gap in the number of books about different faiths, beliefs and celebrations and was keen to address this and to go beyond the faiths represented in the school and school's community to those of the wider city and country.

The physical environment of the school's library was also utilised to promote representation. School libraries can often be a place of refuge and librarians are the stewards of the space that makes them safe and welcoming spaces for all (Wittman and Fisher-Allison, 2020). This idea also applies to teachers and their classrooms, book corners and any other reading spaces they have ownership of and curating this environment takes careful thought. The school library we visited had a wide range of display boards including one on the theme of LGBTQ+ Pride and the librarian discussed that it had previously been a display on the theme of Ramadan. The visual displays extended beyond boards on the wall as there were also hot air balloons inspired by different books hanging from the ceiling. These again promoted books that uplifted the voices and stories of a diverse range of characters.

Figure 5.2 shows the "balloons" that depict different books.

Figure 5.2 Balloon display used to depict different books

Representation in children's literature 81

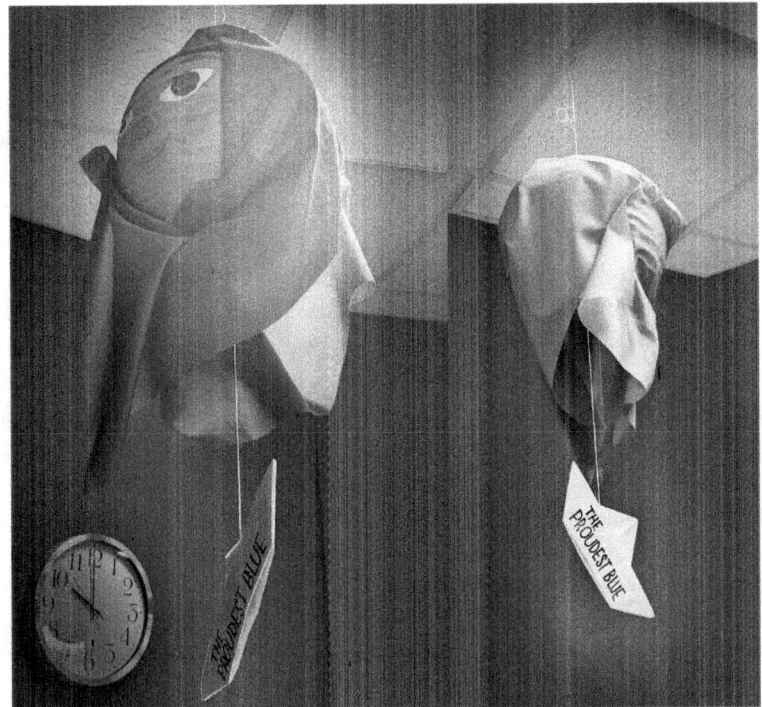

Figure 5.3 Balloon display of the book, "The Proudest Blue" written by Ibihaj Muhammed and S.K. Ali, illustustrated by Hatem Aly

A "balloon" displaying "The Proudest Blue" written by Ibihaj Muhammed and S.K. Ali, illustrated by Hatem Aly (Figure 5.3).

It may be beneficial for teachers to think about the books they display or prioritise and ask the following questions:

- What characters are being portrayed in these books?
- Who are the authors of these books?
- Are there books that challenge or reinforce stereotypes? (Another recommendation of Shaddai Tembo in Thomas, 2022)
- Do these books reflect the backgrounds, positions, and lived experiences of children in my setting?

Beyond the physical spaces of the school library and classrooms, an effective strategy adopted by the school was that of extra book clubs for some learners. The case study school ran a club known as "Books at Breakfast" for their Year 6 Pupil Premium children where they were able to read their books alongside having a healthy breakfast snack. The physical space for this at the school was the school library but is something that could work elsewhere in a school. Pupil Premium funding has meant that the school was able to also provide the eligible children with a book for every year they were in the school so that by the end of their time there they would have seven books of their own. This is a way of using available funding to promote an environment (or climate) of representational reading for pleasure beyond the physical boundaries of the school.

Conclusion and call to action!

As mentioned at the start of this chapter, things are improving with regard to representation in children's texts, largely due to reports from the CLPE (2017-2022) that highlighted the lack of diversity in children's literature and the impact on children as readers. However, despite the percentage of children's books published that featured Black, Brown and minoritised groups rising to 20%, there has not been the same level of attention on representation of other protected characteristics, and this was mirrored in our study with children discussing race over any other protected characteristics. The main take aways from our study were the clear sense of reader identity that the children had, despite their age, as well as the passion and enthusiasm their teachers and staff had for reading and representation. Children were confident in sharing their thoughts about the books, making recommendations, and articulating the reasons for choosing their books. As teachers, we cannot ignore the power of representation in texts. Bishop (1990) highlights the importance of this in how children see themselves and their value but also in the development of their identity as reader and as individual in society.

Most of us will not have the privilege of a dedicated school librarian to support this work. However, all the practices in this chapter can be emulated at a school level or a classroom level through some concerted changes to practice:

- Randomly select 20 books from your bookshelf without looking at the spine or noticing authors or book titles. This will give you a general idea of the types of books available to your children. You can then do a mini audit of what this selection tells you e.g. representations of authors, protagonists, genre, characters and text types, is representation tokenistic?
- The above can be done in year group teams or whole school staff meetings where you can create the space and time for careful thought and planning about what needs to change and why. What do the children in your school need and why?
- Create an opportunity to conduct a book blanket with your own class using the methodology of our case study.
- Literature can be used to expose children to worlds outside their own windows – consider how you can use texts to support children in developing their understanding of other children's lives. Simply having these books is not enough. This will need to be modelled by a knowledgeable adult first followed by sharing and discussing strategies for choosing books (McGeown and Oxley, 2023).
- Cremin et al. (2009) make it clear that teachers' knowledge of children's literature is key in selecting and curating an appropriate collection. Be pro-active here and look for training or join societies such as the United Kingdom Literacy Association to ensure that you are up to date and have access to appropriate texts to support your children. Additional resources such as "In the Reading Corner" podcast by writer and educator Nickie Gamble, book awards including awards such as the Adrien Prize, which focuses on the positive portrayal of a main character with a disability and Matthew Tobin's selection of high-quality picture books using the padlet (see Tobin, 2024).
- Try not to let budget be an issue – start by discarding old texts that are no longer relevant (these can often be sold on websites to create some funds) and build your collection slowly. There are so many good second-hand sources for texts that costs can be lowered

significantly. Use your school newsletter to create wish lists of second-hand books or Facebook groups to request that any used books be given to the school.
- Who are your children's reading role models? You might wish to explore children's perceptions of you as a reader by asking them to draw and annotate a picture of you with things they think are important to you (Cremin et al., 2018) This can be a starting point for you as the teacher to consider how your children see you as a reader.
- Create a space in your classroom or library that showcases a different book each week or month. This can be a way for children to see books that represent their interests, hobbies or protected characteristics. This will likely need to be explored with children to make it purposeful and to guide them through the text and learning involved.
- Children need frequent, regular, and sustained opportunities to talk about texts and engage with reading – this will need to be a sustained part of your classroom practice. Make being a reading advocate in your school your superpower!

References

Equality Act (2010) UK Public General Act. https://www.legislation.gov.uk/ukpga/2010/15/introduction

Biklen, D. and Bogdana, R. (1977) 'Media portrayal of disabled people: A study of stereotypes', *Inter-racial Children's Book Bulletin*, 8(6-7), pp. 4-9 (cited by Roshini, R. and Rajasekaran, V., 2022. More Than an Invalid: A Comparative Study Addressing Disability Portrayal in Children's Fiction. *Theory and Practice in Language Studies*, **12**(3), pp. 551-557).

Bishop, R.S. (1990) 'Mirrors, windows, and sliding glass doors', *Perspectives: Choosing and Using Books for the Classroom*, 6(3), pp. ix-xi. Center for the Study of Multicultural Children's Literature.

Botelho, M.J. and Rudman, M.K. (2009) *Critical multicultural analysis of children's literature: Mirrors, windows, and doors*. New York: Routledge.

CLPE: Centre for Literacy in Primary Education (2018) Reflecting realities: Survey of ethnic representation within UK children's literature 2017. https://clpe.org.uk/system/files/CLPE%20Reflecting%20Realities%20Report%20July%202018.pdf

CLPE: Centre for Literacy in Primary Education (2019) Reflecting realities: Survey of ethnic representation within UK children's literature 2018. https://clpe.org.uk/system/files/CLPE%20Reflecting%20Realities%202019%20-%20Low%20Res%20%28website%29.pdf

CLPE: Centre for Literacy in Primary Education (2020) Reflecting realities: Survey of ethnic representation within UK children's literature 2019. https://clpe.org.uk/system/files/CLPE%20Reflecting%20Realities%202020.pdf

CLPE: Centre for Literacy in Primary Education (2021) Reflecting realities: Survey of ethnic representation within UK children's literature 2020. https://clpe.org.uk/system/files/2021-12/CLPE%20Reflecting%20Realities%20Report%202021_0.pdf

CLPE: Centre for Literacy in Primary Education (2022) Reflecting realities: Survey of ethnic representation within UK Children's literature 2017-2021. https://clpe.org.uk/system/files/2022-11/CLPE%20Reflecting%20Reality%202022%20WEB_0.pdf

CLPE: Centre for Literacy in Primary Education (2023) Reflecting realities: Survey of ethnic representation within UK children's literature 2022. https://clpe.org.uk/system/files/2023-11/CLPE%20Reflecting%20Reality%202023%20v8%20web.pdf

Cooperative Children's Book Centre (CCBC) Diversity Statistics: Primary Character/Subject (2023).

Cremin, T. (2020) Reading for pleasure: Challenges and opportunities. In: Davison, J. and Daly, C. (eds). *Debates in English teaching. Debates in subject teaching*. London: Routledge. https://doi.org/10.4324/9780429506871

Cremin, T., Davis, S., Williams, C. and Thomson, B. (2018) 'Reading teachers: Teachers who read and readers who teach', *UKLA English 4-11*, 62, pp. 9-11.

Cremin, T., Mottram, M., Collins, F., Powell, S. and Safford, K. (2014) *Building communities of engaged readers: Reading for pleasure*. London: Routledge.

Cremin, T., Mottram, M., Collins, F., Powell, S. and Safford, K. (2009) Teachers as readers: Building communities of readers, *Literacy*, 43. pp. 11-19. https://doi.org/10.1111/lit.12115

Elliott, V., Nelson-Addy, L., Chantiluke, R. and Courtney, M. (2021) "Lit in Colour: Diversity in Literature in English Schools." https://wp.penguin.co.uk/wp-content/uploads/2021/08/Lit-in-Colour-research-report.pdf

Ellis, S. and Smith, V. (2017) Assessment, teacher education and the emergence of professional expertise, *Literacy*, 51, pp. 84-93. https://doi.org/10.1111/lit.12115

Enriquez, G. (2021) 'Foggy mirrors, tiny windows, and heavy doors: Beyond diverse books toward meaningful literacy instruction', *Read Teach*, 75(1), pp. 103-106. https://doi.org/10.1002/trtr.2030

Freire, P. (1970) *Pedagogy of the oppressed*. New York: Herder and Herder.

Gaiman, N. (2014) 'Why our future depends on libraries, reading and daydreaming', *The Guardian*, 15 October. https://www.theguardian.com/books/2013/oct/15/neil-gaiman-future-libraries-reading-daydreaming

Johnson-Bailey, J. (2012) 'Positionality and transformative learning: A tale of inclusion and exclusion', in Taylor, E.W. (ed.) *The handbook of transformative learning: Theory, research and practice*. 1st ed. San Francisco: Jossey-Bass, pp. 260-273.

Kidd, D.C. and Castano, E. (2013) 'Reading literary fiction improves theory of mind', *Science*, 342(6156), pp. 377-380.

Koss, M.D. (2015) 'Diversity in contemporary picturebooks: A content analysis', *Journal of Children's Literature*, 41(1), pp. 32-42.

McDonald, M.T. (2018) 'Troubling sympathy: Teaching refugee narratives', *JCT: Journal of Curriculum Theorizing*, 32(3), pp. 61-78.

Mantei, J. and Kervin, L. (2014) *Interpreting the images in a picture book: Students make connections to themselves, their lives and experiences*. Australia: University of Woolongong. https://ro.uow.edu.au/sspapers/1218/

McGeown, S. and Oxley, E. (2023) 'Love to read: Principles to supporting children's reading motivation and engagement', *UKLA English 4-11*, 77, pp. 17-18.

Merga, M. (2022) *School libraries supporting literacy and wellbeing*. London: Facet.

National Literacy Trust (2023) *Reading for pleasure activities: Choice and voice*

Reed, D. (2022) 'Mirrors, windows, and sliding glass doors': The key to diverse library collections.

Saleh, A. (2023) 'Black british literature in the secondary English classroom', *Changing English*, 30(4), pp. 342-358.

Saunders, K. (2000) *Happily ever afters: A story-book code to teaching children about disabilities*. Stoke-on-Trent: Trentham Books Ltd.

Scafe, S. (1989) *Teaching black literature*. London: Virago.

Schneider, C.C. (2009) *The use of children's books as a vehicle for ideological transmission*. Columbus, Ohio: The Ohio State University, ProQuest Dissertations Publishing.

Smith, R., Snow, P., Serry, T. and Hammond, L. (2021) 'The role of background knowledge in reading comprehension: A critical review', *Reading Psychology*, 42(3), pp. 214-240.

Thomas, A. (2022) *Representation matters: How to become an anti-racist educator*. London: Bloomsbury.

Tobin, M. (2024) High quality picture books for cross-curricular planning - padlet. https://padlet.com/p0077346/high-quality-picture-books-for-cross-curricular-planning-eaf5llgdy71d

Traille, K. (2007) *Never too young to know: How young children conceptualize race*. Sterling, VA: Trentham Books.

UK Government. (2023) "School Workforce in England." UK Government. https://explore-education-statistics.service.gov.uk/find-statistics/school-workforce-in-england#dataBlock-0012b04a-43d9-4348-a7c3-843937c7e9d9-tables

Vincent, C. (2021) *Schools, education, and community: Fostering belonging and participation*. London: Routledge.

Wittmann, P. and Fisher-Allison, N. (2020) 'Intentionally creating a safe space for all: The school library as refuge', *Knowledge Quest*, 48(3), pp. 40-49. https://www.proquest.com/docview/2333934396

Zakai, S. (2019) "Bad things happened": How children of the digital age make sense of violent current events', *The Social Studies*, 110(2), pp. 67-85.

6 Engaging and re-engaging readers

Innovative approaches that can help reignite the spark

Ros Steward, Catherine Delor and Leah Dowty

Introduction

In most classes there are children that seem to "drink in" books, that "lap up" suggestions and who are "readers" rather than just children who can read. However, generally speaking, these are therefore not the children you are concerned about. It is the children who, despite your best efforts, seem to be disengaged with reading. These may be children who have never been "into" reading but there are also others who seem to have lost the pleasure in reading they once had. You are not alone! In this chapter, we will discuss the evidence that suggests that children in England are reading for pleasure less than ever before (Clark, Picton and Galway, 2023) and will try to unpick some of the reasons why this is happening. The chapter shares some practical advice and some tried and tested classroom strategies to help make reading connect for more of our children. From reading circles and book clubs to displays and scrapbooks, schools in England are developing a range of innovative ways to make reading for pleasure irresistible for even the most reluctant reader. At the heart of all of these approaches is the importance of reader identity and agency which we will discuss in detail throughout the chapter.

Ellis and Smith (2017) emphasise the importance of getting to know your children's reader identity and their social and cultural capital as well as their "reading level" if we want to really understand them as a reader. This is particularly relevant when we pause to consider engaging and re-engaging the readers that we teach. You might want to return to the introduction and to Chapters 5 and 7 to refresh your memory about this model before continuing with this current chapter.

What is putting children off reading?

Whilst there was a surge in enjoyment of reading during the 2020 COVID-19 pandemic, any ground that had been gained was soon lost (Cole et al., 2022). In 2023 the Progress in International Reading Literacy Study (PIRLS) found that English 10-year-olds were more proficient readers than ever before, but their overall reading enjoyment was on the decline (Lindorff, Stiff and Kayton, 2023). This was further compounded when the National Literacy Trust reported the lowest levels of reading enjoyment in their 18 year history of surveying British children's perceptions of reading (Clark, Picton and Galway, 2023).

DOI: 10.4324/9781003409939-6

So what has changed? In 2023 the National Literacy Trust annual survey (Clark et al., 2023) reported that:

- fewer girls now say that they enjoy reading
- fewer children aged 8-11 now say that they read for pleasure
- there is a particularly marked decline in the enjoyment of reading between Key Stages 1 and 2
- fewer children who receive free school meals said they enjoyed reading compared with their peers who do not receive free school meals
- more boys enjoyed reading at school than reported enjoying reading at home.

The reasons why children are reading for pleasure less are both complex and multifaceted and were often discussed by the children that we interviewed for our case studies. Before continuing to read you might think about the barriers to reading engagement and motivation for the children in your class, Key Stage and school. These questions are a useful starting point for developing your reflections relating to these children:

- Are they given the agency to choose what they would like to read?
- Do they know what type of text they would like to read next?
- Do they know where, when and how to locate their next text?
- Do they have the skills and knowledge needed to make choices – and can they articulate these as they make their choices?
- Do they have access to a suitable environment for reading?
- Do they have the reading proficiency needed to access their chosen text?
- Has developing the *skill* to read been prioritised over nurturing the *will* to read?
- Is there time built into the day for them to read for pleasure and how much agency do children have over when this might be?
- Do they have reading role models that inspire them to read and can they articulate who this may be?
- Do they have opportunities to listen to stories at school and at home and have some choice and agency over what is read to them sometimes?
- Is there time for talking about reading with peers or adults?
- Do they see the value or purpose of their reading, and can they articulate this?
- Do they see themselves as "a reader"?

Those children who are less proficient than many of their peers, often referred to as "struggling" or "vulnerable" readers, can sometimes be those that it is harder to engage in reading for pleasure. It can be useful to think about how we help all children develop both the *skill* and the *will* to read (Cremin et al., 2014) to make sure that we get the right balance and keep as many children engaged in reading as we possibly can. However, we know that it is often the most vulnerable readers in school who tend to spend more time developing reading *skill* through targeted interventions and so can often miss out on experiences that will strengthen their *will* to read (Hempel-Jorgensen et al., 2018; Wyse and Bradbury, 2022). Cremin (2022, p. xiv) argues that this stubborn focus on developing reading proficiency can mean that children become "caught up in a cycle of disadvantage" which is caused by limited experiences of early reading success, constrained access to quality literature and a pedagogy that fails to adequately promote reading for pleasure (Hempel-Jorgensen et al., 2018). Chapter 2 focuses on considering how the *skill* can be developed in a purposefully positive way, trying to ensure that in the endeavour to increase the skills and knowledge needed as a reader, a child's *will* is not broken. Reflect on what interventions look like in your school? Do the teachers, teaching assistants and volunteer readers that support this group of children have reading for meaning, purpose and pleasure at the heart of even the most basic phonics intervention? How can we ensure that we carefully navigate the right balance of *skill* and *will* for all of the children that we teach?

It is worth noting at this stage the correlation that often exists between our less-engaged readers and those who come from families with lower incomes. We know that children from economically disadvantaged backgrounds are more likely to have fewer books at home and are also more likely (although not necessarily) to be less proficient readers than their higher income peers. In Chapter 6 you can read a more detailed discussion on the range of different literacy lives of families as well as a focus on the equally different ways that families and children can be engaged. The key point here is that we need to move from thinking these children or families are "lacking" in some way, or in deficit, but bring their own lives and experiences to reading that may be the same or different to our own but equally valid and valuable for the reading journey.

Whilst there is a growing movement to embed reading-for-pleasure pedagogy into English classrooms with thriving social media communities and growing numbers of teacher-led case studies on the Open University RfP website (OU RfP, no date) we still need to understand how readers who do not currently have the *will* to read can be best supported. By making sure that we fully understand the theory that underpins our actions we can make sure that the approaches we use are as impactful as possible. If we understand "why," we are better able to put into practice the "how." Many of us already know that having a book corner can be a useful strategy and that it makes visible the books that are on offer and entices new readers. However, knowing that this should be an inclusive strategy can help us avoid common pitfalls that can often take place in a busy classroom. For example, using the book corner for children who finish their learning activities quickly without thinking about the impact of this on all children. Considering the equity of book corner use and those children who are given some responsibility in organising the book corner are important considerations when thinking about not just the "what" but also the "why."

What are children's views about how to help them read for pleasure?

Children themselves have responded in a variety of ways when asked, "What would make you want to read more?" As reported in the National Literacy Trust survey (Clark et al., 2023), 38% of children and young people said that **having books recommended to them** would make them want to read more. **Being given books** was also a strong motivational factor, listed by 32% of those in the survey as something that would make them want to read more. Similarly, a third of children and young people said that **having books that represented them** would make them want to read more. Two further factors, that of **having family and friends talk about books** (23%) and **seeing someone they looked up to reading** (18%) were recorded as reasons that respondents would read more.

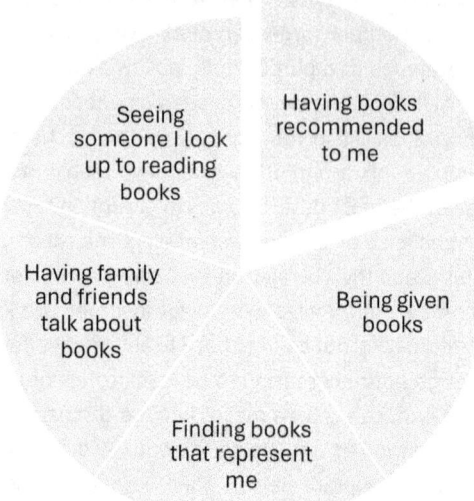

Figure 6.1 What makes me want to read?

What would make you want to read more? (Figure 6.1).

As teachers who want to develop reading for pleasure with our classes, it is important that we act on these wider findings, and whilst ensuring we ask these same questions to our own class of children, acknowledging the differences that exist between schools, classes and individual children. By listening to the perspectives of children we might be less likely to create checklists of reading behaviours we want them to show and instead will bring volitional reading to the heart of the classroom. So, should teachers take responsibility for fostering "readers for life"? (Cremin, 2020) Most of us would hopefully respond affirmatively here but whilst it may appear therefore, as a teacher's duty, we also want to consider how we can encourage the child to develop their own habits of reading and enable the evolution of a child's reading identity.

The Ofsted research review for English (2022) discussed the difficulties of incentives that help with children's "short term motivation" but do not lead to longer-term motivation for reading citing studies by Toste et al. (2020) and Baker and Scher (2002). Chapter 6 will continue this discussion about the role of motivation and its connection to reading for pleasure. However, it is important at this stage to also consider the findings of Hempel-Jorgensen et al. (2018). They found that children responded to reading for pleasure pedagogy in very different ways and that children who were less likely to see themselves as "readers" were less impacted by the focus on reading for pleasure in the classroom. Those children who entered the class not seeing themselves as readers and who did not meet the expected standards for reading, left the classroom at the end of the academic year with similar attitudes to reading than when had entered it. The reading for pleasure practices had not impacted on them in the same way it had for those with a more positive reader identity. Clearly then, the social justice implications of our actions to develop reading for pleasure need to be carefully considered so that we do not inadvertently widen the gap between those that do read and those that do not.

Cremin (2023), in her article *Reading for Motivation: Focusing on Disengaged Readers*, is clear about the distinction between different motivations: Intrinsic Motivation – internal reasons for reading, e.g. deriving enjoyment, involvement and satisfying one's curiosity; Extrinsic Motivation – external reasons for reading e.g. rewards and recognition; and a third type of motivation, which sometimes gets overlooked, Social Motivation – relational reasons for reading, e.g. to connect and interact with others. She suggests that the focus on extrinsic motivators can sometimes dominate our pedagogy, which in the long term might not be as beneficial as one would hope, as the motivation is quickly lost once the rewards are removed. She reflects on the need to develop self-determination by interweaving opportunities for all three elements to enhance a high degree of agency, volition and choice (autonomy), a sense of self-efficacy and a positive reader identity (competence). The sections in this chapter focus on a range of strategies that have been found to encompass all three of these, at times simultaneously, and will provide you with some ideas that you can incorporate into your repertoire to encourage reading for pleasure in your classroom.

What practical steps can we take to help children read for pleasure?

Know your children

At the heart of re-engaging readers is knowing your children and their reading habits (Cremin et al., 2014). Essential to this is moving beyond the "reading level" that a child might have been assessed as working within and instead building in opportunities throughout the reading provision to get to know children's interests, choice, confidence and interaction with the class reading community (Svrcek and AbugaseaHeidt, 2022). Opportunities to get to know more about the children as readers may be as simple as a "reading survey" or observing the children closely during reading time to see how they interact with their chosen text (Open University, no date). There are audits available online, particularly from the Open University Reading for Pleasure website which may be useful for you to identify what your children feel about reading and you can use the data to identify where they might need further support. Activities that allow you to gather more in-depth knowledge of the children's holistic reader identities can be well-placed at the very beginning of the academic year as you are getting to know the motivation and engagement levels of the readers in your class. These will help you understand who needs more help to find books that interest them, who needs to be re-connected with the class reading community or who would benefit from another strategy. Alongside the careful but informal observations and classroom conversations that continue through the school year, it can be useful to repeat the more formal information-gathering processes, such as a survey, to monitor the impact of your actions on children's engagement and reader identity. Just because a particular approach "worked" one year or in another school or is regularly promoted on teachers' social media spaces, does not mean it will resonate with the individual children in your school and class. When we change practice, we want to look for its impacts – both positive, negative and neutral. Whilst knowing change in identity, culture and engagement takes time, checking in on the progress of that change is essential.

Don't be judgemental about texts

Teachers and family members often bring with them an inherent set of judgement values in relation to the texts that children choose to read independently for pleasure. Some may say a picture book is too "babyish," some that a series is too repetitive and some that a longer novel is too challenging. In one case study school, the children referred to books that were considered to be low quality and overly simplistic by their teachers as *"toilet books"* and they were very clear as to which texts would fall under this category. However, these text types were often the texts that were most frequently selected by more reluctant readers – *Diary of a Wimpy Kid,* by Jeff Kinney, *Captain Underpants* and *Dog Man,* by Dav Pilkey – and are therefore crucial in helping all children engage in reading for pleasure. If children repeatedly hear the message that the texts that they would most like to read are not considered to be of value by the adults around them, they will be likely to have any emerging sense of reading volition dampened, if not squashed altogether. Graphic novels are one type of text, that are written in a whole range of genre that can be misunderstood and perhaps judged, often by parents rather than teachers, as of a lower status than the traditional novel. Chapter 2 gives lots more guidance and detail on the role of the graphic novel in reading for pleasure. The Department of Education (2022) have made considerable changes to their advice on reading for pleasure in later iterations of The Reading Framework and one significant alteration is the additional guidance given on the breadth of texts that children can and should be encouraged to read. Teachers are encouraged to provide children with a "feast of books" (p. 93) from a variety of authors and genres and the instruction is clear that *any* text should be considered if it has the potential to "hook" a child into reading for pleasure.

Think for a moment about what you consider to be a "good" read for your class and what other members of the school community and team identify as "appropriate." Even if these views are not voiced to children, how might children pick up on our "judgment"?

Have a variety of reading material to cater to individual reading identities

Children's agency and ability to choose their next text is central to developing a reading-for-pleasure culture. However, they can only choose from what is available to them and so the books, comics, annuals and magazines that we curate for them are key to building irresistible reading opportunities. So what types of reading materials should we be offering to our children? Chapter 3 explores the importance of diverse, inclusive reading materials and the importance of children seeing themselves represented in the texts that they read. But are there other considerations that we need to take into account too?

Reedy and Reedy (2024) note the importance of children's previous reading experiences and their familiarity with a text when choosing a book to read. For some children – often those at the beginning of their independent reading journey – being able to select a book that they have listened to or read independently before is a key factor in their decision-making. Reading the same book over and over again, may for a teacher, feel like "wasted" reading development time, but for a child, it may provide the security and comfort that others find in discovering a new book. Finding a book series works well here and provides a child with the security of knowing the characters and style of the book that a repeated read of the same book offers but enables them to extend their reading range. As you can see from the list of books the less engaged readers gave, these books all are part of a series and so this may be an additional reason that the more reluctant reader is drawn to these books. The desire to revisit the familiar is true for many of us and perhaps enabling children to do this physically is another helpful re-engaging activity: arrange with another class lower down the school, for your class to come on a "down memory lane, book raid." Children can find, in their own year group and old classrooms, some of their well-loved books from their younger years, and have the chance to re-read these, either to a child in that class or to bring them back to their own class to read in the comfort of their own environment. If you are a Key Stage 1 teacher, find out when the reception class is out on a trip and use this as your "book raid" day or if you are in Key Stage 2, find a day that Key Stage 1 is on a trip or out swimming – just remember to replace the books carefully to avoid upset!

Reedy and Reedy (2024) also acknowledge the importance of children choosing texts that represent their own passions and interests, with texts related to football being a particularly powerful area of engagement. We also found this in one of our case study schools in which a recently published football annual was by far the most popular choice. One child, in particular, lamented the fact that this type of text was not usually available to him at school and he would not be able to use it to become a "word millionaire" on the school's bought-in reading programme. You might find it useful at this point to consider what opportunities you have at school to get to know about the passions and interests of the children you work with, and how these feed into the selection of texts that you make available to them. What schemes or incentives do you use in your school and how might these impact on the reading materials available for children to choose from?

Burnett and Merchant (2018) explored how the *range* of reading materials available can enhance engagement as well as being the driver of the "future" benefits of reading, such as increased knowledge, self-improvement and employability. Diversity of literary practices can be sidelined and of course it has become apparent that certain kinds of literacies have traditionally been valued more than others (Street, 2003). The apparent dichotomy between the sustained reading of a single text and the rapid, mobile, socially situated engagements associated with digital media so prevalent today, formed the basis of the Burnett and Merchant (2018) study. However, the study found that it was difficult to correlate digital media practices and educational attainment, as media practices and devices rapidly become obsolete impacting on longitudinal studies. Regardless of this, the implication from their study is that accommodating mobile digital practices *as well as* traditional sources is increasingly essential. This requires us to acknowledge and build on children's out-of-school literacies, with an additional focus on critical literacy e.g. fake news, e-safety concerns. Chapter 7 focuses on this area and demonstrates how we can move children from critical literacy with traditional sources to critical literacy in relation to wider social and news media. The Burnett and Merchant study also highlights the need to have available the range within these multiliteracies e.g. online communities where blogs, manuals and chatscreens, provide additional opportunities for reading. You may like to read Bailey's (2016) study of an after-school Minecraft club which demonstrated how multiliteracy reading was already interwoven into children's everyday lives and so were useful and legitimate reading for pleasure practices. In addition, the format of reading online may suit some children. Online books can provide not just the text of the book, but many have audio available, enabling the book to be read to the child as they read along or listen. The COVID-19 pandemic gave rise to a proliferation of books online and whilst some publishers have withdrawn this "service" they are still many books available on YouTube, TicTok or specific websites such as Epic https://www.getepic.com/, Sooper Books which offers 5 to 10-minute bedtime stories https://sooperbooks.com, Oxford Owl offering a range of online books https://www.oxfordowl.co.uk/for-home/find-a-book/library-page and free children's stories https://www.freechildrenstories.com/. Whilst many teachers use the free first chapter tasters provided by Love Reading 4 Kids, children too may be engaged by both the online nature of these first chapters but also by the brevity of what they have access to. With any luck, a child may then want to read the rest of the book! It is important not to forget the services of the local library here. Most libraries now offer audio and digital books – these are free to borrow, and it is simple to use. Make it a class activity that at the start of the year you all join the local library. If there isn't a "local" enough library, you can do this online and invite a librarian to talk to your class by Zoom.

We need to reassure children that *all* of these different and diverse approaches to reading are part of the rich tapestry of what counts as reading. Our case study children were selected by their teachers to include some children who could read but chose not to and children who found reading hard and so also chose not to read. These groups of children often said they chose a book because it was short – they regularly did this with a wry smile, as if to say, "I don't like reading and so I'll do as little of it as possible." Whilst this may cause us to have an inward sigh, we can see this as an opportunity! We know these children like a "short book" and so sourcing as many of these across a range of genre and interest areas as we can, enables that child to find the books they want and potentially the one "short" book that might inspire them to read another. Some publishers specialise in such books – the wonderful *Barrington Stoke* books use well-known, high-quality authors, to write shorter, dyslexia-friendly books, are one such publisher. Ask your group of children, who like a short book (for whatever reason or motivation), to be in charge of a small pot of money that buys a few books from this or a similar publisher a couple of times a year to ensure your shelves have a range of shorter books, that is being regularly added to. If money is tight in your school and this is not an option, send out lists to willing parents and the wider school community of books to look out for in charity shops or where you have a parent-teacher organisation, request that a small amount of money each year is dedicated to this particular group of children and books. You may be aware that you, as a time-poor teacher, rarely get the chance to read for yourself. The Reading Agency promotes "Quick reads" that can be purchased for just a pound for adults who find themselves in the same position as those children who want something brief. If you have a borrowing collection for parents, ensure that it has some of these "quick reads."

Consider also if these children could be introduced to short story collections. For some children, holding a chunkier book at a time when everyone else in the class is reading a longer novel, and yet knowing they only need to read a few pages to get a whole story, is an incentive. The Book Trust has a useful list of short story anthologies as a good starting point, as does Bloomsbury which has a free, online short story collection with all of the stories written by well-known authors titled *The Book of Hopes:* https://issuu.com/bloomsburypublishing/docs/thebookofhopes_interactivepdf

We can show children that they can choose a book because of a book's brevity, because they want to return to the same book again and again, or because they only want to read the first chapter or even, just read the last chapter! *The Rights of the Reader* (Pennac, 2006) are essential not only to share with children but to live in the classroom. We *should* allow children to decide that some books are boring, after all we do too! Reflecting on our own reading habits can help us to value those that children may be developing too. For example, some of ours include deciding to skip parts of the book, starting with the ending, setting personal targets or deciding whether to read the whole book as quickly as possible or reading several books at the same time! Children could suggest making plans for future reading – as we do with our many mountains of books by our bedsides waiting to be read. The important aspect to take away here is the focus on celebrating and being positive with children, validating their choices; these may not be "good literature" or have "good literary merit" but does it matter? If their choice endorses their culture and interests, then that is a positive. Children have a lifetime to broaden their repertoire once reading becomes more enjoyable and habitual.

Guide children through their book selections

Miller (2009) suggests book selection is also about reading freedoms. Consider how your class chooses a book? What have they been taught about book selection? Do they use the cover or the title? Do they stick to a familiar series, author or illustrator? Do they rely on recommendations – and whose recommendations do they find the most valuable? You may want to ask a sample of children in your class how they go about making their choices and can they articulate their selection process as they look through a shelf of books?

Unsurprisingly, children *do* judge a book by its cover and use this as a key strategy for choosing their next text to read (Reedy and Reedy, 2024). They also consider the level of challenge when they flick through a book, gauging the size and amount of text and considering this in relation to their own reading proficiency (Reedy and Reedy, 2024). Of course, some children may do this in an aspirational way so that they can showboat their confidence as a reader, while others may underplay their reading skills and continually select texts below their instructional level. Some children may begin to utilise the blurb on the back of a book to help them identify what to read, although Reedy and Reedy (2024) suggest that this is a strategy that children are more likely to use towards the end of primary school. It is helpful to introduce strategies for choosing a book from the start of a child's reading journey. This can begin with modelling how you make a choice of a read-aloud for the class, involving the children in perusing the book with a quick flick through and perhaps a read of the first page. As children progress, encourage them to think about making a book choice that suits their interest and purpose for reading but also a book choice that they can comprehend – so a Goldilocks book – one that is not too easy, not too difficult but is just right. Teach children how to read a page from the book, placing a finger on each word they find either difficult to decode or understand. If they have five fingers on the page by the time they have read the whole page, it is possible that the book may present too much of a challenge at this point in the child's reading journey. Of course, if this is a book they plan to read alongside an adult or a book they have a real passion to read, encourage the child to select the book alongside another that may fit with the Goldilocks principle. Suggest to children that reading a couple of pages is a good idea when choosing a book, taking note not only of its interest level for the child but also how the book "feels" for the child in terms of print size, layout, illustration and style. Teach children the different formats they may encounter and how each requires a different type of reading approach, such as the graphic novel or non-fiction text. With non-fiction, teach children how to select which parts of the book they wish to read, perhaps reading the introduction and then using the contents page and index page to decide in which order they wish to read the book and which bits they will choose not to read. Model how to use "what next" websites, that make suggestions of books based on the reader's recent reads. Remind children to try out and experiment with books or other text formats as well as different authors and genre – if they don't like it, they don't have to continue to read it!

As mentioned above, and in detail in Chapter 3, having books that represent us or books we can make personal connections with are a powerful driver of children's book choices. When we see ourselves represented in books, they become more meaningful, we begin to nurture links with literature. This was illustrated in the case study, where the book blanket approach was taken to the focus group, and children were invited to choose a book. One child explained her choice by explaining, *"I like this book and I kind of relate to one of the stories because where I'm from in Cameroon, which is right next to Nigeria, people don't do Halloween there and in this story it's kind of similar in that...it [also] has lots of food [in the book] that we have in Cameroon as well."* Another child made her choice because *"my teacher, last year, he read this book, like for half an hour, to the class – and it reminds me of him. It just sounded fun when he read it."*

Whilst choice is important, Oxley and McGeown (2023) argue that the less experienced the reader, the harder it is for them to make choices, especially if faced with too much variety.

- Take a look at your book corner and consider the number of books made available and how they are displayed.
- Does the number of books mean that few of the books can be displayed in a way that is accessible and appealing?
- How are the books organised?
- Is there a system to the organisation that children have either designed or has been explained/taught to them?
- Is the system similar to or linked in some way to the school library's organisation? If it isn't, is there a clear rationale for this?
- How are recommendations made clear – are there a few books highlighted each week or term that have a recommendation from children in the class, the teacher or another adult in the school?
- Are there post-it notes or bookmarks or similar left in each book someone in the class has read that indicate the reader's views, opinions and ideas – perhaps it is highlighting a "best bit" or something like "the sort of person who would like this book is someone who enjoys …."
- Are there clear parts of the book corner where comics can be found, or a particular text form e.g. graphic novels, short story anthologies, poetry or non-fiction text?
- Are non-fiction text read aloud as a "taster" and then put in the book corner for children to access in the same way as other books?
- Whatever the year group, are there always a range of picture books available for reading and browsing?

There are some excellent lesson plans and activity ideas for scaffolding children's book selections in the "Love to Read" resources and blogs https://blogs.ed.ac.uk/lovetoread/open-research/.

Infectious recommendations

The case studies in this chapter were conducted in two primary schools both with positive Ofsted reports about their reading and particularly their reading for pleasure culture and climate.

Through our discussions with children in our case study schools we discovered that having books recommended to them was a key factor in making children want to read more:

> "Our teacher might, like, recommend a books that they'll think you like. We had the best teachers and he recommended books ...sometimes he even took some books out of my hand and gave me a different one!" (Year 6)

> "In year five, if I had a recommendation for the class [then] they [would take a] picture of me holding the book and you would write [about it]" (Year 5)

> "I used to not like reading but my teacher helped me in the mornings to go and get a book because there's no point really just sitting there. So he gives me books and I really, really enjoy them. I used to not actually read, like I'd pretend, not actually read them. And they he actually got me to read one!" (Year 6)

> "Our teacher will, like, read us a bit of a story to whet our appetite and then say, read as much [of it] this weekend as you can." (Year 5)

Time and again the children told us about the recommendations they had had from knowledgeable teachers at school and how much this had helped them to select their next text. Chapters 2 and 8 gives some advice on how to extend knowledge. They also told us about how looking around at books other children were enjoying supported their selection process. It therefore seems particularly important to consider what opportunities children have within your class, phase or school to hear and respond to reading recommendations from you and peers? How do you build in time for this in an already busy day?

When you choose read alouds for the whole class there are a range of considerations and one is that this book is a "shop front" recommendation for your class as readers. For many children (and their parents) the supermarket is the place where recommendations are made – with their large displays and discounted prices of popular, celebrity authors' books. They tend to stock the "known" authors – many of whom are long since dead – but are remembered by parents and grandparents and so are more likely to sell. Whilst we have argued that all books are good books when it comes to reading for pleasure, there is still a case to be made for widening children's knowledge and repertoire of known authors, genre and styles. The read aloud is a vehicle for introducing children to the classics alongside the new and modern authors. One teacher in one of our case study schools found it beneficial to read the first book of a series as a read aloud and then strategically release multiple copies of the second book within the series into the classroom library. This heightened the interest of less engaged readers, creating a book buzz around independently engaging with the follow up texts. Another year 4 teacher chose *The Iron Man* (by Ted Hughes) as the initial class read aloud as she had recognised that many of the children were quite disengaged from reading and thought that the format of short standalone chapters would enable the children to listen and digest the content in relatively short sittings. In addition, as 65% of the class were boys, she thought perhaps a robot and a boy protagonist might be engaging for them. The children had many opportunities to ask questions or talk about each story together before moving on to the next chapter. They did loosely link the book to other activities linked to reading, for example, building a giant "Iron Man" in the book corner out of junk (this was a team building exercise carried out throughout the rest of each day's timetable, the only rule being that nothing could be undone, only added to) and they used the description of the robot to draw on for their design. Interestingly, after finishing this book, some children had researched the author and found that he had written another book called *"The Iron Woman"* which they wanted to be read next, so the teacher acquired it and started to read- after the first 2 chapters, it became apparent that the children were not as enthusiastic, so having asked their opinion, the teacher suggested they stop where they had reached. To select the next book, the teacher brought together a selection of books with a similar theme to "The Iron Man," reading extracts from each. From this, the class selected their next book. Any child who did want to read on, was able to borrow the "Iron Woman" for their independent reading.

Many social media groups for teachers supporting Reading for Pleasure often show teachers asking for recommendations for read aloud texts that focus on the class topic. This is something also identified in the Ofsted 2024 English subject report. We suggest that this is fine as long as the main consideration of the final choice is the quality of the text as a read aloud – so one that gives the teacher the potential to read the book with some verve and passion, has a fabulous use of language that warrants being spoken out loud or a rip roaring adventure or mystery that can grip and enthral or is a side-splitting laugh out loud romp. How are books chosen to read aloud in your school? How might this limit the "pleasurable" element if texts always link to the topic focus?

Book clubs and scrap books

Book Clubs have existed in different guises for many years. In primary schools they are usually defined as "a group that meets to talk about and share a book." The aim is usually to share one book and act as an interactive platform to discuss the book and perhaps the author. However, the term "book club" is increasingly being used for a wider variety of activities – sharing multiple books, looking at a selection by one author, exploring a theme, using peer recommendations and building a widening repertoire. The one thing that successful Book Clubs need are adults who advocate reading and who have access to a seemingly bottomless treasure trove of books to explore! Sometimes these groups are focused on a particular year group, they are usually facilitated by a member of staff, and they are often run near to transition points in the school day – during register; after lunch; instead of assembly; or just before the end of the day. The more thought that goes into the choosing of the book or books, the more successful the session. At Westbury Park Primary School, a thriving two-class entry primary school, a weekly book club was set up for a small group of year four readers. The Club ran first thing in the morning for thirty minutes, throughout Terms 3 and 4. Each weekly session focused on a different book or small selection of books and each session started with a "Big Question of the Week." The questions were designed to value the pupils' opinions and feelings about reading as well as to guide the facilitator to texts each child might enjoy.

Here are some examples of the "Big Question of the Week":

What don't you like about reading?
What makes you want to read?
Have you ever been "turned off" reading and what switched you on again?
If a new person started in your class what should the teacher do to get them reading?
If you could only keep one book in the world, what would it be?
If you were Shen (in The Magic Paintbrush by Julia Donaldson) what would you paint?
What's your top tip for teachers to inspire children to read?
Have you ever read a book more than once? What was it?

Each Book Club session was set up with care so that when the children arrived there was a sense of anticipation as to what would be unveiled that week. Three of the sessions used the idea of a "feast of books" (starter, main and pudding) – a plate was set in each child's place with a book – a personal recommendation – placed on it, ready to delve into. The chosen books, recommendations and suggested authors for each week were chosen with attention to each child – remembering their opinions and interests which were gathered in the weeks before the Book Club began. These included things like:

> "I like graphic novels and books that are really funny. I like to get through them and go onto the next"

> "I don't really read much even though I'm a free reader. I like puzzles, like Rubik's Cube."

> "I stopped reading when I had other things to do but then I found a book I liked – it started with Flat Stanley, then Harry Potter, then Tom Gates and now I'm reading Rooftoppers."

A fairly recent innovation, where peers are invited to share their reading responses, can be found in the burgeoning use of "reading scrapbooks." These have been widely acclaimed and shared via social media, though there is little robust research around their use currently. Scrapbooks/floorbooks have long been used within the Primary classroom, but generally linked to a subject or topic, and generally used for formative assessment purposes. Scrapbooks enable children to respond to a text in whatever medium they wish or have available. Alexander (2013) suggests an approach like this enables recommendations to be shared through an inclusive approach and, in addition, identified the "pedagogical value" of the scrapbook.

The scrapbooks can be varied in size and style, and have no specific format, other than using a double page spread. Some schools require a child to take the scrapbook home along with the class reader or chosen book and share it with their family before responding. The scrapbook is then returned for the next child to complete. One teacher on social media was very explicit in their instructions: "*I bought a scrap book, put instructions inside it and then did an example page. The children signed up for the waiting list and one child takes it home*

98 Putting Social Justice and Equity at the Heart of Reading for Pleasure

(all voluntary) Monday to Wednesday, Wednesday to Friday or over the weekend so currently getting 3 children doing it. I bought some metallic pens and as our children don't have a lot at home, they request the book cover to be printed and any extras. It is lovely seeing the children (particularly the reluctant readers) wanting to share"!

However, others keep the scrapbooks in class and plan times for children to complete pages during school time, often responding to the class reader which creates a dialogue for the children who can browse the scrapbook alongside listening to the story. For less confident children, this can motivate them to respond with their own ideas through "magpie-ing" from others. This is how we approached their use in practice with pre-service teachers. As a part of the United Kingdom Literacy Association (UKLA) book shadowing awards (2023 and 2024), our pre-service teachers were asked to work in groups, read the selection of books from the short list and decide which one they wanted to respond to further. Groups were then asked to create personal responses either individually or in small groups in an A3 sketchbook, using a wide range of materials provided. They used their creativity and imagination to create some fascinating responses including these below, based on the shortlisted books: *Barbara Throws a Wobbler* by Nadia Shireen; *We're Going to Find the Monster* by Malorie Blackman and illustrated by Dapo Adeola; *Martha Maps it Out* by Leigh Hodgkinson and *Dick the Delightful Duck* by Kaye Umansky and illustrated by Ben Mantle.

Examples of scrapbook entries (Figures 6.2–6.6).

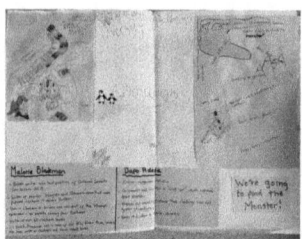

Figure 6.2 Scrapbook example

Figure 6.3 Scrapbook example

Figure 6.4 Scrapbook example

Figure 6.5 Scrapbook example

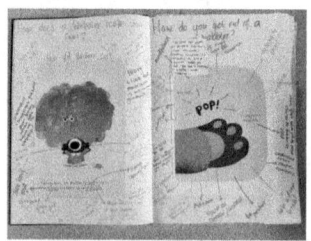

Figure 6.6 Scrapbook example

There are many further examples on social media (Facebook and X) and their use is championed by Jon Biddle (**Jon Biddle https://twitter.com/jonnybid**) who said:

> What goes in these scrapbooks? Anything! Literally anything the child wants to do that links to the books and shows how much they love it. And help them – give them whatever they need in terms of resources. Also, encourage anyone at home to help them - the more people involved, the more people learn about the book, which is a good thing. What books should be chosen? Any! Fiction, non-fiction, poems, graphic novels – you name it, it can be done. Book choices can come from anywhere but remember that this is an opportunity to showcase wonderful books that perhaps don't always get as much attention as they deserve.

What is so lovely about scrapbooks is that there is no specific format to adhere to. If you were to use a scrapbook approach, which of the approaches suggested appeals to you? Would you want to be directly involved as some of the in-service teachers have demonstrated? Or would you prefer to let the children, and possibly their families, hold the reins on how the scrapbook develops? You can be as creative as you like, with minimal resources really required: pencils, paper, crayons to start, with other media used as and when available. Some adults are daunted by their perception of their own artistic skills-but don't be! You don't have to be an artist to draw and write your responses to what you have read as the examples show.

Ultimately the use of reading scrapbooks adheres to the views of Cremin et al. (2014, p. 5) when they say "At its core is the reader's volition, their agency and desire to read, their anticipation of the satisfaction gained through the experience and/or afterwards in interaction with others." So this is possibly an avenue that you might explore further, perhaps with your class or as a whole school focus.

So, having identified some ways in which we can develop a greater interest in books, how can these be brought in in a regular and consistent way into the classroom? The next section considers some strategies alongside some relevant research.

Reading environments (classroom and timetable)

To counter the potential inequalities once children arrive in school, a rich and diverse collection of books is essential in creating an inviting reading environment. Access to a wide range of books, including fiction, non-fiction, and various genres, allows children to explore their interests, discover new topics, and find books that resonate with them. A well-stocked classroom and/or school library provides further opportunities for students to engage in independent reading and choose books that appeal to them. The National Literacy Trust's research report "Children's and Young People's Reading in 2023" highlights the impact of the reading environment on reading enjoyment. The report found that children who have access to a wide range of books at home and in their community, as well as a supportive reading environment in school, are more likely to read for pleasure, stating "Nearly three times as many children and young people who perceived their reading environment to be supportive said they enjoyed reading compared with those who perceived it to be less supportive (63.9% vs. 25.4%), while twice as many read daily in their free time (41.7% vs. 17.7%)."

This emphasizes the role of the reading environment in fostering positive reading attitudes and habits. Guthrie et al. (2007) investigated the impact of classroom libraries on students' reading achievement and engagement. The study found that classrooms with well-stocked libraries, access to a variety of books, and supportive reading practices had higher levels of student reading achievement and greater reading engagement. The presence of a conducive reading environment was identified as a significant factor in promoting reading for pleasure. Mol and Bus (2011) indicated that a classroom environment that is rich in books, provides comfortable reading spaces, and offers opportunities for social interaction and discussion positively impacts students' reading enjoyment and motivation.

However, the use of both classroom reading environments and school libraries may not always be utilised as efficiently as they could. Children, as the key users of a school library are often quick to be critical friends when it comes to talking about what works. Our case study children provided some examples of this:

> "Sometimes it's hard to find the books you want in the library."

> "There are high shelves. I think it's more for years 5 or 6."

> "Sometimes the books are in the wrong place, not chronological. Or the books are all bunched up and it's very confusing."

> "To make it better you could paint the walls. Sometimes the books are a bit ripped."

Miller (2009) identifies the importance of "not labelling" readers. For example, it is not uncommon to hear readers referred to as "struggling," "reluctant" or "more able." Miller (2009) suggests the terms: developing readers, dormant readers and underground readers.

Developing readers can be characterised as having had minimal positive reading experiences. This may be because the child is neurodivergent and has not had appropriate personalised reading guidance, or it could simply be a child who does not regard themselves as a reader for any reason. Frequently these children read less than their peers – anything up to 75% less. These children may have had the same quantity and quality of instruction as others in the "mechanics" of reading but have not transferred the skills of reading into its independent practice. Miller (2009) identifies the importance of providing multiple opportunities across a wide range of text, for independent reading alongside explicit instruction in reading strategies. Very often the opportunities provided for children to make the leap from instruction to independence is through reading scheme books or short, comprehension focused exercises. Whilst there is value in matching text to children's reading attainment, the interest level and purpose for reading are as significant, and hence, it is useful to provide a balance and range of "practice" text.

Dormant readers are those "middle of the road" children who can read and pass tests but remain unmotivated. Reading to this group of children is work, not pleasure. They need experiences to enable them to discover the "magic" of reading again. It may take time to find genres and authors they enjoy, so this is where teachers' knowledge of children's literature is important in selecting texts to read aloud. Spending five minutes daily to read aloud snippets of multiple books, the blurb of new books, flicking through pictures in picture books, reading tempting tasters from non-fiction and exploring different formats of text both on and offline, are all part of this temptation repertoire.

Underground readers are the readers who separate personal reading from the reading required in school. These children will tell you they get bored by the prolonged reading of a class novel, finding the pace too slow. They can be avid readers but experience too few opportunities to read sufficiently for their needs. These readers can be overlooked by teachers and are often underachievers who seem to lack interest and motivation but do not warrant the attention of those readers who are not reaching age-related expectations. Indeed, these are the readers that Moss (2000) identifies as the "can but don't read" children – the disengaged. It is helpful to consider not just the texts we use for teaching – which may hold no interest for the child – but also the approaches used to follow up the reading they are asked to do in school. Worksheets, book reviews, quizzes (online and off), reading diaries are often used to ensure "compliance" and "accountability" of reading but can contribute to negating reading for pleasure.

Reflect on these categories of readers and consider how you address their differing needs. You may also want to consider the work of Cambourne (1995) who looked more holistically at the classroom environment. How does your classroom environment reflect the conditions for reading for pleasure that were explored in this research?

- Immersion – being surrounded by books of all types and in all aspects of classroom learning with the books being central to the learning conversations.
- Demonstrations – being taught purposefully about text features to enable children to access the elements of the text they are most interested in.
- Expectations – ensuring high teacher expectations for the amount of time children can spend reading on daily basis and expecting this to be successful.
- Responsibility – giving children responsibility for making choices about texts.
- Employment – giving children time to practice in real-life contexts.
- Approximations – encouraging children to read texts at any level including below their book grade or band level and so understanding the value and benefits of mastery and confidence.
- Building response – providing children with positive, instant verbal feedback including reading conferences and daily discussion.
- Engagement – recognising that reading must have personal value to children and building confidence so that they see themselves as capable and free from anxiety. Modelling from someone they like, trust and want to emulate is an important part of this.

Reading Incentives (challenges and barriers) Reading challenges are becoming a feature for many schools Having a target, for example, Court's 40 books (Court, 2011) may be motivating for some children. The Summer Reading Challenge which is free via public libraries is cited as a positive: Kennedy and Bearne (2010, p. 71) found that "children who take part are more enthusiastic about reading [and it] can help prevent the summer holiday reading dip." However, when listening to children in our case study schools their comments would seem to contradict their head teacher's view that the reading challenges the school set helped promote reading for pleasure:

> One child in Year 5 said, "We have something called the 100 book challenge in our school and we aim to read them all and it is to encourage us to read different kinds of books. My brother has read them all but did it in five terms and he can't tell me anything about any of them."

> Another child said, "The only thing is there's never 100 books, there's about 20. People lose them and some were never on the bookshelf – maybe they got lost."

> A number of children commented on the list itself, "We need to have more interesting and fun books. Instead of just reading books we could have comics and magazines on the list too."

> "We need more books about sport on the list – at least they'd be something I'm interested in."

> Other children talked about how demotivating a list can appear, "I can't read a 100 books so I won't bother to start."

The use of incentives and rewards to encourage children's reading for pleasure has been a subject of debate in the research. While some studies suggest potential benefits, especially in motivating reluctant readers, others caution against the unintended consequences, particularly when it comes to sustaining long-term reading habits and fostering intrinsic motivation. Gambrell (2001) suggested that extrinsic rewards including such things as being awarded points and prizes, can initially motivate some more reluctant readers to engage. It is possible that this can lead to the development of reading positive reading habits. It is argued that such incentives can act as a bridge to intrinsic motivation, particularly when the rewards are closely tied to reading itself, including books and book tokens. For readers who are struggling to develop reading fluency and automaticity, these incentives can ensure these readers get the "practise" needed to develop fluency. When reading is no longer a "chore" because of the mechanics of reading, these children may then become intrinsically motivated readers, who no longer need the reward because the reward becomes the new pleasure found in reading. This short-term engagement was found by Edmunds and Bauserman (2006) who talked to children (in US classrooms). However, the children were clear that this short-term engagement did not always translate to longer-term reader benefits. This was also reported by Clark and Rumbold (2006) who found that it was intrinsic motivation that was linked to more regular reading, improved literacy outcomes and reading for pleasure. Competitions, praise, marks and grades along with other teacher or school rewards were found to provide only short-term gains and did not sustain reading engagement. Gambrell et al. (2011) identified "Seven Rules of Engagement" when considering motivation and whilst this study is also based in the US it has been influential in the UK. The factors identified were the same factors identified in relation to Reading for Pleasure pedagogies, including giving children choice, providing opportunities for social interaction and making reading materials relevant to children. They also found that reading became associated with the rewards offered driving the desire the read for purpose and pleasure even further out of the reach of the child.

Conclusion and call to action!

Most of us will not have the autonomy to make changes at a whole school level, but nearly all the strategies in this chapter can be embedded through some considered changes to your own practice:

- Look carefully at your classroom environment and consider whether there is a diverse, accessible range of reading materials available catering to *all* the children's interests. How are these displayed? How much autonomy do the children have in choosing and organising books? Is the reading area (if you have one) inviting- if not, how can this be managed with minimal impact on time or cost? Consider encouraging the children to have responsibility for this perhaps?
- Try to avoid making assumptions about whether the strategies you (or the school) currently employ to encourage reading for pleasure are actually having the impact you think they are!
- Role modelling is key to transmitting that energy and enthusiasm for reading. How can you make recommendations in an interesting and engaging way?
- Embed at least one strategy into your weekly timetable that enables children to have some time to read without any pressure, perhaps independently or with a partner, or small group.

References

Alexander, K.P. (2013) Material affordances: The potential of scrapbooks in the composition classroom, *Composition Forum* 27, Spring 2013. https://files.eric.ed.gov/fulltext/EJ1003969.pdf

Bailey, C. (2016) 'Free the sheep: Improvised song and performance in and around a minecraft community', *Literacy*, 50(2), pp. 62-71. https://onlinelibrary.wiley.com/doi/full/10.1111/lit.12076

Baker, L. and Scher, D. (2002) 'Beginning readers' motivation for reading in relation to parental beliefs and home reading experiences', *Reading Psychology*, 23(4), pp. 239-269.

Burnett, C. and Merchant, G. (2018) 'Affective encounters: Enchantment and the possibility of reading for pleasure', *Literacy/UKLA*, 52(2), pp. 62-69 https://onlinelibrary.wiley.com/doi/full/10.1111/lit.12144

Cambourne, B. (1995) 'Towards an educationally relevant theory of literacy learning: Twenty years of enquiry', *Reading Teacher*, 49(3). https://www.jstor.org/stable/i20201581

Clark, C., Picton, I. and Galway, M. (2023) *Children and young people's reading in 2023*. https://www.researchgate.net/publication/381376436_Children_and_young_peoples_reading_in_2023

Clark, C. and Rumbold, K. (2006). *Reading for pleasure: A research overview*. London: National Literacy Trust.

Cole, A., Brown, A., Clark, C. and Picton, I. (2022) *Children and young people's reading engagement in 2022: Continuing insight into the impact of the Covid19 pandemic on reading*. https://cdn.literacytrust.org.uk/media/documents/Reading_trends_2022_-_Final.pdf

Court, J. (ed.) (2011) *Read to succeed*. London: SAGE.

Cremin, T. (2020) 'Reading for pleasure: Tensions and challenges in c', in Davison, J (ed.) *Debates in English teaching*. London: Routledge, pp. 92-102.

Cremin, T. (2023) Reading and motivation: Focusing on dis-engaged readers NATE. https://cdn.ourfp.org/wp-content/uploads/20231212180729/Cremin-2023-NATE-Reading-and-Motivation.pdf?_gl=1*1y95azn*_ga*OTM3MzY5NS4xNzE4MTEwNDc4*_ga_56HENEGN4V*MTcxOTMwOTg1MC4yLjAuMTcxOTMwOTg1MC4wLjAuMA

Cremin, T., Hendry, H., Leon, L.R. and Kucirkova, N. (2023) *Reading teachers: Nurturing reading for pleasure*. London: Routledge.

Cremin, T., Hendry, H., Rodriguez Leon, L. and Kucirkova, N. (Eds) (2022) *Reading teachers: Nurturing reading for pleasure (1st ed.)*. London: Routledge. https://doi.org/10.4324/9781003215615

Cremin, T., Mottram, M., Collins, F., Powell, S. and Safford, K. (2014) *Building communities of engaged readers: Reading for pleasure*. London/New York: Routledge.

Department for Education (2022) *The reading framework*. [Online] Available at: https://assets.publishing.service.gov.uk/media/664f600c05e5fe28788fc437/The_reading_framework_.pdf [Accessed 24 March 2024]

Edmunds, K.M. and Bauserman, K.L. (2006) 'What teachers can learn about reading motivation through conversations with children', *The Reading Teacher*, 59(5), pp. 414-424.

Ellis, S. and Smith, V. (2017) 'Assessment, teacher education and the emergence of professional expertise', *Literacy*, 51, pp. 84-93.

Gambrell, L.B. (2001) 'What we know about motivation to read', in R.F. Flippo (ed.), *Reading researchers in search of common ground.*, pp. 129-143. London: Routledge.

Gambrell, L.B. (2011) ''Seven rules of engagement: What's most important to know about motivation to read', *The Reading Teacher*, 65(3), pp. 172-178. https://doi.org/10.1002/TRTR.01024.

Gioia, D. (2008) Cited by https://www.theguardian.com/technology/2008/feb/07/internet.literacy

Guthrie, J.T., Hoa, A., Wigfield, A., Tonks, S., Humenick, N.M. and Littles, E. (2007) 'Reading motivation and reading comprehension growth in the later elementary years', *Contemporary Educational Psychology*, 32(2007), pp. 282-313.

Hempel-Jorgensen, A., Cremin, T., Harris, D. and Chamberlain, L. (2018) 'Pedagogy for reading for pleasure in low socio-economic primary schools: Beyond 'pedagogy of poverty'? *UKLA Literacy*, 52(2), pp. 86-94. https://cdn.ourfp.org/wp-content/uploads/20210219145940/Hempel-Jorgensen_et_al-2018-Literacy.pdf

Hughes, T. (1968) The Iron Man. London: Faber & Faber.

Kennedy, R. and Bearne, E. (2010) *Summer reading challenge 2009 impact research report*. UKLA

Krashen, S. (2004) *The power of Reading: Insights from the research*. Heinemann.

Lindorff, A., Stiff, J. and Kayton, H. (2023) *PIRLS 2021: National report for England research report*. London: Department for Education. https://www.gov.uk/government/publications/pirls-2021-reading-literacy-performance-in-england

Miller, D. (2009) *The book whisperer*. San Francisco: Jossey-Bass.

Mol, S. and Bus, A. (2011) 'To read or not to read: A meta-analysis of print exposure from infancy to early adulthood', *Psychological Bulletin*, 137, 267-96. https://doi.org/10.1037/a0021890

Moss, G. (2000) 'Raising boys' attainment in reading: Some principles for intervention', *Reading*, 34(3), pp. 101-106.

Open University Reading for Pleasure (no date) *Teachers' knowledge of children's reading practices classroom strategies.* https://cdn.ourfp.org/wp-content/uploads/20210205160528/Teachers_knowledge_of_childrens_reading_practices_Practical_Strategies-final.pdf?_gl=1*d092hl*_ga*MTU4OTU3MzQzOC4xNzE0MDM5Mjk2*_ga_56HENEGN4V*MTcxNDA0NTAyNC4yLjEuMTcxNDA0NTAzMi4wLjAuMA

Oxley, E. and McGeown, S. (2023) 'Reading for pleasure practices in school: Children's perspectives and experiences', *Educational Research*, 65, pp. 375-391.

Pennac, D. (2006) *The rights of the reader*. London: Walker Books.

Reedy, A. and Reedy, D. (2024) 'Because it reminds me of my culture.' 'Because I want to challenge myself.' 'Because I like all the stars and the swirls.' What influences children's independent choice of text?, *Literacy*, In Press, 58(2), pp. 97-110.

Sènèchal, M. and LeFevre, J. (2002) 'Parental involvement in the development of children's reading skill: A five-year longitudinal study', *Child Development*, 73(2), pp. 445-460. https://doi.org/10.1111/1467-8624.00417. PMID: 11949902

Street, B. (2003) 'What's "new" in new literacy studies? Critical approaches to literacy in theory and practice', *Current Issues in Comparative Education*, 5(2), pp. 77-91.

Svrcek, N.S. and AbugaseaHeidt, M. (2022) 'Beyond levels and labels: Applying self-determination theory to support readers', *Literacy*, 56(4), pp. 311-326. https://doi.org/10.1111/lit.12286

Swain, C. (2009) *Reading magazines with a critical eye in the primary school*. London: UKLA.

Topping, K. (2014) Paired reading and related methods for improving fluency. https://files.eric.ed.gov/fulltext/EJ1053797.pdf

Toste, J.R., Didion, L., Peng, P., Filderman, M. and McClelland, A.M. (2020) 'A meta-analytic review of the relations between motivation and reading achievement for K-12 students.' *Review of Educational Research*. https://doi.org/10.3102/0034654320919352

Wyse, D. and Bradbury, A. (2022) Reading wars or reading reconciliation? A critical examination of robust research evidence, curriculum policy and teachers' practices for teaching phonics and reading. https://bera-journals.onlinelibrary.wiley.com/doi/epdf/10.1002/rev3.3314

YouGov (2019) Kids and family reading report: finding their story. https://www.scholastic.com/content/dam/scholastic/site/KFRR/KFRR_7th%20Edtidion.pdf

7 Family engagement
Who are your influencers?
Jane Carter

Introduction

We know that the foundations of attitudes and dispositions for reading are laid down well before the start of formal education: the home literacy environment provides the foundations for a child's identity as a reader, their language and indeed the relationship they build with literacy (Fletcher and Reese, 2005). This chapter will seek to unpick some of what we currently know about the role of the family in reading and, in particular, reading for pleasure, with a focus on what we can learn as teachers from the children in our classes by exploring and expanding on the ideas of "Funds of Knowledge" (González et al., 2005) and children's "Social and Cultural Capital" (Ellis and Smith, 2017). It is worth remembering here that a book or indeed any text, only holds meaning if we engage with it in some way. Our engagement and enjoyment of a book or text (or not) is derived from what we bring to it in relation to our background knowledge, our experiences, likes and dislikes and our view of the world from our place within it. Sometimes a text can widen these perspectives and open new worlds, but we need to have something to build this from, something we can latch on to and understand, in order to extend and develop. As you read this chapter, you will be encouraged to reflect on what you know about the children, families and communities you engage with and the assumptions that might be made about these different groups. You will be encouraged to reflect on what each unique child brings to the reading process. This chapter will also spotlight children and families living in poverty and the Gypsy Roma community, and the potential and specific barriers these families face in relation to reading for pleasure. The chapter will share a case study from one school with an innovative approach to drawing on Funds of Knowledge through community "influencers" to engage and re-engage families with reading. The chapter will finish with a round-up of some of the approaches that have been tried and tested in schools to support a respectful home-school partnership in reading for pleasure.

School and home

For some children their early encounters with language, literacy, reading and books matches the "version" of literacy they find when they arrive in school and so eases their transition to school. This continues as children move through their schooling, with those whose home literacy lives match that of school and curriculum expectations experiencing no disruption or disjuncture between the two. The "reading for pleasure" that they hear talked about in school is something they see in their home environment – someone reading a magazine, a sibling reading a book, someone referring to Google advice when trying to find out why the car won't start! However, for many children, this is not the case for many different reasons (Scherer, 2016). There has been a growing use of the term "school readiness" (Ofsted, 2014) where the expectation is that the family must mirror the school environment and hold and understand the same ideological positioning of reading, language and literacy as a school. What this misses, is the richness of the diversity that home practices and home constructs of literacy and reading, can supply. In addition, it places some families and children in a deficit position because they do not match a fixed view of school literacy and literacies and, in fact, this is not a view that is possible (or desirable) for them to achieve. For some children, therefore, their worlds of home and school are separate, discordant, and potentially confusing. Moll et al. (1992) argue that literacy is culturally and socially constructed and what is often identified by schools as a literacy deficit, is merely a mismatch between the literacies of the home and community and the literacy of school. Thomson and Hall (2008, p. 89) use the wonderful analogy of the school bag. They suggest that all children come to school with a virtual school bag, packed with their "knowledges, experiences and dispositions" but schools tend only to draw "on some children's school bags" those that match the "game of education" and so advantaging certain groups right from the first days at school. This analogy also helps us to see how a child might feel if their school bag is not even allowed into the classroom, never mind opened, shared and explored. They encourage teachers to challenge their ideas of what is considered to be "important knowledge." In this chapter (and in fact throughout this book) we want to think in terms of the reciprocal relationships that need to be built between home and school. Schools need to be "child and family ready" as much as a child and family need to consider school readiness.

This chapter will be using a socio-cognitive model of reading to frame the points being made. This is a model that sees reading as necessarily socially situated and "socially constituted" (Pretorius and Lephalala, 2011, p. 3). The introduction and Chapter 4 explore what is meant by reader identity and it is useful to think again about how identity is also socially situated and forged in the home and community environment. Hall (2012) suggests that identity is formed from how you view yourself in relation to society's norms, your experience of society and how you see or perceive society. When a child moves from home to school, it is easy to see how this can cause a shift in identity. I am sure we can all remember when we first went to school, talking about home traditions around festivals. For me this was Christmas. I suddenly found out that not everyone followed the same customs which until then, I thought were the "facts of the matter": the time of day we had Christmas dinner; when we opened presents; how Father Christmas left presents (or not). I found out too that not everyone celebrates Christmas and for some this winter festival had another name and meaning. The same is true of language. As a family, we have always used a made-up word for when a cat kneads a lap with its paws before curling up to sleep – we call this "freefrumming." When my daughter was talking to her friends using this word (when she had just started at university) she could not understand why no one else seemed to know what she meant. She had assumed it was a technical term. She phoned me to check and was rather indignant that we had made her look rather silly by not telling her that this was a family word rather than a "real" word. In the same way, reader identity is also formed by these personal experiences, synergies and contradictions and so understanding the family environment is a non-negotiable in developing reading for pleasure.

Reading and the family – What the research tells us

The Organisation for Economic Cooperation and Development (OECD, 2014) identified that developing positive attitudes to reading at an early stage secures future attainment success. More significantly, they found that a positive attitude to reading can support children in overcoming the challenges the child may face in relation to socio-economic disadvantage. Flouri and Buchanan (2004) identified that positive attitudes and home engagement with reading had a greater impact on the child than parents' education, family size and socio-economic status.

Whilst policy and curricula have continued to promote one view of reading, seminal studies locate reading as a social and cultural construct (Brice-Heath, 1983; Street, 1984). Most schools have policies and practices that focus on engaging with parents and the community, but Preece and Levy (2020) suggested that many of these approaches ignored the literacy practices that already existed in the home. They argue that in order to really understand family and community literacy practices and to be able to promote book-based shared activities with sensitivity, there is a need to recognise what "reading does for families" including experiences of bonding, closeness, engagement and enjoyment and to promote these alongside the practices shared with families and enabling families to share their own practices, that may be different to those of the school.

We know that many of our families and communities in school are readily engaged – and these families may come from a range of cultural and socio-economic backgrounds but it is those children, families and communities that feel a little "harder to reach" than others that therefore may need an additional focus. Bonevski et al. (2014), in the United States, identify a range of terms used by researchers when referring to groups or individuals that do not readily or easily engage with state institutions. These include: "hard to reach"; "vulnerable"; "disadvantaged groups" and "excluded groups." In medical research, these groups are considered to be "hidden groups" (Lambert and Wiebel, 1990) as they are often not represented in research resulting in outcomes that can be unreliable and potentially skewed. Hannon, Nutbrown and Morgan (2020) acknowledge that there is no single definition of "disadvantaged families" but that they can be characterised as families from 'lower socio-economic levels in society' (p. 311), who are likely to experience multiple disadvantage in relation to income, health, housing and educational outcomes. Whilst recognising that the national data and perhaps your school data, demonstrates that children from these "harder to reach" groups tend to have lower achievement levels in reading than their more advantaged peers, this may be a result of an inability to engage with these groups, to recognise and value "cultural strengths," or perhaps to recognise that these groups cannot always be engaged by the same means as the more advantaged family groups.

Before continuing to read, think about your class, your year group, Key Stage and school in relation to the unique families and communities that are represented. What do you currently know about the home lives of the children in your class? What does literacy in the home look like for these children? Are there books in the home, computers and other electronic devices, TVs, magazines, are the family present on social media, Instagram or Facebook, and so reading "content" in this way? Do families have any traditions, religious or cultural? Do families engage in hobbies or other interests? Which football team, rugby team or other sport does the family follow – if any? What is unique and special about each child and their family? Focus now on those children that you know do not engage in reading for pleasure – what do you know about them, their families and communities? Consider those children in your lowest 20% of attainment – what do you know about them, their families and communities?

For some of your children, one of the greatest impacts on their home lives will be poverty.

What do we know about poverty and reading for pleasure?

As demonstrated in many of the chapters of this book, the 2023 the National Literacy Trust (NLT) reported the decline in reading for pleasure and noted that this decline was most significant in children from lower socio-economic backgrounds. They found that 60% of children who receive Free School Meals (an accepted but imperfect method for identifying children living in poverty) said they did not read for pleasure. We also know that in 2023 the NLT found that "over a third of children on Free School Meals are leaving primary school without reaching the expected level of reading." In 2023, the Child Poverty Action Group reported statistics from the Department for Work and Pensions that show 30% of children are now living in relative poverty and those families that were already considered to be in poverty have fallen more deeply into poverty due, in part, to rising housing costs. 69% of children in poverty come from working families.

Thompson, McNicholl and Menter (2016) found that a cohort of pre-service teachers had little knowledge or understanding of the link between poverty and attainment. Pre-service teachers tended to locate low attainment as a problem of the family and the child, rather than having an understanding of the challenges and barriers faced by children living in poverty that adversely affect attainment. The study also highlighted how pre-service teachers perpetuated low expectations seeing some children and families as inevitably having low attainment, often framing this as a cultural or family issue rather than a poverty of school issue. Mazzoli and Todd (2016, p. 3) evaluated a framework for "Poverty Proofing" schools. The framework engaged schools in auditing how everyday practices, from school uniforms to afterschool clubs and trips, to food availability and homework inadvertently stigmatised children from poorer homes "multiple times" each school day. Another group of children that may either currently or in the past, have been impacted by poverty are Looked After Children, or Children in Care. The local authority has parental responsibility for this group of children and schools will know which children in their school community are within this group. They deserve to have the very best of what a school can offer in relation to reading for pleasure. Petula Bhojwani and Liz Kitts describe their project in the United Kingdom Literacy Association magazine, English 4-11, which engaged a local authority and a group of Children in Care through a multimodal literacy project. They produced a number of multimodal kits that included a number of books around a theme, artefacts linked to the theme, a talking photo album and leaflets about local places of interest linked to the kit's theme. The kit came with some guidance and prompt cards for carers and children, encouraging both the sharing of the books and some approaches to responding to the books. The idea of creating kits is a fabulous one that can enable children and parents together to have the opportunity to create connections, see reading in its broadest sense and to take a more multimodal approach to engagement.

Of course, knowing this and being aware of the alarming statistics around child poverty does not provide us with answers, but merely highlights the issue. Schools cannot eliminate poverty, but they can reflect on the everyday challenges families may encounter and consider how school practice can both support and mitigate. Where possible, schools can also be part of campaigns that address social inequality.

Here are some ideas that your school may already have considered:

1. Think about the events that you put on in relation to reading e.g. World Book Day, book character dressing-up, etc., or afterschool pajama reading evenings. For children and families in poverty, these events can be a real challenge. There will not be money available for costumes, or if the family spends some money on a costume, something else that week will not be paid for. Where there are lots of children in the family, the problem is multiplied. You may notice some children don't come to school on these days and are "ill" or come to school, but their behaviour is poor. Either do not focus on costumes on these days or provide ideas for all parents that involve everyday clothes that do not need adaptation or sewing, or set whole class challenges instead e.g. as a class, dress your classroom door as a character or book; redesign the classroom as a setting from your class's favourite book. These are some of the ideas found here https://www.michellerobinson.co.uk/news/alternative-world-book-day-ideas-for-schools along with a book in a box and book hats. Whilst there are suggestions on websites about making dressing a potato or egg as a character, I would avoid these too. Using food for art can also be an insensitive activity, where we also need to be aware of wider sustainability issues as well as food poverty.

2. Prioritise the school library. If you do not have a school library, consider the reasons why not. As Verity Robson, from Mangotsfield Primary, pointed out, the Prison Rules (1999) state that in every prison there is an obligation to provide a library. This is clearly a good thing, but it raises the question as to why libraries are mandatory in prisons but not schools! We know that the number of books in the home is an indicator of both attainment and likelihood of reading for pleasure (Cole et al., 2022) and that according to the National Literacy Trust (2023) children living in poverty are less likely to own books of their own. Neuman and Moland (2019) highlighted what they called book deserts in areas of the USA. They suggest that as areas of cities become more and more segregated in relation to income, those living in low-income neighbourhoods find themselves with no access to print. Without access and choice, disadvantage grows and so it is this group that needs priority access to the school library. This needs to be handled sensitively – there is nothing worse than singling out children but ensuring these children get the "new in" books perhaps before others, have a voice in deciding which books the library will purchase and perhaps being encouraged to have some responsibilities in the library are all worth considering. This is even better if you have a librarian – rather a rare luxury in most schools, who can get to know children and so be able to make recommendations to children. Verity Robson also made the insightful comment that a library without a librarian is really just a room full of books! If you do or don't have a librarian, reflect on the status given to the teacher who has responsibility for the library – this should be a high-status role if we are valuing reading. Encourage your

school to become members of the School Library Association who offer an amazing network of knowledge alongside resources, training, ideas and awards.

3. Try to make links with your local public library and cultivate a relationship with its librarians. Public libraries are also on the decline, despite campaigns by high-profile authors to make them a priority for public sector spending. School libraries are the stepping stones for children towards lifelong public library membership. Forging these links early is important. Libraries are no longer hushed places that are the preserve of adults, where fines are levied the moment a book is a few hours overdue. Most libraries no longer fine, most libraries no longer demand silence and most libraries offer services and spaces for families. When you do make trips to the local library, make these family trips – perhaps coordinate them at the end of the school day so that parents can come (making sure siblings in other parts of the school are catered for or brought along as well), or hold a school reading event in the library to encourage families to join the library and experience it, if these are unfamiliar places for the family. Keep in touch with the library, letting them know about your topics, children's favourite authors and illustrators as well as school reading activities, competitions and challenges. Advertise your local library in your school newsletter – ask the library to tell you about a new book, audiobook or other resource that they would like you to advertise as well as activities being held at the library, whether these are story times or book clubs. If families living in poverty access their local libraries, they will find a whole range of free resources which they may not know about. Most schools invite the library staff to come to school before the summer holidays to tell children about the annual Summer Reading Challenge (https://summerreadingchallenge.org.uk/) and library activities during the school summer holidays but try to invite the local librarians more frequently so that children know who they are when they visit the library independently. This breaks down one of the barriers that might prevent a child from going to the public library. If we don't use our local libraries, we will lose them!

4. Audit the books you have on offer in school. In Chapter 5 you will have considered issues of representation, but representation matters too when we think about poverty. How many books do you have that have main characters living in poverty, that children can easily identify with? Lovereading4kids.co.uk has a good Blog with reading suggestions, as does Booktrust.org.uk. However, it is essential we are mindful of how such books are perceived by all children – we want to avoid the "less fortunate" label that is often shared when discussing these books with little awareness of how this label will make some children feel. Books that offer simplistic solutions to poverty, or those with paternalistic and patronising approaches or books that suggest, it is just a matter of hard work and determination, should be avoided.

5. It is a misconception to suggest that because a family is living in poverty, they will not support their child with reading however, there are many reasons why parents may not be able to support home reading – work commitments; space in the home environment; time and resources to name a few. Working with parents will enable schools to build a picture of what can best support the family and child. Gay et al. (2020) found in the US that the amount of school reading instruction time was a key factor in supporting the reading of children living in poverty where it was known that parents were not able to

provide this in the home. It could be suggested therefore that a similar outcome could be applied to reading for pleasure.

6   When considering which children have opportunities to read with knowledgeable adults during the school day, focus not only on the children with lower attainment. Consider a focus also on children who may not have the opportunity to practise reading at home and opportunities for reading for pleasure, making the focus on the time, not instruction but reading for pleasure. This dedicated time is for the child to lead the adult, for the child to make choices in what they read or what the adult reads to them. The child may choose to browse and "flick" with the adult, talking about the text or anything connected to the text.

7   Highlight issues of social justice in some of the books you choose to read aloud to children. If you haven't read or shared with children the picture book, *When Angus Rides the Goods Train* by Alan Durant and illustrated by Chris Riddell, then you must! It will awaken debate about social justice that can really enable children to reflect on the sort of world they wish to live in as they grow and develop.

Funds of knowledge and cultural capital

Hopefully, so far this chapter has highlighted the need to really know the children and their families in our classes and school. González et al. (2005) went further in this idea of teacher "knowing." They noted that teachers in their studies made many assumptions about families, particularly those families in poverty and families from cultures different from those of the teacher or the dominant culture of the school. Often these assumptions were based on a deficit model – what the families were perceived to be "lacking." This idea was flipped on its head and González et al. (2005) focused teachers' attention on how home and cultural practices could be affirmed and valued in the school space. They sought to help teachers identify where their curriculum may have unintentionally excluded some and favoured others and also what was valued as "knowledge that counts." They encouraged what they called a funds of knowledge approach which recognises that communities "historically accumulate and culturally develop bodies of knowledge essential for household or individual functioning and well-being" within that community, which may differ from community to community and even family to family. The work of Reyes, Da Silva Iddings and Feller (2016) in the US focused on linguistically minoritised families: families in the UK we may think of as having English as an additional language i.e. in addition to one or more languages. They argue that all families will engage with a wide range of printed, oral, visual, physical (gesture) "text" in order to engage in everyday life both within their family and cultural community but also beyond this, in the wider community and area in which they live. Reyes, Da Silva Iddings and Feller (2016) argue strongly for teachers to deliberately seek out these literacy practices, to know and understand cultural practices and to make clear how these are valued in the school setting. A fund of knowledge approach seeks to demonstrate that linguistic and cultural capital is not fixed and singular but diverse and multifaceted. The term Cultural Capital was used by Bourdieu and Passerson (1977) as referring to what was considered to be "legitimate knowledge," knowledge that is valued by a society, its education systems and culture. Since this point, the term has been used in differing ways, including by Amanda Speilman, the then head of Ofsted (2019) to explain Ofsted's requirement for a broad and rich curriculum. Ellis (2017, p. 4) uses the term as part of their Three Domains Model, citing teacher knowledge of each child's "cultural capital for, and their socio-cultural understanding of, literacy." It is defined as the "child's funds of knowledge from outside school, the frequency and nature of the literacy experiences they have the importance attached to these by people in their family and the wider community." Ellis suggests that as teachers we need to link this knowledge to our understanding of children's interests, their beliefs about what literacy is for, and the sorts of literacy practices they have engaged with. The teacher's role is then to use this as the first building block in literacy teaching and learning within the school context. Chalmers and Crisfield (2019) cite this as an approach that enables the creation of a positive learning culture, one that is inclusive and builds on assets and values the multilingual capital children bring with them.

What might this mean in practice? Here are some ideas that may help get you thinking about practices in your classroom and school.

1. We tend to know the different languages and heritages of children in our class and school, but do we know any songs and rhymes in those languages? Is there someone in our school or community who could teach the class some of them? Even if your school or class is monolingual, it is a great activity to encourage children to hear voices and rhymes from a range of countries. There are some great websites, here are a few:

    https://www.bbc.co.uk/teach/school-radio/articles/zjjkbdm
    https://www.worldnurseryrhymeweek.com/
    https://www.exploreeverywhere.com/about
    https://www.songsforteaching.com/diversitymulticulturalism.htm

2. Do you encourage children to learn poems by heart and perform them for the class? If you do, these poems do not have to be in English. Encourage children to learn a poem that is of value to them or is important for their family, community or culture.
3. Members of children's extended families may be willing to come in and share a favourite book or oral story with the class.
4. How many dual language books do we have in our school? Even if we have very few children who speak languages other than English, dual-language books can ignite conversations about language. Where we have children that speak the language of dual language book, giving them a chance to read this to the class or talk about the text more generally promotes an inclusive learning environment that values multilingualism. A useful place to start is by looking at what the publisher Mantralingua https://uk.mantralingua.com/ offers.
5. Share with parents the benefits of either formally or informally developing the home language. Encourage children to sit with parents or grandparents when they are emailing, writing or posting on social media in the home language to family and friends.
6. Be aware of which children in your school attend home language schooling outside of the school day. Encourage children to bring in any texts they are reading in their home language and feature these alongside other books being promoted as part of a reading-for-pleasure display.
7. Create story sacks for some of the books you have in your library and for all ages. You can use either monolingual or bilingual books for this and in each sack include the book

and some objects that are linked to the story. They can include puppets or other linked texts, either fiction or non-fiction. It can be useful to hold sessions in school where the use of these is modelled – perhaps at the regular sharing assembly where parents are usually invited. This ensures particular parents are not "singled out" and the borrowing of the story sack is a valued activity for all children and parents.

8   Consider the language used about families in school. Often families, intentionally or intentionally, are framed as "in deficit" or "lacking" – this could be in relation to vocabulary and language deficit (we are all familiar with the guidance on the "word gap"). Use a staff meeting to read the work of Ian Cushing as a provocation to thinking. The 2023 article, "Word rich or word poor? Deficit discourses, raciolinguistic ideologies and the resurgence of the 'word gap' in England's education policy," provide an alternative perspective on language. You may not agree with all of what he argues, but challenging thinking is part of the process of being a reflective teacher.

The Gypsy, Roma and Traveller communities

One distinct community that requires thought when considering family engagement with reading for pleasure is the Gypsy, Roma and Traveller communities This community is often part of a demographic that has low socio-economic status and so is impacted by all of the things detailed in the section about poverty. Not only this, but it is also evident that a disproportionate number of children from this community are taken into care, have some of the lowest attainment levels of any minoritised group in the UK and are a community with very high school exclusion rates. This sort of narrative can encourage a deficit model perspective of this community and therefore this group needs special attention and respect when considering reading for pleasure. This is a community who have much to offer when thinking about funds of knowledge approach to engaging with families.

Not one homogenous group but a shared history of discrimination and prejudice

It is important to note at this point that the Gypsy, Roma and Traveller communities are not one homogenous group. Whilst they have many similarities and a shared history of nomadism (although not all groups continue to be nomadic), these groups have different traditions, stories and cultures. The 2024 education pack, published to support Gypsy, Roma and Traveller history month (in June each year since 2008) outlines the range of communities that the term often covers – from the Romany Gypsy to the Roma community to the Irish Travellers to boater and showmen communities. Sweeney and Matthews (2017, p. 2) cite Allen (2015) who made it clear that despite these differences, they do have in common experiences of 'racism, discrimination, poverty [and] social injustice'. If you have children from these communities in your school, do you know which particular heritage group the children belong? What do you know about the distinct group, rather than a more generalised view of the whole community? A good place to start is to consider the language and dialect of the children in your class. There is a wide diversity of languages and dialects spoken including Romani, Scottish Cant and Irish Cant or Gamon language traditions, as well as Eastern European languages such as Polish and Slovak. Alongside this are the different approaches to the use of language. Language and communication can sometimes be the source of prejudices against these communities, as well as language being used about the communities that are racist – and sometimes other children and adults are not always aware of how derogatory some of the names are for different groups of travellers. The term "gypsy" is felt to be a term of abuse for some traveller groups but also a term used by other groups to refer to themselves. Knowing your children, your community, and their preferred "name," is essential to any parental engagement approach. Challenging some of the stereotypes held about these communities is essential, particularly around literacy and education more generally. Devarakonda (2015) makes clear that families value basic literacy for their children and hold a view of education being wider than what can be offered in a school – with skills and responsibilities being part of the education that takes place within the family.

The Gypsy, Roma and Traveller communities and children's literature

As with all children, seeing yourself represented in literature is important. Books that mirror your history, culture and experiences are vital. As with all representation in children's literature, it is as important for the majority of children to read books where there are positive representations of minoritised groups as for the communities themselves. Stick (2017) writing for The Book Trust (2017) noted that many representations of the Gypsy, Roma and Traveller communities were stereotyped, romanticised or negative. Chetty and Sands-O'Connor (2023) in their Blog for "Books for Keeps" provide a brief history of some of the books that have featured characters from these communities and make suggestions as to why some of the books we may have read as children, in fact, may contain stereotypical viewpoints. As considered in Chapter 5, it is not just making a character from a minoritised group the focus of a book just because they are from this group, but important for characters to be well-drawn characters in their own right. Authors Richard O'Neil and Katharine Quarmby have published picture books that aim to address these vital aspects of representation, presenting aspects of traveller life, skills and traditions in a positive light, creating characters that are well-rounded and multi-dimensional, that are not defined simply by their traveller heritage. Chetty and Sands-O'Connor (2023) provide a useful list of more up-to-date books that also do the same.

When thinking about what this may mean for practice, the following may provide you with some starting points. These are not tips on developing reading for pleasure as such but are more about approaches to building trust with children and parents so that many of the other ideas in this book can be used:

1 Be mindful of stereotyping and when thinking about reading for pleasure, be particularly mindful of avoiding an over-romanticised view of communities as storytellers. All communities have their stories, and the Gypsy, Roma and traveller communities are no different, but it is important not to overplay this when engaging with parents.
2 One way to avoid this may be to encourage children to write their own stories where they are the main characters. Make multiple copies of the books your class makes so that children are able to take these home where they can be shared with parents, wider family and siblings but also copies can be made available in school. Where literacy

skills place restrictions on the story a child wants to tell, try to record the child telling their story so that it can be written down by an adult and perhaps then illustrated by the child. You may be interested in the work of Dobson, Stephenson and De Arede (2021, p. 511) who worked with a group of Roma children to create a published story as part of the "Story Makers Press" a university-based publisher which co-construct stories with "under-represented groups of children." They describe the challenges of avoiding stereotypes whilst maintaining validity in the community's eye and the trust of the children.

3   Think about ensuring the reading and writing in the classroom is authentic and has a real audience and purpose and consider what is authentic and real for the Gypsy, Roma and Traveller community children in your class. Enabling children to take their writing home to share (so make copies of what has been done in exercise books) is important.

4   Use the resources and ideas available on the Friends, Families and Travellers website and in particular the resources for Gypsy, Roma and Traveller month that can be accessed all year round.

5   Across your curriculum consider where historical figures from these communities are represented, as well as thinking about the modern history of activism within the community. Look at *Standing on the shoulders of giants: Stories from people who have challenged injustice faced by Gypsy, Roma, Traveller and nomadic communities* a series of short films, some of which could be used with children. Use these alongside stories from other communities, including those stories from majority groups. Children need to feel included rather than "singled out" and this needs to be the message that children communicate to their parents when they get home – strengthening trust between school and home.

6   Racist bullying, prejudice and discrimination are all too common in the experience of these communities. When putting together resources you will use for anti-bullying week, or when you are addressing bullying as part of PHSE, or when you are reading aloud a book to the class that highlights bullying, remember to discuss scenarios that include children and families from these communities. This is important in classes where there are no children from Gypsy, Roma or traveller communities, as anti-racism in all its forms should be a feature of practice.

7   Be mindful that many children do not wish for other children in their class or school to know about their heritage and community for many different reasons. Be respectful of this. If you have established an inclusive classroom children may gradually trust you and the children in the class.

Other useful approaches to family engagement

Thinking more widely, both including and going beyond families in poverty and the particular needs of the Gypsy Roma community, much has been reported and published about effective approaches to engaging families. Use the list below as a tool to audit and reflect on your current school practices.

1   For many families, a simple reframing of reading for pleasure as reading for purpose may enable some families to identify with both the importance of reading but also with the practice we associate with reading for pleasure. This reframing can enable families

to find their role and place in supporting their child's choice of what to read, talking about what is read, offering a pathway to connecting with a community of readers interested in the same subjects and areas as their child and also provide something different that can be read aloud together or by the parent with the child. The Farshore, Reading for Pleasure and Purpose report (2022) identified that "messaging that recognises both [reading for pleasure and reading for purpose] may be a more inclusive way to encourage reading to children." This had some links to another finding from this report that suggested that many parents (and many parents of minoritised children) preferred to read, browse and use non-fiction rather than fiction. Tapping into this reading is one way to connect with and engage parents.

2. This same report also highlighted that school messaging and often school homework focuses on the skill of reading. This results in both children and parents seeing reading as "work." This dominant narrative around reading therefore can make children associate reading with schoolwork and so in spare time, children reach for the computer game or other activity that to them, represents "down-time." It is useful to look at the school website, homework messages, newsletters, etc., to see just how reading is most dominantly represented and seek a greater balance.

3. Many school websites contain some super messaging about reading and reading for pleasure. However, text-heavy websites can be a barrier for some parents – whether this is about time, access or parents' own literacy confidence. Some schools have created short videos, sent via the schools' text messaging services or links in newsletters, that exemplify reading-for-pleasure practices or myth-busting clips about reading. It was found that some parents had very set views on reading and gender, suggesting that boys were "naturally more active" than girls and so, therefore, parental expectations around boys' interest in books were reduced (this was another interesting finding from the Farshore report). These ideas are useful to explore not just with parents but also with children. If children can be involved in researching and creating short films for parents, there will be a wider group of beneficiaries!

4. Many schools already host bedtime reading events, where parents and children come to school in the evening dressed in pyjamas with their teddy bears and enjoy an evening of story and warm drinks! If you know some families are unable to join with this, I know of one school that makes a special trip to the home of the family (pre-arranged) to read a bedtime story to the child at home – this models both the joy of the bedtime story and "how to do it."

5. Verity Robson, librarian at Mangotsfield Primary held Booknics (rather than picnic) at the end of a school day in the summer, where children and parents brought blanket, snacks and books to the school playground, for an after-school "book-in." It is worth teachers knowing their class well and offering their own blanket, snacks and books to those children whose parents are unable to come for whatever reason, so the children do not miss out. If photos can be shared with the families of those children, then parents can be helped to feel part of the reading community even if they are not able to attend.

6. Book swap events have become increasingly popular. Ask parents to bring any books their children no longer want to school on a particular day. If you have a school library,

make sure you take a look at the books before putting them out for the book swap event as this is a good way to increase the choice available in the library and to keep it stocked with new books. Again, if you know some parents are unable to come, try to support the children to find books for themselves at these events and encourage children to then tell their parents what they have chosen. These events are better when they are not about having to have something to swap – these are "re-distribution" events – from those who have to those that do not! Hold events on different days of the week and times of year to ensure that the same parents are not always prevented from attending by work commitments on particular days.

7. Use every opportunity to talk to parents about reading for pleasure. Announcements at the school fayre or sports day; child-led "adverts" at the end of the school play; displays and if possible "free books" at parents' evenings. Really reflect on these messages – messages need to be designed not to engender guilt or sound like more "school-work" but need to provide information on the benefits of reading for pleasure for both the parent and child, as well as promoting activities like reading aloud to children or using audiobooks if reading aloud is not an option for a parent. Does your school have audiobooks for some of the most popular titles in your class or school library? These may be a way in for parental engagement. In the same way that all parents are different, different types and styles of messaging are needed. Some messages need to focus on the benefits for both parents and children – so perhaps reading for pleasure's ability to support parental bonding and children's well-being. Other messages may be more powerful for some parents if the focus is on the benefits of academic attainment.

8. Another key part of messaging is to ensure parents are aware that reading for pleasure is not just about traditional books. Reading comics, magazines, graphic novels, audiobooks, online books, song lyrics – is all reading! YouTube has a whole host of books being read aloud. Feature one or two of these each week in the newsletter, along with book recommendations (that can be found in your class or school library if possible).

9. Consider sport as a way in to engaging some families. This can either be through local clubs or players of popular sports or using a sports theme for some reading activities and events for the wider community.

10. Breakfast reading clubs, reading cafes, stay and reads, parent/grandparent-led story times, parents' own reading clubs (of both adult and children's literature) are all common features of many schools' repertoire of reading for pleasure offers.

Whilst all of these approaches may be useful, it is always important to consider the very particular needs of your specific school community. The case study that follows provides an example of one school's approach to engaging with its community.

A case study based in the Somali community

This case study focused on a large inner-city primary school and is reported in the study by Carter, Mohammad and Aidid (2022). The school had tried hard to work alongside its community with a large Somali population and had much success in engaging families with learning to read in English and reading for pleasure. However, as with many schools, there was a small group of families that rarely came to school reading events or reading information evenings.

The school was keenly aware that these families did not always have easy access to children's books and so the opportunities to share informally in book chat, and saw this alongside the growing threat of closure of local public libraries, children's centres and the reduced funding for library outreach. The school had already established a library at the school with dedicated parent and teacher volunteers who staffed the library at different points during the school day. This case study project sought to find new ways of reaching families and share messages about the value, benefits and enjoyment of reading and encourage families to browse and borrow books from the school library when it was to be opened for families after school, twice a week for the period of the project.

The school had many channels of communication with its families, from the newsletter to its Twitter feed (now X) and class WhatsApp groups. The question was then posed: if families were receiving these messages but some families were not acting on them, who or what might be more effective at getting the messages across and how could messages be designed to ensure they had impact?

The term "influencer" is perhaps most strongly associated with the world of marketing products and services: motivations, customer networks and word-of-mouth marketing. Briggs et al. (2012) define influencers as "Individuals who have significant contact with, and influence on, [the subject in question]. They may include, but are not limited to, role models, mentors, parents, and peers [as well as] other, more general cultural influences that impact beliefs, attitudes, and behaviors." Marketing seeks to identify these individuals or groups who are able to distribute product or service messages based on the range, scope and nature of their networks or spheres of influence. The school was aware that the "product" they had to sell was the joy of book sharing and reading! More recently, the term influencer has become more strongly associated with social media. "Social media influencers are prominent social media users who accumulated a dedicated following by crafting an authentic online persona" (Tafesse and Wood, 2021, p.1). Social influence theory identifies three aspects of social influence: compliance, identification, and internalization (Kelman, 2006). Internalisation suggests the follower internalises the message of the influencer because the values and message resonate with those of the follower. The follower is more likely to take on new behaviours recommended by the influencer if they see the influencer as a trusted and credible person. These ideas were the foundation of the project and case study.

First steps for the project

The first step was to find out who the influencers were within and beyond the school and community and in the Somali community in particular. This needed the insight of school and community members. They began by identifying people in the community who were considered to be influential. This process was conducted by the community researchers, first by identifying specific groups that were significant to the area i.e. community and religious groups as well as from the neighbourhood networks. The community researchers then approached people that they identified within these groupings. There was a group of male influencers: a local Imam; an elder; a community organiser and a school governor, and also a female group, made up of elders; a teacher; community organisers and a parent.

The community

An essential starting point for any project that aims to develop parent and community engagement, is to explore the background and funds of knowledge of that community. The school knew that its Somali community was highly engaged with education and had high expectations. They also knew that children from the Somali community often faced multiple barriers including poverty and housing disadvantage. Abikar (2021) also highlighted that in the education system Somali families often faced racism, trauma and lack of information about the English school systems. It was also highlighted here that schools often lacked knowledge about the Somali culture and in addition families faced the challenges that come for parents who have a different language to the one used in school. Demie, Lewis and McLean (2007) and Stokes et al. (2015) also highlighted that some in the community feared the loss of community identity and language. Parents or grandparents within the community were likely to have experienced a drastic reduction in formal education during the war in the 1990s, although literacy continued to be taught through the family and religious networks. This made oral traditions and the reading of the Qur'an important literacy drivers. Matthheisen (2017) cautioned against viewing these multiple barriers as a deficit to be countered and suggested that greater effort needed to be made by schools to recognise the benefits of dual language and of the cultural capital that comes with the Somali heritage.

Finding out more - Funds of knowledge

Focus groups were undertaken with the influencers to identify what they felt were current barriers to the engagement of families, as well as considering the most effective approaches to messaging and how to frame messaging about book sharing, reading and engaging with the school library.

Some of the key themes from these groups were: the importance of the family, community and religion; the significance of identity in terms of heritage and in relation to the city and representation in children's literature; the importance of the oral tradition rather than just a book based focus; the importance for parents and families to have control and avoid what is perceived as a "deficit model" that is felt was inherent in the more general messaging about reading and education the community received. The influencers recognised the challenges faced by many community members in relation to time and space for families to share books. They identified the differences many families felt between their children's development as readers and their own - with many having their education disrupted as children, managing multiple languages as they grew up and having a view of reading bound by education and employment rather than relaxation and pleasure.

Next steps

The school identified two, weekly, fifteen-minute sessions when the school library could be opened to families after school for browsing and book borrowing. A parent volunteer and a school Teaching Assistant volunteered to staff the session and facilitate book borrowing. The researcher, the school's deputy head and community worker were also available during the session to talk to families and guide, book selection.

The school also worked on the book selection that would be available in the library – so an additional "selling point" for the project. A group of children were taken to purchase more books for the library with a focus on representation as well as different types of books, including graphic novels and Manga. A number of short messages were created that could be sent out every few days during the term the library was open after school for families. Different messages were created by the researcher with the community influencers using the focus group data as the basis for the messages. The influencers then selected the messages they would send out via their own channels of communication – whether WhatsApp, social media channels or word of mouth. These were sent out a couple of times a week in English and Somali. The school also sent out messages via the school newsletter or verbally – when teachers were "on the gate."

> **Example of the messages sent out by the community influencers in the half term week before the opening of the library:**
>
> We all know that reading to our children and with our children from when they are very young, is important. To help with access to lots of books to do this, the school is opening its library after school every Tuesday and Friday for families to look at books and borrow one if they wish. Encourage all your friends who have children at the school to go along on the first Tuesday the library is open at 3.15
>
> During half term, tell your children some of the stories your parents told you when you were a child. Oral story-telling is just as important as reading a book to your child. Perhaps you remember your parent or grandparent telling you the scary story of Dhegdheer! When you return to school, remember that the library is open to families after school every Tuesday and Friday next term.

> **Example of the messages sent out by the community influencers during the term the library was open for families:**
>
> The first words of the Quran tell us to "Read, read, read." Help your child to fulfil this message by supporting their reading by choosing a book from the school library every Tuesday and Friday after school.
>
> Exploring and sharing your culture with your children is a great way to keep you and your children connected to their heritage but also help them grow in confidence. Can you remember the songs and rhymes you were taught when you were a child? Share them with your child and then perhaps see if you can find books in the school library that tell the stories of your childhood.
>
> Have you noticed recently how much time we all spend on our phones? This week could you perhaps decide that there will be no phones on Tuesday after school? Or Friday after school? In this time you and your child could visit the school library 3.15 to 3.30 when it is open for families to look at books, talk about what is offered in the library and to borrow a book if you want.

> "Reading is Free!" This is a famous saying of Abbas Mahmoud al- Aqqad. Our children often don't read because there are so many other things they would rather do but the key to unlocking reading is finding a book that your child really enjoys. It doesn't have to be a book! It could be a comic or a magazine. It could be an information book or a story. Find out what your child might enjoy by visiting the school library with you child. It is open for families every Tuesday and Friday after school.

Family engagement

The Hub Library saw a wide range of families visit the library a number of times over the pilot six weeks. Children who had been on the new book shopping trip were some of the first visitors with their families to borrow books – with a waiting list growing for some of the really sought-after graphic novels. Children were heard talking to their parents about the sorts of books they were interested in and what they were looking for. Favourite authors were shared and parents and children browsed together to make their book choices, although some children's indecision was clearly difficult for parents with limited time!

Outcomes – Who came and why?

The library opening saw 69 children borrowing a total of 144 books alongside a parent, guardian or family member during the six weeks that the Library was opened after school. Of these children, 43 were with parents that would not usually come to after-school activities with their child when advertised in the usual school newsletter format. 31 of the children were of Somali heritage (from 26 families) and so these families were followed up by the school's community development co-ordinator through a quick telephone call. 14 parents responded to this providing some useful information about how they heard about the library being open after school, why they came and what they thought could be done further by the school to reach families and encourage engagement with the library.

In terms of the "influencer" messages, it is possible therefore that eight of the families were influenced to come along to the hub library. Almost as influential was the "good old" personal touch at the school gate.

Why parents came

Families offered a range of reasons as to why they came to the library after school. The most frequent response was that their children wanted to come (nine parents reported this) whilst four others talked about it as a way for them to get more books for their children to read. Two parents were persuaded to come along, either by other parents or a friend at the school.

There were lots of suggestions about how the school could better promote reading and the library including

- Opening before school one day a week as the after-school opening was often a rush for some parents who had work or other commitments at the end of the school day.
- More text reminders and reminders in Somali as well as English.

- More regular contact and reminders on the school gate.
- Sending reminder letters home with the children each week.

Other recommendations related to the book stock in the library with some parents asking for more bilingual books, books that had a more diverse representation and texts in Somali. One parent suggested that the children could be more involved with the selection of books for the library and another asked for there to be a story time in the library with books being read aloud during some of the school Library opening times.

This project was certainly not conclusive in terms of the value of the "influencer" network but provided the school with some important messages about the variety of methods for communication and the recognition that it is rarely one approach that works but a combination of approaches that work together to "influence" the actions of families.

Reflections

Having read this case study, take some time to reflect on the approaches your school currently takes. It is useful to think about the variety of modes of communication that are used; how do you currently use community role models and elders to support messaging about reading; what you know about the literacy histories and lives of your different communities; what the biggest influences are on your community – be it religious, community or friendship based. Could your school try some sort of "influencer" project of your own? How would you change and adapt the approach to make it suitable for your school? If you would like to find out a little more about this case study, it was published first by Jane Carter, Hibo Mohammad and Fathia Aidid, in the UKLA English 4 to 11 in 2022 and also in the journal, Educational Futures.

Conclusion and call to action!

We know that parental engagement is a key to children's success as readers and equally their development as readers who read for pleasure and purpose. Knowing each child and understanding their "homeplace" lens in which they view the world, is the first step to engaging with their parents.

1. Find out about the communities that your school serves – do this in relation to your knowledge of the culture, heritage, histories and traditions. Use this to support you in making connections with parents.
2. Build trust through your messaging about reading and reading for pleasure, recognising that the idea of reading for pleasure may not be something the family recognises. Build a myriad of message channels as well as messages to support communication with parents.
3. There are no "hard to reach" families, just families that need to be "engaged differently."

References

Abikar, S. (2021) 'Addressing English reading comprehension difficulties by Somali origin pupils in England primary schools: Using parents as resources', *International Journal of Education and Learning*, 3(1), pp. 56-64.

Bhojwani, P. and Kitts, L. (2014) *The multimodal literacy project: Supporting looked after children*. English 4-11. 52, pp. 14-18.

Bonevski, B., Randell, M., Paul, C., Chapman, K., Twyman, L., Bryant, J., Brozek, I. and Hughes, C. (2014) 'Reaching the hard-to-reach: A systematic review of strategies for improving health and medical research with socially disadvantaged groups', *Medical Research Methodology*, 14 (42), pp. 1-29. Available from https://pubmed.ncbi.nlm.nih.gov/24669751/

Bourdieu, P. and Passerson, J.C. (1977) Reproduction in education, society and culture. R. Nice (Trans). London: Sage.

Brice-Heath, S. (1983) *Ways with words*. Cambridge, UK: Cambridge University Press.

Briggs, M., Grella, L., Burton, T.A., Yarmuth, M. and Taylor, T. (2012) 'Understanding and engaging key influencers of youth in high-risk urban communities: A review of the literature', *Social Marketing Quarterly*, 18(3), pp. 203-220.

Carter, J., Mohammad, H. and Aidid, F. (2022) Somali 'influencers' in and beyond a school community using funds of knowledge to influence family and children's reading engagement. Educational Futures, 13(2). Available from https://uwe-repository.worktribe.com/output/10142067

Chalmers, H. and Crisfield, E. (2019) 'Drawing on linguistic and cultural capital to create positive learning cultures for EAL learners', *Impact*, 5, pp. 40-42.

Chetty, D. and Sands-O'Connor, K. (2023) Beyond the secret garden: Gypsy, Roma and traveller representation in children's literature. Books for Keep. Available from https://booksforkeeps.co.uk/article/gypsy-roma-and-traveller-representation-in-childrens-literature/

Cole, A., Brown, A., Clark, C. and Picton, I. (2022) Children and young people's reading engagement in 2022. Available online https://files.eric.ed.gov/fulltext/ED627073.pdf

Cushing, I. (2023) 'Word rich or word poor? Deficit discourses, raciolinguistic ideologies and the resurgence of the 'word gap' in England's education policy', *Critical Inquiry in Language Studies*, 20(4), pp. 305-331.

Demie, F., Lewis, K. and McLean, C. (2007) *Raising the achievement of Somali pupils: Challenges and schools responses*. London: Lambeth Research and Statistics Unit.

Devarakonda, C. (2015) *Diversity & inclusion in early childhood: An introduction*. SAGE Publications Ltd. https://doi.org/10.4135/9781473957725

Dobson, T., Stephenson, L. and De Arede, A. (2021) Writing a novel with Roma primary school children: Tensions in disrupting aetonormativity. *Children's Literature in Education* 52, 511-527. https://doi.org/10.1007/s10583-020-09428-3

Ellis, S. (2017) The Strathclyde literacy clinic: Developing student teacher values, knowledge and identity as inclusive practitioners. In: *A companion to research in teacher education*. Singapore: Springer Publishing Company, pp. 121-134. http://dx.doi.org/10.1007/978-981-10-4075-7

Ellis, S. and Smith, V. (2017) 'Assessment, teacher education and the emergence of professional expertise', *Literacy*, 51(2), pp. 84-93.

Farshore (2022) Reading for Pleasure and Purpose. Available from https://www.farshore.co.uk/wp-content/uploads/sites/46/2022/03/Reading-for-Pleasure-and-Purpose-Report-Farshore.pdf

Fletcher, K.L. and Reese, E. (2005) 'Picture book reading with young children: A conceptual framework', *Developmental Review*, 25(1), pp. 64-103.

Flouri, E. and Buchanan, A. (2004) 'Early father's and mother's involvement and child's later educational outcomes', *British Journal of Educational Psychology*, 74(2), pp. 141-153. https://doi.org/10.1348/000709904773839806

Gay, B., Sonnenschein, S., Sun, S. and Baker, L. (2020) Poverty, parent involvement, and children's reading skills: Testing the compensatory effect of the amount of classroom reading instruction, early education and development.

González, N., Moll, L.C. and Amanti, C. (2005) *Funds of knowledge: Theorizing practices in households, communities, and classrooms*. Mahwah, NJ: Lawrence Erlbaum.

Gypsy, Roma and Travellers History Month (2024) Available from https://www.gypsy-traveller.org/grthm/

Hall, M. (2012) *Personal identity as access to perception of equity. Paper presented at the international congress of qualitative inquiry*. University of Illinois at Urbana-Champaign.

Hannon, P., Nutbrown, C. and Morgan, A. (2020) 'Effects of extending disadvantaged families' teaching of emergent literacy', *Research Papers in Education*, 35(3), pp. 310-336.

Kelman, H.C. (2006) 'Interests, relationships, identities: Three central issues for individuals and groups in negotiating their social environment', *Annual Review Psychology*, 57(1), pp. 1-26.

Lambert, E.Y. and Wiebel, W.W.. (1990) The collection and interpretation of data from hidden populations. Washington, DC: United States National Institute on Drug Abuse; 1990. Online. Available from https://archives.nida.nih.gov/sites/default/files/monograph98.pdf

Matthheisen, N.C.L. (2017) 'Working together in a deficit logic: Home-school partnerships with Somali diaspora parents', *Race, Ethnicity and Education*, 20(4), pp. 495–507.

Mazzoli Smith, L. and Todd, L. (2016) 'Poverty proofing the school day: Evaluation and development report.', Project Report. Research Centre for Learning and Teaching, Newcastle University, Newcastle upon Tyne.

Moll, L.C., Amanti, C., Neff, D. and González, N. (1992) 'Funds of knowledge for teaching: Using a qualitative approach to connect homes and classrooms', *Theory into Practice*, 31(2), pp. 132–141.

National Literacy Trust (2023) Book ownership in 2023. Available from https://literacytrust.org.uk/research-services/research-reports/book-ownership-in-2023/

Neuman, S.B. and Moland, N. (2019) 'Book deserts: The consequences of income segregation on Children's access to print', *Urban Education*, 54(1), pp. 126–147. https://doi.org/10.1177/0042085916654525

Office for Standards in Education, Children's Services and Skills [Ofsted] (2014) Are you ready? Good practice in school readiness. Ofsted: London. Available from https://www.gov.uk/government/publications/are-you-ready-good-practice-in-school-readiness

Organisation for Economic Cooperation and Development (2014) *Education at a glance: Education indicators*. Paris: OECD.

Preece, J. and Levy, R.A. (2020) 'Understanding the barriers and motivations to shared reading with young children: The role of enjoyment and feedback', *Journal of Early Childhood Literacy*, 20(4), pp. 631–654.

Pretorius, E.J. and Lephalala, M. (2011) 'Reading Comprehension in high-poverty schools: How should it be taught and how well does it work?', *Per Linguam: A Journal of Language*, 27(2), pp. 1–24.

Reyes, I., Da Silva Iddings, A.C. and Feller, N. (2016) 'Building relationships with diverse students and families: A funds of knowledge perspective', *Journal of Early Childhood Literacy*, 16(1), pp. 8–33. https://doi.org/10.1177/1468798415584692

Scherer, L. (2016) *Children, literacy and ethnicity: Reading Identities in the primary school*. Basingstoke: Palgrave Macmillan.

Stokes, L., Rolfe, H., Hudson-Sharp, N. and Stevens, S. (2015) *A compendium of evidence on ethnic minority resilience to the effects of deprivation on attainment*. London: Department for Education.

Street, B. (1984) *Literacy in theory and practice*. New York: Cambridge University Press.

Stick, A. (2017) Celebrating Roma, Gypsy and Traveller stories. Available from https://www.booktrust.org.uk/news-and-features/features/2017/april/celebrating-roma-gypsy-and-traveller-stories/ [Accessed on 21 November 2024].

Sweeney, S. and Matthews, Z. (2017) *Friends, family and travellers: A guide for professionals working with Gypsyies, Roma and Travellers in Children's Services*. Available from https://www.gypsy-traveller.org/wp-content/uploads/2017/03/A-guide-for-professionals-working-with-Gypsies-and-Travellers-in-the-public-care-system.pdf [Accessed on 21 November 2024].

Tafesse, W. and Wood, B.P. (2021) Followers' engagement with Instagram influencers: The role of influencers' content and engagement strategy. *Journal of Retailing and Consumer Services*, 58. Online. Available from https://doi.org/10.1016/j.jretconser.2020.102303 [Accessed 20 July 2022].

The Prison Rules 1999 (SI 1999/728). Available from https://www.legislation.gov.uk/uksi/1999/728/part/II/crossheading/education-and-library [Accessed 21 November 2024].

Thompson, I., McNicholl, J. and Menter, I. (2016) 'Student teachers' perceptions of poverty and educational achievement', *Oxford Review of Education*, 42(2), 214–229.

Thomson, P. and Hall, C. (2008) 'Opportunities missed and/or thwarted?: 'Funds of knowledge' meet the English national curriculum', *The Curriculum Journal*, 19(2), pp. 87–103.

8 The importance of teachers' knowledge of children's literature to develop children's reading for pleasure

Ann Cowling, Ros Steward and Laura Manison

Introduction

Gamble (2019) asserts the need for teachers to be knowledgeable about children's literature in order to effectively deploy this expertise through their teaching. Ensuring that this knowledge addresses issues of inclusion and diversity is key to Reading for Pleasure for all. In this chapter, readers will be invited to reflect on how their own reading experiences have shaped their engagement with children's literature and how this can be translated into pedagogical practice. Cremin et al. (2014) developed a range of pedagogical principles through their research project *Teachers as Readers* (TARs) which highlighted the crucial importance of ensuring teachers have a developed and developing knowledge of children's literature to enhance their confidence and pedagogical understanding of reading in the classroom and beyond. This research will be discussed, together with case studies and opportunities to reflect on personal practice. It will also consider how children are influenced by their perceptions of the adults with whom they interact, both in and outside of school, and how this impacts their feelings of inclusion or exclusion as reader. Case studies will suggest practical approaches to engage and embed these principles into teaching, alongside a reflective discussion about the potential barriers to all children feeling included as developing readers.

Research (Applegate and Applegate, 2004) has suggested over a period of time that huge numbers of pre-service teachers are functionally alliterate; that is, they can read but choose not to do so. Pre-service teachers are expected to promote and encourage the development of the ideal and deeply engaged readers that they themselves are not; Nathanson, Pruslow and Levitt (2008) reported similar findings among practising teachers. This puts them squarely into the unfortunate position described as the "Peter Effect." The term "Peter Effect" is drawn from a New Testament story of a beggar who approaches St. Peter and asks him for money. Peter replies that he 'cannot give what he does not have' (Acts 3:5) and this appears to hold true in terms of knowledge of children's literature.

When discussing with first-year undergraduate pre-service teachers their "reading journeys" many profess to have enjoyed reading at home with parents or siblings, with most carrying on their enthusiasm in Key Stage 1 and lower Key Stage 2. It is interesting to see how many read the same books at a similar age to their peers. It was noticeable too how popular reading scheme series e.g. The *Oxford Reading Tree* and *Biff and Chip* books engendered fond memories – perhaps this is reading for pleasure in retrospect, rather than reading for pleasure at the time of reading. Summerfield (2004) considered the role of revisiting personal narratives and how this shaped emotional responses and pleasure. Ross's (1999) study about revisiting text as part of reading for pleasure is useful to consider for children – do we give children planned opportunities to revisit texts from their past, recent or otherwise. These affective responses can perhaps reignite children's engagement with reading.

Pre-service teachers reported that the pleasure in reading dissipated during upper Key Stage 2 when reading became a definite academic or school subject. When they talked about reading the set books for GCSE and beyond, pleasure disappeared rapidly. Many stated that they had not recovered their love of reading and now merely read *because they have to for coursework.*' Pre-service teachers also said they read more on social media and magazines but they did not see this as the "reading" they were being asked about when they were asked to share their reading journeys. They seemed to confine "reading" to novels and dispelling this myth is an essential part of any teacher education programme in relation to developing them as teachers of both readers for pleasure and teachers of reading for pleasure.

When discussing children's literature with a range of teachers and teaching assistants in our research case study schools, it became apparent that many of those interviewed had been encouraged to read at home when children and their formative experiences still resonated:

> One said, "*I can still remember the class book my teacher read to me*" and another "*Reading was promoted to us in through our teachers in primary school, who showed that they enjoyed reading. I want to be like that teacher I had when I was younger and make the children excited and not just 'I'm going to sit and read you a page of this because I have to and it's the end of the day.'*"

> Interestingly, one participant suggested that they learned to love reading despite their school experiences: "*I hated primary school with a passion but my dad always used to read to me at night and as I got older he used to read me the Hobbit and Lord of the Rings. It took a very long time but every night, without fail my dad read to me and that was what we did but primary ....no, I don't have good memories or reading and school.*"

These responses demonstrate that our early experiences do indeed shape the way we interact with reading as adults, and hence its importance for us as teachers. It underlines the need to widen our knowledge of children's literature in order to engage and enthuse each child we teach. Knowledge of children's literature allows the facilitation of discussions that guide children to explore the themes, characters, and moral dilemmas present in books. This collaborative process of meaning-making enables children to actively construct their understanding of the text and its relevance to their own lives. There is an intersection here between guided and modelled instruction and pleasure, with children actively constructing knowledge and understanding rather than passively receiving information. Children's enjoyment and engagement with literature are also influenced by their prior knowledge, experiences and their environment (including the teacher and their peers), all of which can be developed in a variety of ways e.g. through book clubs, reading cafes, or shared read-aloud sessions. By facilitating this active engagement, meaningful interactions and social learning experiences, teachers can create an environment where students construct their own understanding of texts and develop a lifelong love for reading.

Insights from our case study

Data collected in our case study schools referred to some strategies employed by teachers to share their knowledge of children's literature with their classes:

- Train track displays in the book corner that suggest "next books to read" or "if you like this, you will love this."
- These displays were placed on classroom windows facing out onto the areas where parents were likely to see and so create possible conversations between parents.
- Children were encouraged to add to these displays based on their own reading experience.
- One display shared was a spider diagram based on one book: including other books by the same authors; similar settings or plot lines or genre; books with the same "subject" focus by other authors and books the author themselves, has recommended and promoted.

By offering a diverse range of engaging books, teachers can capture children's attention and cater to their individual preferences, which is vital for cultivating a love for reading (Gamble, 2019). A teacher's knowledge of children's literature allows them to handpick books that not only entertain but also inspire young minds (Cremin et al., 2008). Secondly, teachers who possess a deep understanding of children's literature can guide children in making meaningful connections between the stories they read and their own lives. They can facilitate discussions and reflections on characters, themes, and moral dilemmas, encouraging critical thinking and empathy in children. By drawing parallels between literature and real-life situations, teachers help children relate to the stories and develop a personal connection with the material, ultimately enhancing their reading enjoyment.

The United Kingdom Literacy Association (UKLA) carried out a *Teachers as Readers* (TARS) research project (2007-2008), involving responses from over 1000 teachers in the U.K., which revealed that there were some significantly popular authors e.g. Roald Dahl, Jacqueline Wilson and JK Rowling, and, more recently, David Walliams, but little mention was made of more newly published authors. Similarly, a more recent study by Baker (2024), sought to identify how strong teachers' subject knowledge around diverse authors really was by creating an online survey which included a list of 28 authors, 4 of which were made up (for added validity). All the real authors were recently published and were prize winners, including poets and author-illustrators. The aim was to identify how many English-speaking authors from other countries were being overlooked due to a narrow lens. Despite being a small-scale study, the results were interesting although perhaps not surprising: writers are more likely to be well-known if they are from the country where the teacher is working. Put simply, in the US the best-known writers were Kate DiCamillo, Katherine Applegate and Jacqueline Woodson (all American), in Australia (Morris Gleitzman, Shan Tan and Emily Rodda) and the best-known British authors were Neil Gaiman and Emily Gravett. Shaun Tan was also known to teachers across all the groups, as was Neil Gaiman. Other writers were acknowledged by more experienced teachers e.g. Michael Morpurgo, Katherine Rundell and JK Rowling, which suggests that length of service may also play a part in the acquisition of knowledge of children's literature- but also may present an issue in ensuring that this is constantly refreshed with more recent authors. It would be interesting to replicate this study across a range of schools, or even individual schools to identify any emerging patterns.

Some pre-service teachers' knowledge of poetry was even more limited than their awareness of prose. This was reflected in a recent session with first-year trainees in an undergraduate Initial Teacher Education English seminar who, when asked what children's poets they could name, were unable to name even one. Teachers' knowledge of poetry has been found to be linked to the school exam system and the problem may start here, where poetry teaching may come down to spotting metaphors, underlining powerful verbs, identifying rhyming patterns and analysis. As Pie Corbett (NATE, 2022) asks, "I wonder what would happen if children were steeped in poetry so that from the nursery class onwards, it was an everyday occurrence, something that we enjoyed like music or singing?" However, the resources available for primary teachers wanting to incorporate poetry into their lessons are rapidly growing – looking at the numerous ideas for teaching poetry in the 2022 NATE Special Poetry Edition (https://www.nate.org.uk/wp-content/uploads/2023/10/Primary-Matters-special-poetry-edition-Autumn-2022.pdf) or the CLPE, Centre for Literacy in Primary Poetry Award, teaching sequences (https://clpe.org.uk/poetry/clippa-teaching-sequences) will give anyone who may be a little uncertain about including poetry in their Reading for Pleasure approaches just the helping hand they need. Michael Rosen reminds us that, "poetry is the sound of words in your ears, it's the look of poets in motion and that can be you. Make your poems sing, whisper, shout and float."

Some of our research participants did show some awareness of how book choice impacted children's understanding of diversity and representation. One teacher shared that when they studied slavery, she selected a book carefully, avoiding the many books that stereotyped and promoted common myths. *'My class found the message really powerful, that it wasn't something about pity, it was about people fighting for their rights. I had to make sure there was accurate representation, and I was not just picking up (thinking) that looks like it's a story about slavery, but really considering the message of the book and what it is telling children about people in the past or the world or what happened. Children who didn't read were picking up books that had similar themes, including books like "Windrush Child." Children were empowered.'*

It is these exchanges brought about by our choices in the classroom that can widen a child's repertoire and open more doors into the wealth of children's literature available today.

McGeown, Norgate and Warhurst (2012) investigated the relationship between teachers' knowledge of children's literature and students' reading achievement and enjoyment. They found that teachers who had a wide and varied knowledge of children's literature were more successful in promoting reading engagement and fostering positive attitudes towards reading among their students, echoed by Palinscar and Duke (2004). Lockwood (2008) reiterates this, also noting that a key factor in promoting Reading for Pleasure in the classroom is being an active role model as a keen reader. If teachers state, "I'm not a keen reader but…." this clearly suggests the opposite to children! Another negative message teachers may inadvertently give about reading is where reading is perceived as a punishment and part of the "hidden curriculum" of a school. Examples would be where pupils have to stay in and read instead of going out to play, and another is where reading is used as a holding activity at transition times, or where children are "forced" to read, particularly when the environment may not be conducive to pleasurable reading in the first place, all of which can have negative impacts on attitudes to reading.

Teachers who are well-versed in children's literature can serve as reading role models, inspiring their students by sharing their own enthusiasm for books. By discussing their favourite authors, genres, and series, teachers demonstrate their personal connection to reading, which can motivate children to explore literature independently. When students witness their teachers' passion for reading, it both counters the Peter Effect and reinforces the idea that reading is enjoyable, fostering a positive attitude towards books. Clark and Rumbold (2006) also examined the impact of teachers' knowledge of children's literature on reading achievement. The findings indicated that teachers who had extensive knowledge of children's literature were more effective in promoting reading comprehension skills, vocabulary development, and overall reading achievement among their students.

Teachers equipped with comprehensive knowledge of children's literature can create a supportive reading environment:

- By establishing classroom libraries with a wide array of books representing diverse cultures, genres and perspectives;
- By displaying teachers' favourite books;
- By creating displays about reading around the school and the grounds – outside spaces are often underused, so use notice boards to share with the wider school community;
- By making a particular teacher's favourite books available to read in the playground at breaktimes – each week with a different teacher's favourite books;
- By using the school's website to promote each teacher's top picks;
- By having a reading afternoon where children tour around the school, visiting different teachers who are reading from their favourite book.

Think about how children in your class know you are a reader – what are the visible and verbal signals you give? How do children know each teacher in the school is a unique reader with their own preferences and approaches to reading? What strategies does your school currently use to share this? How do parents know this and how is it communicated at each "open event," "school tour for new or prospective parents" or school event such as sports day or class assemblies? Is the diversity of reading preferences profiled – from social media to magazines to novels to graphic novels – to ensure no parent is made to feel their experiences are somehow "not enough"?

The children's voice from our research study made this quite clear with some children providing many examples of how their teacher had shared book preferences, ideas for books a child might enjoy, or just how well they read a class novel. However, many children said their teacher never shared anything about themselves as a reader – never disclosing if they read at home or sharing recommendations and suggestions for reading. The contrast between teachers was noted, with one child saying that it was *obvious* a particular teacher was a reader because displayed on their classroom door was a sign that said, *'this teacher is reading...along with a picture of the cover of the book.'*

As Gill, Stephenson and Waugh (2021) state that teachers' knowledge of texts and the interests and preferences of their children enables teachers to make appropriate book matches or recommendations to children. Whilst children's choice is essential the teachers in our study had an awareness of the need to introduce books to children that they otherwise might not have found independently. For example, some children will confine themselves to a specific genre (which is not a problem in itself) but can be awakened to other genres that they perhaps did not initially think they would like. Linking to the subject or content can be a useful approach to this.

Primary teachers can update their knowledge of children's literature through various methods and resources. Below are some strategies that have been employed by the case study schools in this research that they felt to be successful.

Professional development workshops

Teachers attended workshops and training sessions e.g. Centre for Literacy in Primary Education (CLPE) which were specifically designed for enhancing knowledge of children's literature. These workshops often covered topics like new releases, diverse literature, and strategies for promoting reading in the classroom. The CLPE also have resources available to non-subscribers. (https://clpe.org.uk/).

Teachers attended twilight workshops provided in conjunction with the Open University's Reading for Pleasure group through a local university or Teacher Training Provider or Department for Education English Hub. These groups enabled teachers to foster children's Reading For Pleasure through the sharing of research-informed practice as well as supporting teachers by building communities of practice both on and off line. Teachers were able to share their experiences through the website as well as in person.

Nikki Gamble's "Just Imagine" company (https://justimagine.co.uk/) regularly holds podcasts with well-known authors in the evening, and the website provides teachers with a mine of information providing content, resources and courses that promote excellent practice in the teaching of reading, writing, and oracy. Some of these were accessed by teachers free of charge, with others that needed to be budgeted for as part of the school's staff development programme.

However, many resources are free such as the recommended book lists and book reviews. The United Kingdom Literacy Association (UKLA) (https://ukla.org/) involved some of the study schools in their annual book awards, including the "Our Class Loves This Book" award. For the Book Awards, schools are invited to share some of the long-listed books with their children and vote for the most popular – these are then short-listed and ultimately the winner is chosen.

Becoming involved with schemes such as UKLA's book awards or CLPE's CLiPPA (poetry) awards not only enhanced the teachers' knowledge but included their children in reading, discussing and voting for their favourite book from the long and shortlists. There is a useful list of some of the best children's book awards that can be found here https://schoolreadinglist.co.uk/resources/childrens-literature-awards/ Looking also at book awards from other countries and in particular books that have been translated, can widen children's perspectives. Of course, UK book awards also include books in translation with some superb examples from the Carnegie medal – with a book in translation winning in 2023 (Manon Steffan Ros's young adult novel *The Blue Book of Nebo* being translated from Welsh) and the UKLA Book Awards regularly make awards to books authored in the US and other countries. Some schools in our case studies picked one award a year to shadow as a staff team – purchasing the books as a school and reading the books collaboratively. Each teacher took their favourite book back to their class and children were entertained by the "battle of the books" in an assembly, with different teachers "pitching" their favourite book as the winner of the award.

Other things the participants mentioned were:

- Slots in staff meetings for staff to share their "good reads";
- Pairing of new colleagues with more experienced members of staff with the specific purpose of book sharing;
- Teachers using social media as a source of book recommendations – especially the following of teacher groups and authors;
- Regular book shops, inviting staff, children and parents to swap and share books.

Interestingly one teacher highlighted the role of the children in developing her knowledge, *'Kids have moved on since we were children – I listen to the children. I find out what kids are 'into' and what is popular or trending. I then use social media to find books that will engage them.'*

This teacher also encouraged the children in her class to take turns to update the book display, with their own suggestions for reading materials – making it clear to children that they did not have to recommend just books but the whole plethora of reading materials that had interested them.

Online resources

Teachers mentioned numerous websites, blogs, and online communities dedicated to children's literature. Teachers followed these resources to access book reviews, recommendations, and discussions about current trends in children's literature. As well as those mentioned above The British Library https://www.bl.uk/learning/ was used by some of the teachers in the study. They cited the range of free exciting resources available for teachers to use, providing themes and resources for planning. Each year teachers joined in the different competitions and campaigns which celebrated inclusivity and representation in children's books, with podcasts from authors and free livestreamed events. Teachers attended the online events and talked about how these sparked the creative juices!

Libraries and bookshops

Regular visits to public libraries helped the teachers in our study discover new titles and stay updated on the latest releases. Teachers valued the expertise of librarians and bookstore staff. Often a relationship with a shop or local library was initiated by one member of staff who developed a long-lasting school partnership. The data we collected suggested that both teachers and children are aware of public libraries near them, yet they did not appear to be utilised to their fullest extent by all of the participants. One teacher said, *'We have always done the Summer Reading Challenge but that is our only contact with the library.'* And another, *'We used to take children to the library each term but we haven't done so for a while now.'*

As stated by Alison Tarrant and Mary Rose Grieve, joint chairs of The Great School Libraries Campaign, there is evidence that a school library supports children's academic attainment and well-being. And yet, it is not statutory in England for a school to have a library. Interestingly, British prisons are required to have a library, but schools are not. Data about public library use would suggest that many children do not access one, making the school library even more important. Roy James, writing for Just Imagine, stated, "If there isn't a dedicated room or area, you can display books just about anywhere. Wall shelves in corridors, outside classrooms, inside classrooms and in school halls (The one room where the whole school gathers for assemblies and lunch but has zero books). But you do need someone to maintain these, keep them fresh, visible and exciting. A 'librarian' doesn't need to be qualified but the role does require a figure with a great deal of enthusiasm and who also doesn't have to be confined to a room of books – becoming a visible presence around the school will raise their profile and, therefore the books."

One school librarian in our study commented that without a librarian, a library is just a room with books!

Becoming a book reviewer

One way the teachers in the study extended their knowledge of children's literature was through becoming a book reviewer for one of the teacher websites they used regularly. Teachers were sent books to review at regular intervals across the year, and their reviews were published online. The teachers were able then to keep the books, which was a nice bonus. One teacher reviewed the Just Imagine website, https://justimagine.co.uk/childrens-books-reviews/having selected the age group and genre of books she was interested in reviewing. Another review for Books for Topics https://www.booksfortopics.com/.

Book clubs

Through collaborative learning, teachers can participate in professional learning communities or join book clubs with other educators to discuss and share their knowledge of children's literature. Collaborating with colleagues can help expand your understanding and expose you to different perspectives. This is something that the research team have found extremely effective with pre-service teachers within our PGCE/Undergraduate English ITE programmes.

Children's literature book clubs for pre-service teachers

We had been running Children's Literature Book Clubs for pre-service teachers at the University of the West of England, Bristol for several years before the first Covid-19 lockdown began in March 2020. They met in small groups of between 1-15, every couple of weeks, and shared their ideas about a variety of picture books, chapter books, poetry and non-fiction for primary-age children which were provided for them by the university to borrow. The sessions were friendly and informal, allowing pre-service teachers to share their opinions and ideas about using such texts in the classroom, but were mainly focused on building their knowledge of children's authors and new titles and encouraging their confidence to speak out in a group setting.

Once the university closed to face-to-face teaching, it began to seem as though the Book Club sessions would have to end until "things got back to normal." Running a Book Club without direct access to lots of books which could be borrowed for a period seemed impossible. However, as time went on, and every teacher became increasingly familiar with a variety of software for online teaching, Book Clubs too came back to life thanks to the use of Teams, Padlet and YouTube. This enforced change in the way Book Clubs were organised prompted a rethink in the choice of texts and how students were asked to become involved and provoked some strong reactions, both negative and positive.

In this section, I will be examining the reasons behind the inclusion of Book Clubs, the choice of children's literature suggested for pre-service teachers to read, and their responses and preferences. Although this is based on activities with pre-service teachers, the concept of a Book Club is one that has been developed amongst school staff in informal meetings or as a brief part of routine staff meetings. See Chapter 6 for a discussion of Children's Book Clubs in primary schools.

Why include children's literature book clubs on an ITE course?

As Cremin et al. (2008, p. 459) remarked, "To become effective reading professionals, student teachers arguably need to understand the significance of developing their knowledge about and pleasure in literature and need to become well acquainted with the widest possible range of children's authors." An over-reliance on the works of Roald Dahl and other well-known authors in the classroom and the persuasive marketing of children's books by celebrity authors seems to have caused a kind of stagnation in the choice of children's literature by many teachers. University-based initial teacher education (ITE) has the potential to offer a vital space in which to interrupt cycles of limited teacher knowledge by broadening their students' awareness of more contemporary authors and more culturally diverse texts for children (Farrah, 2021).

Burgess et al. (2011) concluded that teachers who knew more about children's books were more likely to implement effective literacy strategies than those who were solely reliant on their childhood reading memories. In particular, children with little or developing reading skills need a teacher who is a mentor and role model for fostering a positive attitude and love for reading, who can recommend appropriate titles and authors and communicate their own passion for reading. As ITE UG and especially PG courses have a considerable amount of pedagogical content to cover, finding a space for pre-service teachers to explore contemporary children's literature in any depth is difficult but the addition of several short series of brief Book Club meetings has been found to be helpful and popular with many students, linking effectively with the main English curriculum and also with other subject specialisms. A recent UWE graduate commented *'I have really enjoyed and benefitted from these sessions as I was able to explore different and broader areas for children to read. It was a great way to learn about introducing new books into the classroom.'*

For those pre-service teachers who had not studied English Literature since GCSE and may not read very much in their own time, it is vital to give them the opportunity to express their own views, listen to those of their peers, and think about how a children's book may be used in the classroom. We have always considered it important for such readers to feel confident enough to respond truthfully; to acknowledge that they disliked a text, felt the theme to be inappropriate for primary-age children or found the layout of a picture book distracting. Defending their views and being surprised by those of their peers can introduce them to the type of classroom discussions they may be leading in the future; reading for pleasure doesn't necessarily mean that a reader will enjoy or value every text equally. After all, *The Rights of the Reader* (2006) by Daniel Pennac opens with "The Right Not to Read." Giving agency to readers to choose what they want to read is one of the keys to reading for pleasure; pre-service teachers were offered several texts and could decide for themselves which to read or listen to.

The chance to meet face to face or online, with the simple intention of discussing a book, author, poet or picture book and hearing what others think about it too, can have a beneficial social effect for pre-service teachers at the outset of a course. As Longden et al.

found 'Participation in shared reading groups is linked to enhanced relaxation, calmness, concentration, quality of life, confidence and self-esteem, as well as feelings of shared community and common purpose' (2015, p. 113). The social aspects of reading often seem to be overlooked in higher education but it has been clear that both face-to-face and online Book Clubs have helped build bonds and friendship groups. Reading can certainly be a communal endeavour. It is through creating a sense of community that pre-service teachers can nurture the culture of reading among themselves and consequently see how to apply their passion in their future classrooms. Pre-service teachers may want to ask themselves how much knowledge of children's literature they have gained from their course.

Which books to use?

The choice of texts to use in a limited number of meetings was very important in the pre-service teacher Book Clubs and there were several factors considered when the move came to using digital resources for online Clubs. Firstly, the availability of the desired text as an e-book, secondly whether extracts were available to download from chapter books and thirdly whether authors, teachers or others have provided videos of the story being read aloud. It can also be useful to provide links to other relevant resources for teaching alongside the book, such as lesson plans, links to authors' websites and reviews. These practical issues are useful to consider but the choice of the individual book will also be shaped by whether it has been included in Book Award listings and is therefore quite contemporary and judged to be of high quality, and how well it fits with others to be discussed in the same session. For example, one PG session discussed the following picture books:

Titles	If All the World Were …	Sulwe	It's a No Money Day
Authors	Joseph Coelho	Lupita Nyong'o and Vashti Harrison	Kate Milner
Student views	A very profound and emotional book. I liked that it used such vibrant and beautiful illustrations to accompany some difficult themes. I agree that this might be beneficial to help children who are grieving and encourage them to focus on positive memories.	A beautifully illustrated book about self-acceptance and identity. Important to have in schools for both those with a large representation of BME pupils and for those schools that do not. I also like that it challenges the misconception that Black people may only compare themselves to White people, as opposed to other Black people with lighter skin.	I love how this was read – all the questions, and queries. It's a very detailed book, and I think captures the emotions of the little girl and the mum really well too. It's quite sad and might hit quite close to home for a lot of children.

Choosing representative texts

Being familiar with a wide range of the best contemporary children's books that pre-service teachers may not be familiar with is a good place to start, as is the inclusion of different genres but the publication of the *Reflecting Realities* reports from 2018 onwards (CLPE) provoked an even more thoughtful examination of which books would offer the most valuable experiences for their pre-service teacher readers. We began to think even more carefully about the choice of authors, the characters and themes in their books, and the settings involved, being careful to choose literature which might reflect every child's experiences to include: different genders, racial and religious backgrounds, the LGBTQ community, and those with a range of disabilities and mental health issues, refugee and immigrant families, those caught in the net of poverty and homelessness and books set in other countries, as well as England, and in other historical time periods.

Pre-service teachers engaged with many of these choices, perhaps more easily than with an explicit class debate on such difficult areas as racism or homophobia; as Thomas (2017) speculates '... a book club is a non-threatening way to discuss topics that would probably never be talked about in the school context. Florio-Ruane labels these as 'hot lava' topics, such as race or politics that stir up passion from participants and may cause them to be uncomfortable' (Florio-Ruane, 2001, p. 116).

Akins et al. (2018, p. 66) stress that '... teachers must seek books that represent the backgrounds of the children they teach. Culturally relevant books allow both the child and the teacher to see the world through different lenses. It is crucial for teachers to recognise that relevant texts used in classrooms change with each generation and with each demographic area;' a clear reason to avoid focussing on only those books we remember from our own childhoods. Of course, it is just as important to open the eyes of children to the diversity of the country as a whole – especially if the school is a mono-cultural and mono-lingual environment. Book Clubs enable the challenging of stereotypes and tropes within a safe and supportive space.

With all these reasons to choose a text for discussion to be considered, it could become easy to forget the concept of Reading for Pleasure. We tried to include a variety of funny, serious and silly, and informative books with different messages and themes. Ultimately, the books suggested need to be "good" above all else; their words and illustrations should express the authors' thoughts with a light touch and appeal to the reader through their creative beauty. The best children's books to share contain a simple and original idea which stays with the reader long afterwards and creates a complete and unique world.

Pre-service teachers' views

Pre-service teachers were asked about their views of the online Book Clubs. Here is a sample of some responses:

- 'Yes! Especially the disability-themed week, opened my eyes to a whole new genre'!
- 'It was nice to hear everybody else's viewpoints too. I also loved having the challenge of reading children's literature in between sessions.
- *Online meetings allowed for alternative reading options for those who find reading difficult (dyslexia).'*

- *'The sessions are fantastic and help people expand their knowledge on the range of books available to children. These sessions are so beneficial to our professional practice.'*
- *'I liked that with the books we didn't read, and other people did, we still had an understanding of them.'*

Scheffel, Cameron and Dolmage (2018) discussed a similar use of pre-service teachers Book Clubs at Nipissing University, Canada and found that the use of certain books like *Journey* by Aaron Becker (2014) led to a consideration of how books that leave you with questions may be the best of all. The theme of curiosity stands out for all keen readers; haven't we all been desperate to find out what happens next?

We hope that our pre-service teachers would agree with those in Canada, *'Although we have graduated, our journey has not concluded'* (Scheffel, Cameron and Dolmage, 2018, p. 14).

It could be a potential innovation to consider setting up a Book Club for *your* children. Cost may be an implication but if it is designed as a carousel, fewer books would be required. For example, in an MA study (2018), Steward investigated how picture books could develop empathy for others with whole classes of 30 children. This was managed by using three sets of three books at a time.

Year 3 Spiritual Development – Who you are matters, those around you matter and it is our business in life to matter to each other.	Year 4 Moral Development – No person is an island; coexistence is built on finding and agreeing on a common ground.	Year 5 Social Development – Finding the "i" in community and working together to determine our core values.	Year 6 Tolerance – the word "tolerance" is used in the official guidance, but tolerance is just the starting line. To truly win the race we must aspire towards mutual respect.
Something Else (Kathryn Cave & Chris Riddell)	*Croc and Bird* (Alexis Deacon)	*I am Henry Finch* (Alexis Deacon & Viviane Schwartz)	*The Promise* (Nicola Davies & Laura Carlin)
Beegu (Alexis Deacon)	*Gregory Cool* (Caroline Binch)	*The Yes* (Sarah Bee & Satoshi Kitamura)	*The Lost Thing* (Shaun Tan)
Oliver (Birgitta Sif)	*Tusk Tusk* (David McKee)	*The Journey* (Francesca Sanna)	*The Island* (Armin Greder)

Children in groups were asked to read these one at a time, (approximately 30 minutes each book) and then completed a very brief book review as a way of making notes on each book. In total this stage took less than 2 hours. The next stage involved the children, in their groups, discussing what they thought of each book, which enabled some interesting dialogue to evolve, with diverse opinions about the characters and content. Finally, the children were asked to "vote with their feet" to ascertain which was their favourite book, which wasn't always what their teachers and the researcher expected! Favourites were: *Beegu, Tusk Tusk, I am Henry Finch and The Island*. This generated much excitement amongst the children as it was an innovative activity and introduced them (and the teachers) to some new literature for their repertoire.

You may want to think about how you could set up your own Book Club for children? Consider:

1. Who is it for – a specific year group, "reluctant readers," KS1 or KS2, or just one class?
2. Where will it take place – somewhere quiet and comfortable?
3. How will you choose the books to read – will children be involved?
4. When will you meet – lunchtime, after school, and how frequently?
5. How can it be financed – do you need multiple copies of books to lend?
6. How will you facilitate the discussion – will children enjoy the Book Club?

For further suggestions – see the link below:

https://fdslive.oup.com/www.oup.com/oxed/primary/pathways/ReadingforPleasure/Bookclub%20pp%20FINAL.pdf?region=uk

Conclusion and call to action!

So, what issues might be encountered in ensuring teachers regularly update their knowledge of children's literature? This is an ongoing process, and teachers should try to continuously explore new books, genres, and authors to enrich their teaching practices. However, it is recognised by the research team that this can be problematic considering all that teachers have to contend with, and all teachers should be supported in having the availability of sufficient time and resource to be able to do this, and leadership, particularly from the English Subject Lead, is crucial in this regard.

- Look around your school and identify the ways in which teachers and adults demonstrate recommendations of interesting books for their children – which ones would work best for your class? What innovative ways could you explore?
- Ask the children what sort of reading materials they would be interested in (and why) – find out how you and your school can develop the range of texts on offer: do you have a range of interests, genres and digital resources? Are they accessible to all the children?
- Set up a book club: maybe one for staff and one for the children. Identify the best place, time and style that would suit your context best.
- Find out what Continuing Professional Development opportunities there might be for you: online or in person.
- Become a children's book reviewer! Not only are you introduced to a wide range of recent children's literature, you also get to keep them!

References

Akins, M., Tichenor, M., Heins, E. and Piechura, K. (2018) 'Teachers knowledge of children's literature: What genres do teachers read?, *Reading Improvement*, [online] 55(2), pp. 63-68. [Accessed 24 March 2024].

Applegate, A. J., & Applegate, M. D. (2004). The Peter Effect: Reading habits and attitudes of preservice teachers. *The Reading Teacher*, 57(6), 554-563

Baker, C. (2024) Broadening the Bookshelf. *UKLA English 4-11* [online]. Spring 2024 no.80. [Accessed 24 June 2024].

Becker, A. (2014) *Journey*. London: Walker Books.

Burgess, S.R., Sargent, S., Smith, M., Hill, N. and Morrison, S. (2011) "Teachers' leisure Reading habits and knowledge of Children's books: Do they relate to the teaching practices of elementary school teachers?', *Reading Improvement*, [online]. 48, pp. 88-102. [Accessed 31 May 2024].

Clark, C. and Rumbold, K. (2006) [online]. *Reading for pleasure: a research overview*. National Literacy Trust. Available at https://files.eric.ed.gov/fulltext/ED496343.pdf [Accessed 27 March 2024].

CLPE (2024) *Reflecting realities research*. Available from: *https://clpe.org.uk/research/reflecting-realities* [Accessed 31 May 2024].

Coelho, J. (2019) *If all the world were*. London: Frances Lincoln Children's Books.

Cremin, T., Hendry, H., Leon, L.R. and Kucirkova, N. (eds.) (2023) *Reading teachers: nurturing reading for pleasure*. Abingdon: Routledge.

Cremin, T., Mottram, M., Bearne, E. and Goodwin, P. (2008) 'Exploring teachers' knowledge of children's literature', *Cambridge Journal of Education*, [online]. 38(4), pp. 449-464. [Accessed 18 March 2024].

Cremin, T. Mottram, M., Powell, S., Collins, R. and Safford, K. (2014) *Building communities of engaged readers: Reading for pleasure*. London and NY: Routledge.

Farrah, J. (2021) "I don't really have a reason to read children's literature": Enquiring into primary student Teachers' knowledge of Children's literature', *Journal of Literary Education*, [online]. 4, pp. 6-25. [Accessed 31 May 2024].

Florio-Ruane, S. and DeTar, J. (2001) *Teacher education and the cultural imagination: Autobiography, conversation, and narrative*. Mahwah, NJ: Lawrence Erlbaum Associates.

Gamble, N. (2019) *Exploring children's literature: Reading for knowledge, understanding and pleasure*. 4th ed. London: Sage Publications Ltd.

Gill, A., Stephenson, M. and Waugh, D. (2021) *Developing a love of reading and books*. Exeter: Learning Matters.

Lockwood, M. (2008) *Promoting Reading for pleasure in the primary school*. London: Sage Publications Ltd.

Longden, E., Davis, P., Billington, J., Lampropoulou, S., Farrington, G., Magee, F., Walsh, E. and Corcoran, R. (2015) 'Shared Reading: Assessing the intrinsic value of a literature-based intervention', *Medical Humanities*, [online]. 41(2), pp. 113-20. [Accessed 31 May 2024].

McGeown, S.P., Norgate, R. and Warhurst, A. (2012) 'Exploring intrinsic and extrinsic reading motivation among very good and very poor readers', *Educational Research*, 54(3), pp. 309-322. [Accessed 31 May 2024].

Milner, K. (2019) *It's a no money day*. Edinburgh: Barrington Stoke. National Council for Teacher Education.

Nathanson, S., Pruslow, J. and Levitt, R. (2008) 'The Reading habits and literacy attitudes of inservice and prospective teachers: Results of a questionnaire survey', *Journal of Teacher Education*, [online]. 59(4), pp. 313-321. [Accessed 24 Jun 2024].

National Association of the Teachers of English (2022) Many miles to Babylon - a reading poetry journey into the known and unknown. *Primary Matters* [online]. https://www.nate.org.uk/wp-content/uploads/2023/10/Primary-Matters-special-poetry-edition-Autumn-2022.pdf [Accessed 24 June 2024].

Nyong'o, L. and Harrison, V. (2021) *Sulwe*. London: Puffin.

Palinscar, A.S. and Duke, N.K. (2004) 'The role of text and text-reader interactions in young children's reading development and achievement', *The Elementary School Journal*, [online]. 105(2), pp. 183-197 [Accessed 19 July 2023].

Pennac, D. (2006) *The rights of the reader*. London: Walker Books.

Ross, C.S. (1999) 'Finding without seeking: What readers say about the role of pleasure reading as a source of information', *Australian Library Journal*, 48(3), pp. 241-252.

Scheffel, T.-L., Cameron, C. and Dolmage, L. (2018) 'A collaborative Children's literature book club for teacher candidates', *Reading Horizons,* [online]*,* 57(1), pp. 1-14. [Accessed 31 May 2024].

Summerfield, P. (2004) 'Culture and composure: Creating narratives of the gendered self in oral history interviews', *Cultural and Social History*, 1(1), pp. 65-93.

Thomas, T. (2017) Engaging teachers in a book club to discuss issues of cultural diversity. Dissertation [online]. Doctorate, University of Pittsburgh. Available from https://core.ac.uk/download/pdf/95407298.pdf [Accessed 7 June 2024].

Topping, K.J. and Lindsay, G.A. (1992) 'The structure and development of the paired reading technique', *Journal of Research in Reading*, 15, pp. 120-136. [Accessed 31 May 2024].

Vygotsky, L. (1978) *Mind in society*. Cambridge, MA: Harvard University Press.

9 The pleasure of reading against
Embedding lifelong critical literacy from picturebooks to social media

Ann Alston and Jane Carter

Introduction

As this is a book about reading, and often reading stories, let me begin by telling one. My journey into critical literacy was instigated by a conversation with my then-seven-year-old. We were enjoying a rare one-to-one moment (he has two sisters) sitting in the window seat of a local coffee shop watching the world go by. Across the road, the workmen were putting the finishing touches to a new fish and chip shop and my son excitedly pointed out that we would *have* to buy our next chippy tea from there. I suggested we could, but that we could also keep going to our usual, at which point, unable to sit still, he pointed his finger exclaiming, "But the sign says it's the *finest* fish and chips. That means they will be better than the others. We *have* to go!" Luckily for this chapter, not to mention my son's critical literacy, when we collected our tea one night the following week from this establishment, the chips, it turned out were fine, though no "finer" than anywhere else. A discussion then arose about *why* they might say it's the "finest," about *who* decided it was the "finest," and of course about *whose* words and stories you might or might not trust.

This example was very much set in the world beyond the classroom, for as Cremin et al. (2014) observe, reading for pleasure can involve multiple types of texts and can take place anywhere. Reading for pleasure, is for many, about reading for purpose – pleasure is found in finding out, interrogating, exploring and can be as much functional as "fun." This chapter aims to demonstrate the benefits of teaching children not simply the *mechanics* of reading, but both the pleasure and the agency that comes from teaching them to read all texts critically; from picturebooks to novels, from social media posts to newspaper headlines, and, as it turns out, to signs above fish and chip shop doors. The purpose of this chapter is to show you a variety of ways in which critical literacy can be embedded across both age ranges and subjects, from literature to science to PHSE and from reception onwards. Essentially children will learn that words are tricky, that they are not always trustworthy and that being able to read, as in decoding the words, is simply not enough. More importantly, children need to learn the "subversive" message that they do not have to, and in fact, should not, take words at face value. Reading after the chip shop encounter, was no longer something passive, where the child read the words and had a surface understanding, reading became something much more political, where the child questioned the words, added his/her own voice to them, and enjoyed a new agency. As Roche (2014, p. 11) argues, "critical thinking is necessary for making sense and meaning of our lives and our world. Without it, we risk being mere receivers and consumers of others' knowledge." Reading critically, this chapter will argue, is also an important factor for many readers in reading for pleasure – to analyse, to question, to add your own voice to the voices in the text, can be both empowering and hugely enjoyable as McGillis (1998, p. 204) asserts, "reading critically is a liberating activity. It is also fun." This chapter offers ways to read with children that will open up conversations and possibilities; it will demonstrate how you can teach children to read and simultaneously to question, so that they can then apply the skill of "reading against" to all the narratives they are set to encounter, from picturebooks to social media posts to political speeches and everything in between. You may be wondering if this is really about reading for pleasure and whilst it may not be a feature of many traditional reading-for-pleasure strategies, it is argued that an inclusive approach does not limit what can be pleasurable. It also recognises that some children may only become readers who read for pleasure and purpose with some guidance from teachers into ways of reading that might most ignite their interest. Nodelman and Reimer (2003, p. 156 and pp. 22-26) discuss at length the phrase "reading against" in their text on the "pleasures" of children's fiction. They argue (p. 156) that the closer texts are aligned to readers' own ideologies and experiences then the harder it is to 'read against [...] But even then the attempt to do so is worthwhile – and pleasurable – for doing so gives readers some control of what happens to them- as they read.' If readers feel in control of what they read and are encouraged to ask questions, to unpick, almost we suggest "unread" through finding the gaps within texts, then this provides a solid foundation to create active citizens interested in social justice. Social justice requires generations of readers to take pleasure in asking questions of the materials they read as Janks (2012, p. 158) concludes the need for critical literacy remains strong: 'In the world in which I live, critical engagement with the ways in which we produce and consume meaning, whose meanings count and whose are dismissed, who speaks and who is silenced, who benefits and who is disadvantaged – continue to suggest the importance of an education in critical literacy [...]'

Why critical literacy and social justice are such good bedfellows

Mary Roche (2014, p. 29) in her excellent work on critical literacy and picturebooks argues that we teach comprehension so children:

> ... can question the assumptions made in a text; so they can challenge the ideology inherent in the text, so they can live an examined life; so that they can have agency; so they can ask what Brookfield (2012, p. 9) calls "the big questions."

These "big questions" can also be both pleasurable and empowering, and it is for the most part adults who have, over my years as a literature specialist, complained to me about "ruining a story" by going through it line by line. In my experience though, done well, with booktalk in the classroom, children have welcomed the opportunity to engage in critical literacy. This makes sense to me as looking at literature critically liberates children, for here there are no wrong answers, and the best readings will simply breed more questions, more, as Cremin (2018) would say, "book blether." If we stop and explain that words are not always truths set in stone, that the words of adult authors and narrators, once read, are ours to be called out and questioned, then we are making room at the critical table for the voice of the child, and it is crucial that we as adults lower our voices so we can hear those of the next generation loud and clear.

As Carter and Ghelani stated in their introduction to this book, it is essential that our classrooms model social reading environments and critical literacy affords the perfect opportunities to embed such discussions. Many have observed that critical literacy is helpful in addressing social injustice, encouraging children's agency and in ensuring they become active citizens within democracies, ready to call out dominant voices (Friere, 1972; Roche, 2014). Jon Callow (2022, p. 231) insists that critical literacy has an important role to play in the classroom to encourage advocacy to aid children's understanding of global literacy, "where the political nature of any text from a nursery rhyme to a country's political constitution can be explored and challenged." To be globally literate, Dwyer (2016, p. 131) argues students must be "open-minded, empathetic" and be able to "analyse the complexity of global issues" they must be "critical consumers of media" and to "honour human diversity, languages and cultures." The research into how critical literacy can begin to help address social justice is clear with Meek (1991, p. 10) going so far as to declare that until "all children in school have access to, and are empowered by, critical literacy...then we are failing to educate the next generation properly." However, what this chapter argues is that not only is the pursuit of critical literacy important in the light of all the above research but that it can also form an intrinsic part of reading for pleasure within the classroom. This chapter demonstrates that it is in the classroom that we have the best opportunities to not only foster a lifelong love of reading, but a lifelong love of reading against. And that fiction, rich in secrets and lies, as all the best stories are, affords us the perfect medium to perfect critical skills that will enrich not just individuals but democracy more widely, as we educate the next generations to ask questions of the narratives they hear and read. Facilitating this agency is key if we are to help children to navigate a world that will be filtered to them through their own personal algorithms including all the stories that they are fated to be at the mercy of, and some excellent research currently exists on social media and critical literacy in the classroom (Govender and Farrar, 2023).

Time to start with you – The teachers – and your journeys into critical literacy

If we are to teach critical literacy effectively, then we have to, as with all things, begin with our own reading experiences and approaches. Hollindale (2011, p. 52) argues that "every reading is a negotiation and a reciprocal exchange, since all readers, including children, bring to the text their own armoury of conscious and hidden ideological predispositions." When talking to teachers and students about teaching critical literacy effectively, I often begin to unpack Hollindale's observation with the help of the author Paula Fox's observation in Hearne and Kaye (1981, p. 24):

> When you read to a child, when you put a book in a child's hands, you are bringing that child news of the infinitely varied nature of life. You are an awakener.

If I'm reading *with* Fox's observation, as a teacher, a mother and a book lover, I perhaps sigh nostalgically and reflect on the pleasures of sharing a book with a small child, I might think of a specific sofa, a specific child, or even a moment of book sharing from my own childhood. I, and I suspect many like-minded teachers or pre-service teachers, as Hollindale suggests, bring my own "armoury" of experiences and ideologies to it. In another fantastical moment, I can almost picture myself in a superhero cape awakening the once unconscious class of children into a world of literature and wonder, as if in a teacher training advert. If I am reading *with* the text, then this is straightforward, I can read, sigh, and move on to my next task. What is more demanding, though ultimately more productive, and therefore more pleasurable, is to read *against*. So, when we begin to discuss this quotation, when we engage in what is essentially "book talk" in a social environment, we begin to read differently. Look back at this quotation and ask yourself, who is active and who is passive here? When I present this question to teachers and pre-service teachers they usually observe that the child is passive, that it is the adult who is reading *"to"* the child, that it is the adult who is *"putting"* the book in the child's hands, that it is the adult who is *"awakening"* the child. You might then go on to link this with children's literature publishing more generally, as somewhat inevitably, it is the adults who write, edit, publish and often choose the books. In both instances, the child seems voiceless and without agency, but in discussing the texts, and in writing their own responses and stories that build on the existing foundations of children's literature, teachers can enable children to regain centrality.

Take time to pick up an old favourite

The next step is to question what kind of a world is represented by the specific book we might place in the child's hands. It can be valuable, in order to ignite discussion amongst pre-service teachers or teachers, to use traditional picturebooks such as Holabird's (1983) *Angelina Ballerina* or Murphy's (1987) *All in One Piece*, but if you are looking for yourself or delivering staff training then it is a useful exercise to take a look at what is on your library shelves in what we might deem "traditional" or "classic" and pick off a few for closer inspection. Both Holabird's and Murphy's books have been turned into animations for TV and have been, and continue to be, hugely impactful in terms of the numbers of readers they reach, and both texts/series tend to instigate sighs of recognition and nostalgia from educators – initially at least. The first spread in *All in one Piece* however, shows Mrs Large, on what is traditionally seen as the adult side of the text (where the words are), separated from her children and disdainfully observing them eating breakfast, while she drinks what we assume to be strong tea or coffee. The text (Murphy, 1987) reads "The children were having breakfast. This was not a pleasant sight." This is a line written for the adult reader, I doubt there are many children who reflect on their mealtimes and remark that "it wasn't a pleasant sight" or in fact many children who think that their family needs a break from them. Indeed, the premise for this story and many of the others in this series, is that the adults want to escape from their children. The keen-eyed teachers then respond to the question of what kind of world the illustration in the book shows to readers. The family may be eating messily, but children are sitting together at the table to eat, rather than say, in front of the telly, they are eating traditional breakfast fare – Kellogs' branded cornflakes or eggs for example, their artwork has been lovingly displayed on the wall, the Welsh dresser, a signifier of a "good family" in children's literature, is neat and tidy with a dinner service and books on display (Alston, 2008). Through images and texts such as these, readers internalise what makes a "good" family: eating around the table (though the mother interestingly does not eat), a mother who is almost always inside, a father who in a later spread is pictured getting ready for work, putting on his blue shirt and tie (on the adult side of the text). The mother in this series is firmly encased in the domestic, and when she does venture out it is to Mr Large's "office dinner dance." In Holabird's *Angelina Ballerina,* similar signifiers can be noted; the mother is also situated in the domestic, albeit it a cottage of oak beamed ceilings with herbs hanging down, she provides perfect-looking loaves with tea, and wears an apron, while the father – reads his newspaper. Angelina is pictured knocking things down, disrupting the domestic harmony as she dances around the house. Again, readers note that it is the father who has the bright idea to send her to ballet lessons, after which readers are told she then tidies her room, is no longer late for school and remarkably now "lets the boys catch her at kiss chase."

Take time to select a few picturebooks, those published pre-1990 tend to have particularly rich pickings and spend some time in the staff room thinking about how the fathers or mothers are drawn, what they wear, what kind of houses they might live in and then think about how that might relate to your own family experiences and then to children in your class. If you do have pre-1990 books in your school, consider how they could serve to support critical literacy.

Then, you can ask children in your class or a focus group of children, to do something similar, and perhaps compare more recent books and consider what has and hasn't changed and why this might be important.

The depiction of family and gender in many books of this period is a reflection of their time – but hopefully not a reflection of the world our children are growing up in. I am not in any way suggesting we rid library shelves of these books, but rather suggesting that teachers and children are aware of the ideological bias of the books, and are able to locate it and discuss it rather than it becoming something that is internalised as another thing that separates their own lives from school. Children need to be able to feel both pleasure and empowerment in being able to call it out. As Chambers (2011, p. 98) argues:

> [...] talking well about books is [...] the best rehearsal there is for talking well about other things. So in helping children to talk about their reading, we help them to be articulate about the rest of their lives. In a talkative age, what could be more useful?

Lissa Paul (1998) writes about the "intellectual pleasure" her undergraduates find from turning back to a text repeatedly in order to interpret it and how they enjoy discovering textual secrets. My own experience is that children also benefit from this intellectual pleasure, but that teachers first have to experience calling out their old favourites, and this can be an uncomfortable experience. An initial focus on picture books makes for an efficient beginning. Try to find time as a group of teachers to explore a critical approach before exploring the texts with children, using the same techniques which can also be applied to longer texts. Roald Dahl, for example, came out as the most regularly cited "good" author as rated by teachers in a National Literacy Trust's survey (Clark and Teravainen, 2015), and while I suspect this might not be quite the case in 2024, his texts are continually being retold through various adaptations and they tend to fill the shelves of schools, homes and libraries. However, if children have learnt to call out gender bias in picturebooks in their early social reading experiences, then they will carry this knowledge with them throughout their reading experiences, and may well ask of Dahl's texts, why women who are single and childless are depicted as witches, or why characters are continually body shamed? (Alston, 2020). If this critical reading is encouraged and facilitated in the classroom, then they may well also call out other popular authors, such as David Walliams, who has certainly benefitted from clinging on to Roald Dahl's coattails in terms of both the marketing and the dubious ideologies imparted in the texts. As Hollindale (2011, p. 9) argues:

> Helping children to become alert and expert storytellers and listeners is very important, because it is part of helping them to take control [...] the internet has suddenly made these storytelling and story reading skills more important [...] because we have learned [...] how vulnerable young people can be in what they believe [...]

If we equip readers to read critically, from picturebooks in reception, to novels in KS2 and beyond, then we contend that children will grow up equipped to some extent, to analyse and question what they encounter on social media and elsewhere. Paul (1998, p. 16) notes that 'as a teacher and critic I am learning slowly to take notice of texts and ideas I couldn't see or didn't notice before; to question the approaches to analysis I used to accept as 'natural.' Questioning what is considered "natural" is, of course, the bread and butter of critical literacy, to stop and ask why. To take one example, fathers might be pictured behind newspapers while mothers make the tea, or why, to consider the bigger picture, the majority of characters in children's fiction are still white and that gypsy Roma children are rarely seen, and children with disabilities are somewhere in the background. Paul goes on to offer an invaluable list of questions she used to enhance the critical literacy skills of her literature undergraduates. These same questions were used with children, as part of two case studies, and it was found, that they work equally well in the primary classroom.

Consider how you might incorporate a selection of Paul's (1998, p. 16) questions into your book talk:

- Whose story is this?
- Who is the reader?
- Who is named? And who is not?
- Who is on top?
- Who gets punished? And who gets praised?
- Who speaks? And who is silenced?
- Who acts and who is acted upon?
- Who looks? And who is observed?

Picking out and using three or four of these questions, heightens young readers' analysis skills. If focusing on a picturebook, the conversation is enhanced by asking who is physically pictured "on top" – who is leading, or who is taller? In Anthony Browne's picturebook retelling of *Hansel and Gretel* (1981) for example, the stepmother is clearly pictured leading the family into the forest, and her high-heeled long boots ensure she is taller than her small and seemingly impotent husband. Think for a moment what this image alone tells you about who is in charge? The stepmother is on top in two ways – she is leading the family and she is the tallest. You might then take this observation to a new level, by asking why a woman leading and being on top can be read as a "bad" thing, a thing that a wicked stepmother might do and what this might suggest about how women are constructed more generally in culture? If you do this then you are already instigating critical literacy, igniting curiosity and enabling children to call out their stories. In addition, I found that asking who was and wasn't named and who has, and doesn't have a voice, were portal questions that led to a whole world of delicious debate. The opening of Browne's (1981) *Hansel and Gretel* reads as follows:

> At the edge of a large forest lived a poor woodcutter with his two children and their stepmother. The boy's name was Hansel and the girl's name was Gretel.

If you are reading with the story then you will pass over this in a moment, but if you stop to read against, then you will reap the rewards. Consider, and ask your children to consider, the following:

- Why is the woodcutter "poor"? Is this a financial comment, an empathetic one or both?
- Why is the father the first character in the story?
- Why does the stepmother come after the woodcutter and the two children?
- Why are only children named, and why does the boy get named before the girl?

These questions can be applied to any text and instantly ensure that both you and your children will be equipped to be critically aware of how stories, language and images can never be ideologically neutral. It is not "natural" that the father is the first to be named, or that the boy is named before the girl. This kind of reading enables children and adults to, "take notice" of ideas they 'couldn't see [...] before' (Paul, 1998). If you wish to foster a critical awareness of texts, a first simple step would be to print out some of Paul's questions above, place them in your book corners and classroom displays and ask children to refer to them both in their shared and independent reading.

In Continuing Professional Development (CPD) sessions I ask teachers, or pre-service teachers, to conduct a survey of the books on their shelves in terms of representation. Chetty (2017) suggests teachers in their classrooms ask children to pick out 25 children's book characters and then consider "how many of those characters are white (and look for other patterns too such as gender and disability." More often than not, given the nature of the history of children's publishing, the world represented in our children's books is predominantly white, middle class and western. If we equip children to read critically, to ask these questions about who speaks and who is silenced, educators can first apply such questions to individual texts and images but can move from them to ask the bigger questions about how society functions and who is and isn't represented more generally.

These CPD sessions sometimes mark the first steps for many adults who I've taught into critical literacy, and discussions often continue over what they read as children. From Fox's observation about placing a book in a child's hands, to an analysis of the traditional picturebooks, to questioning Dahl and Walliams, to considering what kind of world the books on the shelves represent, it is clear that reading critically takes effort, it forces us to stop and read against the flow; but it is also enriching, pleasurable and essential in a world fraught with injustice where we are bombarded with information from a variety of often questionable sources. Indeed, it is ultimately essential in a world, where PISA (2018) found that only 1 in 10 students in OECD countries could distinguish between fact and opinion and went on to assert that "tomorrow"s schools will need to help students to think for themselves."

Secrets, lies and tall tales

It seems that PISA (2018) speaks to Hollindale's (2011, p. 47) assertion that a teacher's task is "to teach children how to read so that to the limits of each child's capacity that child will not be at the mercy of *what* she reads." Indeed, it is Hollindale's theories that remain at the very heart of this chapter as he continues to argue that 'by teaching children how to develop an alert enjoyment of stories, we are also equipping them to meet linguistic malpractices of more consequential kinds …' (p. 41). That "alert" enjoyment of stories can be facilitated when classrooms become social reading environments, where children come together to ask questions about the stories they have shared, where "linguistic malpractices" may well be renamed "tall tales." In almost all children's literature somebody lies. The protagonists, and the readers who embark on the journey with them, have to learn to "distinguish fact from fiction" and as such, literature, is the perfect place to begin to answer PISA's (2018) call to ensure students "think for themselves." The first lie that Harry Potter is told by the Dursleys, (in a whole host of deceitful twists and turns in Rowling's (1997-2007) Harry Potter series) is that his parents died in a car accident, Lyra in Pullman's *Northern Lights* (1995) believes Lord Asriel to be her uncle, Mary in Hodgson Burnett's ([1911] 1994) *The Secret Garden* is told the faraway crying she can hear is simply the wind. All of these examples are from texts that readers might typically experience in KS2, and are indeed, useful for discussions of critical literacy. What this chapter demonstrates, however, is that critical literacy skills can be taught from reception onwards, that a critical literacy framework can be applied to any fictional texts, and perhaps most significantly of all, that reading critically can form a key part of reading for pleasure, which, in turn, serves to promote social justice.

Where to begin – An example

Reception teachers can ignite a spark for critical reading with a seemingly simple text like Hutchins'(1968) classic *Rosie's Walk*. Just as Harry, Lyra and Mary in the above examples are lied to, the narrator in this text omits important information. Readers follow Rosie the hen as she "went for a walk/across the yard" (Hutchins, 1968) and if we only take note of the words the narrator tells us, then the story is entirely uneventful, as Rosie continues "around the pond/over the haycock/past the mill/through the fence/under the beehives/and got back in time for dinner." (Hutchins, 1968) However, as in many good picturebooks, words and images offer contradictions, and children reading the images will note that Rosie the hen is pursued throughout her walk by a fox. This fox meets various accidents which prevent him pouncing on Rosie, and Rosie returns home oblivious both to his presence, and to her own close brush with death. *Rosie's Walk* is a perfect early example of a text which alerts readers to the fact that narrators can be untrustworthy. It works precisely because the child reader, who is focused on the images, detects something that the main protagonist is unaware of, and that the adult storyteller does not tell him/her. The pleasure of the text rests in not being fully informed by the narrator, and this text can be used as a sound foundation for introducing the skills to enable readers to read *against*. Try this out with children in your class by asking them what the narrator omits to tell them and why? If you do this, then you will have taken the first steps in instilling the notion that the storyteller is not always all-seeing, all-knowing, or all-telling. This invaluable skill can be carried by readers on to numerous other texts, from children's fiction to adult fiction, from social media accounts to newspaper reports, from questioning their friends' stories in the playground to critiquing political manifestos in later life.

Two case study examples

We asked teachers in two very different primary schools, one in Wales and one in England, to complete a sequence of teaching on critical literacy with years 5/6 and then provide some feedback with examples of work and/or pupil comments. Primary school one was an inner city, two form entry school where 95% of the pupils were identified as from minoritised groups and 45 different languages were spoken. Primary school two was a village school with approximately 300 pupils with the large majority being of White British heritage.

The lessons sought to develop reading comprehension including inference and evaluation and to extend readers to become adept at critiquing image and text. The aim of our case study was to consider not only how effectively our resources could instil critical literacy skills but also how critical literacy could become a vehicle for some children to develop pleasure in reading.

The activities were not reading for pleasure activities but perhaps fit into the "purposefully positive" characterisation of the teaching of reading found in Chapter 2. The lessons had learning objectives, and these included:

- To recognise that not everything that is read is true.
- Facts are few and far between.
- Storytellers don't always have all the information.
- Authors tell stories from a particular perspective.
- Characters have a perspective.
- To encourage children to question these perspectives.

The text used for the session was Zee and Innocenti's (2004) *Erika's Story* (2003) a picturebook that addresses a sensitive and significant historical event, the holocaust. This is a picture book aimed at late KS2 based on the true story of a woman who, as a baby, was thrown out of a train destined for the Nazi concentration camps and taken in and brought up by a bystander. If texts like this are to be used, teachers need to know their class well – the histories and sensitivities of both children and the families of children in the class and based on this, make a decision as to whether the text is appropriate to use.

The first lesson focuses on one picture in the text. It is a watercolour image that shows two hands in the gap at the top of a windowless concentration camp train, a baby mid-air in a pink blanket, and two cyclists whose faces are barely visible. The colours are muted and the landscape is relatively rural. This is an excellent image to initiate a discussion of how to read an image from a variety of perspectives and to consider who has the "truth." Initially, teachers asked pupils to describe what they saw in the image and then to ask themselves further suggested critical questions:

- Who don't you see?
- Why do you only see the hands?
- Whose hands might these be?

- Why can't we see the cyclist's faces?
- What is the weather like and how do we know? Does this matter? (The cyclists are wearing coats)

Teachers then offered a hypothetical newspaper headline "Irresponsible Mother Throws Baby from Train," and children discussed whether they agreed or disagreed. The teacher then gave the context of the story and asked if anyone might change their mind about the headline or be able to offer an alternative one. This "warm-up" exercise was intended to spark classroom discussion and to suggest that perspectives and truths are changeable, that stories and newspaper headlines can be manipulative, and that the pleasure of reading is entwined with the enjoyment of questioning.

The lesson was then introduced with a slide entitled '"Stop telling tales": Spotting the gaps' with images of the book covers for Haworth-Booth's (2018) *The King who Banned the Dark (TKWBTD)* and Scieszka and Smith's (1991) *The True Story of the Three Little Pigs*. These texts show different perspectives and invite readers to question the narrator, or in the case of *The True Story of the Three Little Pigs*, a story (The Three Little Pigs) readers *thought* they knew (for further information on the analysis of this particular text see Gamble, 2019, p. 49). Although again, the teacher needs to reflect on children in their class. Is this a traditional story the class will know? Or/and are there similar or equivalent traditional stories in the cultural heritage of children in the class that they can share? Teachers explained that the lesson would show them how to read more deeply by focusing on how we identify different perspectives in fiction and how we might question all forms of narratives to ascertain if we are being told the whole story. This fed into the next slide of an image from Martineau and Barker's (2020) *Question Everything: An Investigator's Toolkit*. This short non-fiction text is a useful tool for all teachers as the blurb states that it inspires the reader to 'Think for yourself and Question Everything.' Figure 9.1 shows three different stories about the same shark attack and asks provocative questions, as you can see, that can be used to question all kinds of narratives.

Figure 9.1 shows a spread from *Question Everything* with different articles about shark attacks.

The text draws our attention to sharing stories on social media and this gave teachers the opportunity to promote further discussion by asking about stories that children read online, for example when they "liked" posts, whether they thought they might have ever shared a story that wasn't true and what websites they might get their news or sports' stories from? Teachers were also encouraged to ask children about, the stories we tell every day, from accounts of what happened in the playground at breaktime to family stories with an emphasis on critical reflection and on the pleasure of both telling and hearing these stories, as well as the agency involved in the process of questioning them. The lesson, moved fluidly from fictional literature, to non-fiction, to news reports, and to personal anecdote and rumour. As well as focusing on the pleasure of reading stories, regardless of the format in which they are told (oral and written in this case), children can be reminded that who tells their story, and frames other people's, returns us to notions of social justice, which should remind you of Paul's (1998) earlier questions: "whose story is this?" and "who speaks and who is silenced?" Children were asked to consider books or films where a character was maligned, an example might be *The Prisoner of Azkaban*'s Sirius Black who begins the text as a dangerous criminal

Figure 9.1 Image from Question Everything (Martineau and Barker, 2020. pp. 4-5)

and concludes it as a much-loved godparent, or where a character had not been told the truth, for example, Luke Skywalker's discovery that Darth Vader was his father. Teachers and children can enjoy discussing their favourite examples, while simultaneously warming up their analytical skills, focusing on what they already know, and applying that experience to this lesson. Before moving on to a picture book, teachers presented children with two photographs of a harbour (see Figures 9.2 and 9.3) that were identical, except that one had been edited with a filter. In groups, children were asked:

Which image is true? Does it matter?
What does the filter add?
Does the filter take away the truth?
Why might someone add a filter?
Which image would you prefer to send/have published?

Figures 9.2 and 9.3 show 2 versions of a photograph of a harbour.

After further group discussion on perspective, where there were no "wrong" answers, the teacher read Klassen's (2012) *This is Not my Hat* to the class. This text won both the Caldecott Medal and the Kate Greenaway medal and is an example of what, Nikolajeva and Scott (2006) term a "counterpoint" text, where, as in *Rosie's Walk*, the words and the pictures tell contradictory stories. In summary, the small fish offers a first-person narrative, opening with the statement "This hat is not mine/I just stole it." The small fish has stolen the hat from a big fish, and while the text makes statements such as "And he probably won't wake up for a long time" the accompanying illustration shows the big fish with wide-open eyes. The text concludes, unusually enough for a children's book, with a silence from the narrator accompanied

The pleasure of reading against 151

Figure 9.2 Bangor harbour 2020

by an illustration showing the big fish wearing the hat, the implication being that the big fish has indeed found, and potentially eaten (and certainly silenced!) the small fish. *This is Not my Hat* consequently presents the perfect opportunity to introduce readers to critical literacy. Children were given three statements to consider as the teacher read the story, and the teacher paused the reading where they felt it was appropriate in order to allow children time for reflection and discussion.

The fish is telling the truth.
The fish is lying to us.
The fish is lying to us but isn't aware he's lying.

Figure 9.3 Bangor harbour 2020 with filter

Once the teacher had finished the reading, children were given time in groups, to share their views on the three statements. Teachers listened in to each group and identified where children had differing perspectives. When bringing the class together, these differing perspectives were shared, with children justifying their viewpoints and actively persuading other children to their position.

Children were then asked about the crab's role in the text and if they considered his behaviour (he showed the big fish which direction the little fish went in) to be right or wrong. They were asked to think how a newspaper headline might side with the little fish or the big fish, and if either or both stories would be true. Teachers then suggested that one of the main purposes of this text was to show readers that they need to be cautious about which stories they believe. Teachers posed the statement: "Storytellers (narrators of the story rather than the author) know everything about the story" and asked children to discuss this firstly in the light of the text and then regarding other stories they might know. Many of Klassen's picturebooks lend themselves to this exercise in terms of narrators who omit information, and therefore, children can be encouraged to apply the skills developed here to his other texts, (2011) *I Want my Hat Back* for example would progress fluidly from here.

Having consolidated critical literacy skills from the picturebook(s), children were shown how to transfer these skills to non-fictional texts. In this instance, they were given newspaper headlines which covered different perspectives on Kate Middleton and Meghan Markle (though any celebrities could be used here). Children were asked how they felt about each woman, why they thought this, and what words the papers used to frame their perspectives. Children were encouraged to consider how the headlines framed these women by asking who spoke and who was silenced? The children could then begin to discuss how the Press was telling the story of these women without consulting them.

In a follow-up lesson, teachers read Haworth-Booth's (2018) *The King who Banned the Dark* and Greder's (2007) *The Island*. *The King who Banned the Dark i*s a text about news and politics. As a boy, the King was afraid of the dark and vowed to "ban" it when he became King. The King's advisors suggest that the people would revolt if this should occur unless "you make them think it's their idea" and consequently the advisors "started to spread rumours about the dark." The images show the different mediums through which the rumours are spread, including word of mouth, newspapers and even slogans on vans. The people campaign to ban the dark, but of course once the people have got "what they thought they wanted" they begin to tire of the constant light. The King's celebratory fireworks do not show in the light sky, and eventually, once the characters turn away from their newspapers and begin to talk to each other, they plot to turn off the official light, the King's fireworks look beautiful in the night sky and the King realises the error of his ways and lifts the ban on the dark. On the one hand, this is a text about the importance of embracing nature rather than artificial light, on the other it is concerned with the power that stories have to mislead and how the crowd can be (Haworth-Booth, quoted in Salisbury and Styles, 2022 p. 123) 'a force of both stupidity and wisdom, so easily manipulated and yet so powerful.' Children were asked to focus on the words that were being used to describe the dark such as "boring" "scary" "stealing" and "taking" and to consider how the dark, which is a natural phase, was framed as an active monster-like being. Children were also encouraged to analyse the illustrations to consider how the King looked down on his advisors in a light open room and to contrast this with the small snippets of information/rumours that the public received about the dark in small cartoon-like boxes on black page, symbolising perhaps that the public were not getting all the information – quite literally they were being left in the dark. Group discussion centred around asking if the advisors were just doing their jobs/trustworthy/untrustworthy/clever and concluding with "What do you think this story is trying to warn us about with regard to stories and to headlines?"

The Island (Greder, 2007) is a far darker text, suitable only for high KS2 classes. The illustrations are dark, as the text charts the story of when "the people of the island found a man on the beach." Children were initially asked whose story this was – the man's or the islanders'? As the narrative begins with the people of the island it can be deduced that this is not the story of the man so much as it is the islanders' story of him. This led to a discussion about perspective and returned children to the essential notion of who tells whose story. This text again alerts readers to who speaks and who is silenced. Similarly to *The King who Banned the Dark* the characters all create a rumour about this silenced figure and the newspaper headline reads "Foreigner Spreads Fear in Town." The children had been given examples of several picturebooks, and non-fiction texts which complimented each other in terms of encouraging readers to "read against."

In terms of progression, however, we were keen to ensure that children knew that critical thinking skills could be applied to all the texts in their repertoire. All the classes in the schools had previously read Rauf's (2018) *The Boy at the Back of the Class* and therefore teachers returned them to the depiction of Jennie in two pages of this text (pp. 17-18). The narrator explains that Jennie "likes to spy on people and tell stories about them to other people. Sometimes the stories are true, but most of the time they are only half true because she makes things up." Children were asked to underline which words they thought were important here – true/half-true/makes things up and relate them back to the narrators and characters in the other texts they had looked at. They were asked to compare Jennie starting a rumour to the King's advisors in *The King who Banned the Dark*, or if Jennie might be compared to the Klassen's little fish, asking if she has all the information, or if Jennie might be compared to some of the characters in *The Island* who also created a story about an outsider who did not or could not yet speak for himself. Children were asked to consolidate their knowledge by considering the following extract:

> Sometimes I think everyone likes to believe a lie even when they know it's a lie because it's more exciting than the truth. And they especially like to believe it if it's printed in a newspaper [...] we heard Jennie telling everyone that the new boy had [...] done something bad [...]

(Rauf, 2018, p. 18)

Children were encouraged to consider how the author encourages her readers to ask questions about the characters, as well as more broadly about the media and that often fiction forces readers to become detectives because they do not know the whole story yet. As the children were already familiar with this text, they were able to call out Jennie's lies and to consider how the "new boy" was powerless and vulnerable because Jennie was telling his story to him. The teachers concluded with some key findings:

- Stories try to give us different perspectives.
- Sometimes our narrators can't be trusted.
- Sometimes we might not like or trust our authors/narrators.

In terms of voice, agency and social justice children were reminded that literature invited readers to detect lies, and to read critically. Teachers concluded with a slide containing an image of the boy in the back of the class, the man from *The Island* and asked what these texts had in common in terms of their story? Children were encouraged to deduce that all of the characters in these examples had been silenced while someone else told their story to them. There is ample opportunity to develop this finding throughout the curriculum to ensure children are aware of whose voices are championed, and whose stories and histories are told, and by whom, as children were left with the questions:

- Why is it important that you can tell your own story?
- What might happen if someone else tell your story?

Feedback

Teacher feedback was overwhelmingly positive across both schools and all the teachers stated that they would refer back to the lesson, embed critical literacy into their teaching and they were keen to consider how it could be rolled out across the schools. The children had found pleasure in "reading against" with one teacher noting a conversation between two years 5 children:

> *Anna:* I always just trusted the storyteller to tell the truth before. I suppose I just didn't think about it really. I just thought they always told you all the things I needed to know for the story.'
> *Billy:* Yeah me too. I liked finding the lies though.

While teachers noted that some children commented that they had found it hard not to just read *with* the story, the majority had said they enjoyed the reading but found the questioning the most liberating part of the experience. Children observed that they felt during the lesson that they were doing something new, where they felt that their opinions mattered almost more than the characters' or the author's and they embraced this agency. One teacher observed that there was a "real buzz in the classroom" and that children asked to look at other texts written by Klassen as some children had commented that usually they might think that book was for "little children" but it "is fun to look at it like a detective story." Children across the schools embraced the agency that reading critically gave.

The teacher noted that children went on to relate this concept to other stories in their repertoire, citing J.K. Rowling's "Harry Potter" series and the potential contrast between Malfoy and Harry Potter's accounts and then neatly concluded their discussion through comparing this difference in perception to real-life disagreements in the playground, with the teacher noting the following *'like a tackle in the football or something – not everyone sees it in the same way.'* Teachers observed that children were especially animated about their personal experiences of injustice, citing times when someone had *'told on me'* and cases where they thought someone had told lies about them. One teacher commented that the lesson "was great for making them think about telling stories, who 'tells on you' and how much power the person telling the story has." It is not such a jump from this observation then to encourage children to think about what they read or hear on social media and to begin to answer the OECD's calls for children to question.

One teacher noted that the images of the harbour (one with and one without a filter) prompted a rich discussion of how we read images and truths and the differences between lies and exaggerations. All children were animated and involved in this discussion, bringing in their experiences and interests in celebrities using soft focus and the debate moved on to consider how genuine social media posts were with one child stating: *'It creates a better image, but is it the right image? Is that image really you'?* Children in this class went on to consider the Kardashians and image, what gets cropped in or out of images, and most critically who oversees the release of that particular image. The teacher noted that children showed a *'good awareness of bias'* and that the depiction of Meghan Markle and Kate Middleton catalysed these conversations. Teachers remarked that children enjoyed discussing clickbait in relation to exaggeration in terms of headlines and that the opening activity to consider and reconsider a headline for the image where the baby is being thrown from the train set the tone in terms of bias and perception. Children in one school noted that the headline *'framed the way you read the story – it told you what to expect.'* Children in this classroom then made up their own provocative and biased headlines which they accompanied with a less sensational explanation; examples of their work included:

"Epic Scenes on School Field in Football Drama" – Someone kicked the ball over the fence, and everyone got into an argument.

These headlines stemmed from reading a combination of factual text, *Question Everything* and fictional picturebook, *The King who Banned the Dark*. All the teachers agreed that they could have spent a whole lesson on just this one text with one stating he had used this book with younger children but *'hadn't really noticed how useful it could be with older children in terms of teasing out conversations about lies, the media and propaganda.'* This teacher asked children to pick out 20 words in relation to propaganda from a combination of fictional text and newspaper headlines. The children noticed a "step-up" in each image in *The King who Banned the Dark* in terms of the rumour being spread, beginning with passive comments such as the dark is *'scary'* or *'boring'* and then graduating to active claims such as the dark is *'stealing your toys.'* The teacher feedback stated that the *'exercises helped children understand and recognise different layers of truth and lies. Children could pick out the differences between an exaggeration and a lie and enjoyed doing so. Children liked being asked to question something that was written down.'*

Teachers noted that moving across genres embedded both the pleasure of reading critically and its importance for children. All children were engaged in different aspects of the lessons from the images and social media celebrity-focused examples to personal experiences of rumours and injustices, to their own fictional reading journeys, including the texts they had shared as class reads. Teachers remarked that children *'considered more carefully whether they always get a truth when they read something and this enabled them to think about reading more widely […] children were keen to think up examples of unreliable characters and narrators and could bring together many texts using this thread in a way they hadn't previously considered. For example, they enjoyed the examples from The Boy at The Back of the Class as they had read this in year 4, but they also drew on detective fiction – spinning out stories and versions of events – they talked about they were surprised to discover who the murderer* was in Jackson's (2019) High Rise Mystery. They discussed the naivety of Felix in Gleitzman's Holocaust fiction Once and whether the adults should have told him what was going on, why the adults lied to him, and some even discussed Calvin and Hobbes in terms of pondering if Calvin's perception of Hobbes is true, and if he is real or simply real to Calvin? We went from picturebooks to class reads to personal choice.'

It was clear in the feedback from teachers who were kind enough to deliver these lessons that children found pleasure in reading critically, that discussing the power of voice and storytelling, searching for lies and misinformation, was both liberating and pleasurable.

Conclusion and call to action!

Critical literacy, reading for pleasure and agency go hand in hand and should be a fundamental part of the school experience. Children's literature offers the perfect springboard for a full discussion of critical literacy throughout the curriculum. I passed this lesson on to a high school English teacher who used it as a foundation, adding further age-appropriate resources, specifically on narratives concerning climate change, for her KS3 classes. The principle is to begin with picturebooks, but that you can apply these searching questions to *all* texts, from middle-grade novels to adult fiction, to newspaper articles and to the stories passed on in the playground and over generations. There is bias, secrecy and lying in all good stories, and if we want to empower the next generations then it is essential that we point out these nuances, show them that their stories and opinions matter, and instil in children the power they hold in telling their own stories so that others can't frame them for them.

Teacher feedback was clear and positive as it demonstrated that critical literacy was: fundamental not just in itself but has a part to play in reading for pleasure; key in terms of social justice as it enables children to actively question and critique; useful to embed across the school, not just in literacy classes, but could be highly beneficial in relation to discussions of internet safety. In your future practice:

- Pick out some of Paul's (1998) questions and display them in your classroom/library/reading corner. Ask children to refer to them when you read together and then when they read independently.
- Browse your shelves as staff, or as a class. Pick out some old favourites and practise reading against them. What do the good parents wear? What do the kitchens look like? Which characters stay on the inside and who goes outdoors? How do the worlds depicted in these books relate to yours and your children's experiences? To what extent have contemporary texts changed?
- Take a Klassen book or something similar and look for the "counterpoint" – where the words and pictures tell you a different story. Discuss this relationship with your class.
- Go back over any class reads and think about them with regard to reading against. Where did the characters or narrators lie in one way or another?
- Remember that critical literacy applies to all texts. So feel free to move from fiction to fact, from the youngest to the eldest in school, between the arts and sciences, from the written to the oral, from paper to screen, from images to words.

References

Alston, A. (2008) *The family in English Children's literature*. New York and London: Routledge.
Alston, A. (2020) 'It's time to talk about Roald', *Primary Matters*. Manchester: NATE.
Browne, A. (1981) *Hansel and gretel*. London and New York: Julia Macrae Books.
Burnett, F. H. (1911) *The secret garden*. London. Puffin.
Callow, J. (2022) '"Nobody spoke like I did": Picture books, critical literacy, and global contexts', *The Reading Teacher*, 71(2), 231–237. https://doi.org/10.1002/trtr.1626; https://www.researchgate.net/publication/319435780_Nobody_Spoke_Like_I_Did_Picture_Books_Critical_Literacy_and_Global_Contexts
Chambers, A. (2011) *Tell me children, Reading and talk with the Reading environment*. Stroud: The Thimble Press.
Chetty, D. (2017) 'You Can't say that!" Stories have to be about white people', in Shukla, N. (ed.) *The good immigrant*. London: Unbound.
Clark, C. and Teravainen, A. (2015) *Teachers and literacy: Their perceptions, understanding, confidence and awareness*. London: National Literacy Trust.
Cremin, T. (2018) *'Building Reading communities and 'books in common'*. NAAE. https://oro.open.ac.uk/53606/3/Reading_communities_and_books_in_Common_NAAE.pdf
Cremin, T., Mottram, M., Collins, F., Powell, S. and Safford, K. (2014) *Building communities of engaged readers: Reading For pleasure*. Abingdon: Routledge. https://doi.org/10.4324/9781315772585
Dwyer, B. (2016) 'Teaching and learning in the global village: Connect, create, collaborate, and communicate', *The Reading Teacher*, 70(1), pp. 131–136. https://doi.org/10.1002/trtr.1500
Friere, P. (1972) *Pedagogy of the oppressed*. Harmondsworth: Penguin.
Gamble, N. (2019) *Exploring children's literature: Reading for knowledge, understanding and pleasure*. 4th ed. London: Sage.
Gleitzman, M. (2006) *Once*. London: Puffin.
Govender, N. and Farrar, J. (2023) 'Introduction to critical literacies & social media', *English in Education*, 57(4), pp. 252–261.
Greder, A. (2007) *The island*. Crows Nest: Allen and Unwin.
Haworth-Booth, E. (2018) *The king who banned the dark*. London: Pavilion.
Hearne, B. and Kaye, M. (1981) *Celebrating children's books*. New York: Lothrop, Lee and Shepard.
Holabird, K. (1983) *Angelina ballerina*. Illus. Craig, H. Harmondsworth: Puffin.
Hollindale, P. (2011) *The hidden teacher: Ideology and children's reading*. Stroud: The Thimble Press.
Hutchins, P. (1968) *Rosie's walk*. London. The Bodley Head.
Jackson, S. (2019) *High rise mystery*. London: Knights Of.
Janks, H. (2012) 'The importance of critical literacy', *English Teaching*, 11(1), pp. 150–158.
Klassen, J. (2011) *I want my hat back*. London: Walker Books.
Klassen, J. (2012) *This is not my hat*. London: Walker Books.
Martineau, S. and Barker, V. (2020) *Question everything: An investigator's toolkit*. London: b small.
McGillis, R. (1998) 'The delights of impossibility: no children, no books, only theory', *Children's Literature Association Quarterly*, 23(4), pp. 202–208.
Meek, M. (1991) *On being literate*. Portsmouth: Heinemann.
Murphy, J. (1986) *Five minutes peace*. London: Walker Books, 1998.
Murphy, J. (1987) *All in one piece*. London: Walker Books, 1998.
Nikolajeva, M. and Scott, C. (2006) *How picturebooks work*. New York and London: Garland.
Nodelman, P. and Reimer, M. (2003) *The pleasures of Children's literature*. 3rd ed. Boston and New York: Allyn and Bacon.
PISA (2018) 'Analysis', *Education Journal*. (429) October 27 2020. 30. https://www.oecd.org/education/pisa-2018-assessment-and-analytical-framework-b25efab8-en.htm
Paul, L. (1998) *Reading otherways*. Stroud: The Thimble Press.
Pullman, P. (2019) *Northern lights*. London: Scholastic. [1995].
Rauf, O.Q. (2018) *The boy at the back of the class*. London: Orion Children's Books.
Roche, M. (2014) *Developing children's critical thinking through picturebooks: A guide for primary and early years students and teachers*. 1st ed. London. Routledge. https://doi-org.uwe.idm.oclc.org/10.4324/9781315760605
Rowling, J.K. (1998) *Harry Potter and the Philosopher's Stone*. London: Bloomsbury. [1997].

Rowling, J.K. (1999) *Harry Potter and the prisoner of Azkaban*. London: Bloomsbury.
Salisbury, M. and Styles, M. (2022) *Children's picturebooks: The art of visual storytelling*. 2nd ed. London: Laurence King.
Sanna, F. (2016) *The Journey*. London: Flying Eye Books.
Scieszka, J. and Smith, L. (1991) *The true story of the three little pigs*. London: Puffin.
Wilson, J. (1991) *The story of tracy beaker*. London: Doubleday.
Zee, R.V. and Innocenti, R. (2004) *Erika's story*. London: Jonathan Cape.

10 Conclusion

A call to action for social justice and equity in reading for pleasure

Jane Carter and Ann Cowling

As we reach the conclusion of this book, it is useful to reflect on the key messages. From the outset of the book, we have sought to reframe reading for pleasure with a focus on what it is, what it is not and how children can be supported to become the readers they wish to become. In this sense, each author has argued, from their particular perspective, that the pursuit of reading for pleasure cannot be separated from the broader context of social justice and equity. Reading empowers, it opens minds to the good and not so good in the world and offers children the chance to critically engage with text as a springboard to critically engage with the world.

As noted in the chapter focusing on family, children arrive at school with a metaphorical rucksack, packed with their experiences of home, community and the world beyond the school gates. These diverse experiences shape the identities of children, and we have argued the importance of teachers developing knowledge of each child as a person and so their needs can be explored and met, as readers. This thread runs through each chapter in the book.

The current National Curriculum (2013) and countless Ofsted reports have tended to present a single story of not only what it means to be a reader but also what counts as reading. Promoted approaches to the teaching and learning of reading, and those underpinned by the accountability machine, have sometimes run counter to other policies and guidance around reading for pleasure, or at least, they have dominated the narrative of the teaching of reading. We reap what we sow. Years of restricted versions of what it means to be a reader have led us to comparatively high levels of attainment in international league tables, and historically low levels of reading enjoyment and engagement. The tide is turning though, and we hope this book will support you in developing a culture of reading and reading for pleasure in your classroom and school.

We hope that you will be taking a fresh look at reading – from the perspective of thinking about the "purposefully positive" approach that supports the creation of a reading classroom as the foundation from which we can develop reading for pleasure. We felt it was important to make the distinction between some of the amazing units of work and school-centred literature-based schemes that we encountered in many of the case study schools and, reading for pleasure. Many of the units and schemes were designed collaboratively with children, with children supporting the choices of texts to be studied – but ultimately the purpose was about instruction of the skills and knowledge of reading and writing. Reading for pleasure, even with a child's agency at its core, is only about instruction if this is what the child is choosing (and some children do choose text that will enable them to grow and develop academically but, they are in control of the time, place and content when they choose this).

Chapter 2 encouraged you to widen what counts as reading, reflecting first on your own reading histories and preferences and then encouraging children to do the same. The message is that we are all different and so we are bound to have different interests, habits and reading preferences – as teachers we need to ensure we do not favour and promote those reading practices that most align with our own, or align with a particular viewpoint of the "ideal reader." It still makes me smile when I tell the pre-service teachers I teach, that I like to read the last page of a book once I have read the first few chapters. They are horrified. But this is what I need to do – I need to find out if it will all be okay, or even who "did it." Of course, this does sometimes ruin the book for me a little, but I'm prepared to accept that for my reader peace of mind, and it gives me pleasure. I actually realise I read a lot of things like this, blogs, newspaper articles, academic papers, webpages – I read the start, skim a bit and read the end, before deciding if I want to read the rest. Hopefully, through this book, we have encouraged you to reflect on yourself as a reader as a way of acknowledging the breadth and range of what it means to read for pleasure and what counts as reading.

We have suggested a lot of books, websites and resources – clearly, these go out of date, with new books being published daily, but the book intends to whet your appetite for finding your own approaches to keeping up to date and to finding the right books for each child in your class.

Each chapter has either been discussed in detail or has been woven through, representation in children's literature. Representation matters. Our case studies were drawn from a range of schools, some where the majority of children were from minoritised groups; some where children were living in homes of socio-economic disadvantage and others where classrooms were diverse in relation to heritage and economic status. Some schools were largely white and monolingual, others were schools where many languages were spoken. All schools had children with differing academic attainment, some with large numbers of children with Special Educational Needs. All of these children deserve to see themselves reflected in the texts they are introduced to, as well as have the opportunity to see the world through the eyes of children who are not like them. All of these children in our case studies had a view on reading, reading for pleasure and how well their school was doing in encouraging them to be readers. We have taken some of their suggestions and promoted them in the book, as well as highlighted where children have identified the gaps between what teachers think they are doing by promoting a particular strategy or approach and how children view them. The voices of the children in this book should encourage us all to remember to ask the experts – ask the children.

However, given the teachers' responsibility for choosing the majority of the various texts available for children to read in school, we also echo the voices of the teachers in our study who have tried to consider the quality of the literature they share. C.S. Lewis said, "A children's story that can only be enjoyed by children is not a good children's story in the slightest." As an adult, we need to be able to respond in a genuine manner whilst reading a chosen text, whether laughing at the plot of a comic, learning something new from a non-fiction book, empathising with the feelings of a character with dyslexia in a chapter book, or even shedding the occasional tear, just as your children may.

Our writing team was not as diverse as the children and teachers in the case, and we are aware it should have been, but as a team of Initial Teacher Education tutors, we do reflect much of the primary teaching population. We have tried to hold the tensions here and develop our self-awareness of our own identities, heritages, ages and genders. The writing process included regular writing retreats to enable us to share our writing, learn from each other and provide critical feedback on the positions we had taken.

Engagement is the cornerstone of reading for pleasure, and this book has explored various strategies to engage and re-engage young readers both in specific chapters but also in the suggestions about other ways to approach reading for pleasure – through the lens of critical literacy or through links with the environment and sustainability. We have delved into the challenges that some children face in developing a love for reading, whether due to disinterest, difficulty, or previous negative experiences with reading. Of course, it is quite possible that many of these approaches you already know about but hopefully the book serves as a reminder of things you have heard about on your teacher training course, a website you have visited, another book read, or a CPD event you attended.

Whilst we have highlighted the importance of the influence of the individual teacher, it is also evident that the wider school community and home environment impacts significantly on a child's identity as a reader. There are many myths that often go unchallenged about families who are living in poverty, multilingual families, families from particular heritage backgrounds and different family make-ups, and we have tried to challenge these and encourage different thinking around family engagement, recognising again, that literacy is not a single thing that only exists in relation to the curricular. We have encouraged you to "go out" into your communities rather than just "invite them in" to our own school world.

There are many additional chapters that perhaps this book needs – we had hoped to include a chapter about poetry for example and a chapter about how to read aloud well, including the community as part of the read-aloud repertoire of the school. Some of us felt our chapters could be twice as long and some ruthless editing took place! We hope there is enough here to inspire you as you move forwards.

As we look to the future, the work doesn't stop here. The principles and practices discussed in this book are starting points – tools to be adapted and expanded upon as we continue to learn from the children in our classes and from each other. By keeping social justice at the heart of our teaching, we can ensure that reading for pleasure is truly inclusive, benefiting all children, regardless of their background or circumstances.

Call to action!

Each chapter has concluded with a "call to action" with key points to take away and act on. Being a teacher is the best job in the world and it is also the hardest – one where you are asked to do the impossible each day. The list of "jobs" to do each week is a persistent challenge in both its length and breadth. But teachers make a difference in the lives of their class – both teachers and children in our case studies told us this time and time again. For pre-service teachers, this book offers a foundation upon which to build a teaching practice that is rooted in social justice and equity. As you enter the classroom, you will have the opportunity to put these ideas into practice, creating a reading culture that is inclusive, empowering, and reflective of the diverse identities and experiences of your students. The strategies and tools presented in this book are designed to support you in this endeavour, offering practical guidance and inspiration as you embark on your teaching journey. Developing as an excellent teacher of reading who understands the challenge of the basic cognitive skills and knowledge of reading as well as the importance of the environment they create when they do that, which can either foster or squash a pleasure in reading, is not an easy task. It is one however, that is worthwhile in pursuing, remembering always that it is a journey towards social justice and equity. The ideas, strategies, and tools presented in this book are not a final destination but rather a starting point for continued reflection, growth, and action. The work of fostering a love of reading in all children requires every child to be seen, heard, and valued. This book is just one resource among many, and we encourage you to continue to seek out new ideas, perspectives, and strategies as you work to create a reading culture that is inclusive, equitable, and centred on the joy of reading.

In closing, it is worth reflecting on the profound impact that reading for pleasure can have on a child's life. Carl Sagan famously remarked, 'What an astonishing thing a book is. It's a flat object made from a tree with flexible parts on which are imprinted lots of funny dark squiggles. But one glance at it, and you're inside the mind of another person ...' Reading for pleasure is not just about developing literacy skills or academic achievement; it is about opening up new worlds, fostering imagination and creativity, and nurturing a lifelong love of learning. It is about empowering children to see themselves as capable, curious and confident readers and to recognise the power of their own voices in the world of literature. But perhaps most importantly, reading for pleasure is about creating a more just and equitable world. By ensuring that all children have access to literature that reflects their identities and experiences, by teaching them to think critically about the texts they read, and by fostering a love of reading that is inclusive and empowering, we are helping to build a future where every child has the opportunity to thrive – as Joyce Carol Oates suggested, "Reading is the sole means by which we slip, involuntarily, often helplessly, into another's skin, another's voice, another's soul."

As you move forward in your teaching practice, I hope that the ideas and strategies presented in this book will inspire you to continue to place social justice and equity at the heart of your work with young readers. Together, we can create a world where every child has the opportunity to experience the joy of reading, and where every child's voice is valued, respected, and heard.

Thank you for your commitment to this important work, and for your dedication to the children you serve. The future of reading for pleasure is in your hands, and I have no doubt that you will rise to the challenge, creating classrooms which are full of a multiplicity of text and where every child can discover the power and joy of reading:

> A book is a dream that you hold in your hand.
>
> (Neil Gaiman)

Appendices

Dr Jane Carter, Dr Karan Vickers-Hulse and Kalpa Ghelani

Our case study approach

Methodology

The methodology used was a case study with semi-structured interviews being used as our method of data collection, which were incorporated within a small group activity. A case study is an effective way to capture and understand classroom practice and the impact this practice has on children. This method allowed us to gather multiple perspectives and put children's voices at the core of the study (Hamilton and Corbett-Whitier, 2013). A case study holds appeal for classroom practitioners and is 'fit for purpose' which Menter et al. (2011) highlight as an important consideration when conducting small-scale research within your own classrooms. Our approach gave us the opportunity to unpick the particularities of representation in reading (Yin, 2013) and study its complexities within contemporary primary classrooms. Perhaps most simply, a case study as a design frame means concentrating on one element and looking at it in detail rather than parts (Thomas, 2016). Data collected was analysed using a process of thematic analysis with the identification and ongoing review of themes as outlined by Braun and Clarke (2006). Braun and Clarke's (2006) model of thematic analysis offers an accessible and flexible approach to analysing qualitative data and uses the identification of patterns and themes to select those of interest to report to the reader.

Methods and approach

As we conducted this research within settings outside of our own working environment, we ensured that we chose methods that allowed us to work alongside children in a way that was not overtly disruptive to their regular learning schedule. We were conscious of the power dynamics that may have been in play as visiting adults in an educational setting. To mitigate this, we ensured that the research activity was conducted in the children's space, and we positioned ourselves as visitors (Gallagher, 2008). The research method used was a series of semi-structured interviews conducted during a 'book blanket' activity with small groups of primary-age children. Cremin (2020) highlights that these 'book blankets' are an effective pedagogic practice to support a love of reading. Using Cremin's (2020) 'book blanket' approach, we spread a range of books out on a blanket and invited children to browse the selection. This selection included a variety of books which reflected diversity as outlined in the protected characteristics of the Equality Act (2010) and literature outlined in the introduction of Chapters 2 and 5. The books selected were from a range of genres and formats (e.g.: graphic novels, non-fiction, magazines, picture books, chapter books, comics).

Participants

We acknowledge that reading for pleasure begins from the Early Years Foundation Stage (EYFS) and is something that teachers nurture throughout a child's education. We approached schools in a range of locations and contexts with an aim to work with children across a broad spectrum of experiences and age ranges. The authors of this book selected different schools, to use as a case study for this chapter, in which to gather our data. However, as every school is unique, we wanted to reflect this as best as possible through our presentation of data and, for that reason, individual names have been removed to allow generic findings to be used. We acknowledge that these are small-scale case studies, but we hope that this is something that can easily be replicated within your own settings to support you in widening the range of literature that your children have access to and to develop your own knowledge of your pupils as readers.

Children's focus group schedule

Activity 1

'Book blanket' ready with space all around it for children to browse the selection (24-32 books)
   Name labels on; voice recorder on

- **5 mins welcome** - Who we are; what we're doing and why; and what the session involves. Discuss the meaning of consent as a research participant.
- **10 mins browsing time** - Observations made as children browse the selection, sharing books and talking about what they find, what they like and what they don't like.
- **10 mins sharing books** - Children to select a favourite book (or two) and talk about why it is a favourite to the group.
Researcher to make a note of the books chosen and record children's explanations.
- **15 mins question time** - Researchers ask a selection of questions to the whole group.

Child	Favourite book	Reasons

Indicative prompts for children's focus group discussion (from which a selection was made)

Can you tell me if you ever read just for pleasure when you are at home and so not because you have been told to read but because you want to?
Can you tell me about a book you have read that is a favourite?

What things would you like your school to do to help you enjoy reading more?

What do you think of reading – at home and school? Do you read the same things at home and school?

What sorts of things do you read most often e.g. magazines, books, online things?

You have/haven't mentioned poetry. Can you tell me a bit more?

What sorts of things does your Teacher do to help you enjoy reading? Does it work? What else could they do?

Can you think of a book you have read or has been read to you, where the main character is just like you – acts like you, does the sorts of things you would do and is someone you would really like?

Can you think of a book you have read or has been read to you, where you really do not like the character? What is character like?

What advice would you give an author about the sort of characters they should put in their books?

What sorts of things are you interested in (other than reading)? Do you ever read about things you are interested in?

Do you get the chance in school to talk in class (with your friends and teacher) about what you have read at home and/or about what interests you at home?

Can you tell us a bit about the book your teacher is reading aloud to you at the moment in school (with younger children, a book they enjoyed their teacher reading aloud to them)?

Do you have the chance to choose what you read when you are in school? What sorts of things do you/would you choose to read?

When you are at home do you see anyone at home reading? Online, a magazine, a book?

When you are at home, do you ever talk about what you are reading or what your teacher is reading to you? Or perhaps what someone at home is reading (mum, dad, brother, sister)?

Does anyone read aloud to you in school – just for you to enjoy the story of the information? Depending on the answer: Does anyone other than your teacher read aloud to you?

Do you have a favourite book/poem your teacher has read aloud to you?

Does anyone read aloud to you at home? Do you have a favourite that is read to you at home?

Does your teacher ever tell you about what she/he is reading? What about your head teacher? And any of the other staff in school – TAs, dinner staff etc?

What sorts of things does anyone at home do to help you enjoy reading?

Does anyone at school or home give you suggestions for what you could read? Do they just tell you, or the whole class or do they write it somewhere?

How do you use your school library? Do you use the school library to choose books? Who do you do this with?

Do you ever visit the local library with your school or with someone from home?

Have you ever 'gone off' reading? Did anything change your mind back again?

Teachers' focus group schedule

Share the research aims and purposes before reconfirming consent to participate.

Activity 1

Provide a 'book blanket' (books spread out on a blanket) for teachers to browse the selection. The selection will include a range of books, including books which reflect the diversity of Bristol (to include, heritage, disability, gender) and are from a range of genre and formats e.g. graphic novels, non-fiction, magazines, picture books, chapter books, comics.

Put out more than one book blanket for this – different age group books.

Observations will be made as teachers browse the selection. They will be asked to browse, talking about what they find, what they like and what they don't like.

Indicative prompts for teachers' focus group discussion (from which a selection was made)

Teachers will be asked to select a favourite book (or two) and talk about why it is a favourite.

- Are these the sorts of books you are likely to find in your school?
- When I say 'reading for pleasure' what does it mean to you as a teacher and as a reader in your own right?
- Does your school promote reading for pleasure and if it does, how does it do this?
- What are your top hints and tips for promoting reading for pleasure that you would like to share with other teachers?
- How do you encourage families to develop a reading for pleasure climate at home? What has been most successful for your families in your school?
- What strategies have you found to be successful in re-engaging/re-motivating readers particularly in upper KS2?
- Some teachers identify the tricky balancing act of teaching reading for the purpose of assessment, progress and attainment and developing reading for pleasure. Would you say this was something you had to manage in your school? How do you do it?
- Is there one thing that would make the greatest difference to your children as readers who read for pleasure and purpose – what is it?
- Have any personal experiences shaped your knowledge and appreciation of children's literature?
- Do you think these experiences have impacted on your current pedagogy?
- How much autonomy do you have in integrating reading and reading for pleasure in particular, into your planning/timetable?
- What opportunities do you have, if any, and where do you find, supportive CPD opportunities to develop your subject knowledge of children's literature?

Ethics

Ethical approval was sought and was given by the Ethics Committee of the University of the West of England. As part of this process, participants were given information sheets about the research and consent was sought formally (with children this was also from their parents/carers) and the research process and consent were shared at the start of each focus group.

References

Braun, V. and Clarke, V. (2006) 'Using thematic analysis in psychology', *Qualitative Research in Psychology*, 3(2), pp. 77–101.

Cremin, T. (2020) 'Reading for pleasure: Challenges and opportunities', in: Davison, J. and Daly, C. (eds). *Debates in English teaching. Debates in subject teaching*. London: Routledge. https://doi.org/10.4324/9780429506871

Gallagher, S. (2008) 'Intersubjectivity in perception', *Continental Philosophy Review*, 41 (2), pp. 163–178†

Hamilton, L. and Corbett-Whittier, C. (2013) *Using case study in education research*. London: Sage.

Menter, I., Elliot, D., Hall, J., Hall, S., Hulme, M., Lewin, J. and Lowden, K. (2011) *A guide to practitioner research in education*. London: Sage.

Thomas, G. (2016) *How to do your case study*. 2nd ed. London: Sage.

Yin, R. (2013) *Case study research: Design and methods*. London: SAGE Publications.

Index

agency 19, 56, 58, 74, 85, 86, 140-143, 149, 154, 156
audiobooks 30

belonging 69-70, 73-74, 77
book blanket 72, 82, 94
book corner 80, 96, 136
book clubs 81, 96, 133-146
book talk 46, 51, 57, 58, 75, 143
boys 64, 86, 117

children's voice 10-11, 72, 138
choice 57, 65, 72, 74-75, 129, 137-138, 141-142
choosing texts 24, 51, 70-71, 135
cli-fi narrative 62
climate change 55-59, 61-63, 156
comics 29-30
community literacy practices 108-120, 138, 143-144
counterpoint 150, 156
Covid-19 133
critical literacy 79, 136, 140-156
cultural capital 112-113

decodable books 46
disabilities 39, 51, 60, 69, 136, 144, 146
diversity 6, 59, 62, 65, 69-71, 91, 137-138, 144, 146

early years 39-40, 77
eco-pedagogy 55, 59
ecological emergency 55, 64, 66
empathy 56, 61, 66, 78, 136, 142, 145

English as an additional language 58-59, 73
enjoyment 55, 62, 64-65, 66, 135-137
environment 55-56, 58-62, 80, 99-100, 135-138, 144
environmental empathy 61
evaluation 11

families 77-78, 99, 112-114, 122, 143-4, 145-6,
fluency 102
freeze framing 50
funds of knowledge 65, 73, 106, 112-113, 120

gaming 30
graphic novels 29-30, 62, 77, 138
Gypsy Roma Traveller 114-116

hot seating 50

identity 9, 70-71, 74-76, 90, 106
incentives 88, 102
inclusion 6, 8-9, 58-59, 74, 134, 141, 144
influencers 112-113
insects 55, 58, 60-62, 64

library 57-58, 75-76, 92, 119, 132, 140-141, 143, 144

Matthew Effect 37
methodology 11, 82
motivation 42, 89

narrative fiction 26-27
national curriculum 10, 56
National Literacy Trust 25, 58, 75, 144
non-fiction 31-32, 63-64, 74, 117, 149, 152, 153

parents 77-78, 90, 92, 95, 134, 136, 138, 139
passion 45, 82, 135, 138, 142-144
pedagogy 55, 62, 134, 142
Peter Effect 126, 134, 138
phonics 3, 40-41, 44, 87
phonics screening check 40-41
picture books 27-28, 62, 78, 82, 140-156
planet 55, 57, 59, 62-66
poetry 32-33, 64, 137
poverty 109-110, 144
professional development 139, 141-142, 145-146
purposefully positive 37, 43

reading aloud 58, 118, 135
reading for purpose 18
reading instruction 20
reading online 92
reading rivers 18
reflecting realities 16, 20-24, 69, 78, 136, 144
representation 69-83, 87, 136, 137, 143, 146
rights of a reader 20, 93, 142

school librarian 58, 73-74, 80, 117, 141
scrapbooks 85, 97, 98

SEND 8, 73
sequencing 50
simple view 3, 39
small world enactment 49
song lyrics 33
standards agenda 37
stereotypes 69, 77, 80, 115, 144
subject knowledge 136
sustainability 55-57, 62

targets 40
teachers 56-58, 60, 62-64, 66, 88, 90, 92, 134-146, 156
teaching reading 2
tempting talk 64
texts that tempt 25, 62
theory of mind 71
three domains 4, 42, 74
tiny windows 23, 70,

vocabulary 48, 138
volition 15

windows and mirrors 7, 70-71, 78
wordless books 27-28

For Product Safety Concerns and Information please contact our EU
representative GPSR@taylorandfrancis.com
Taylor & Francis Verlag GmbH, Kaufingerstraße 24, 80331 München, Germany

www.ingramcontent.com/pod-product-compliance
Lightning Source LLC
Chambersburg PA
CBHW060301240426
43661CB00060B/2855